by ROBERT BRUSTEIN

SEASONS OF DISCONTENT

THE THEATRE OF REVOLT

SEASONS OF DISCONTENT

DRAMATIC OPINIONS

1959-1965

BY ROBERT BRUSTEIN

SIMON AND SCHUSTER
NEW YORK

FIRST PAPERBACK PRINTING, 1967

LIBRARY OF CONGRESS CATALOG CARD NUMBER: 65–22268
MANUFACTURED IN THE UNITED STATES OF AMERICA

DESIGNED BY EDITH FOWLER

"Aspirin and Surgery" first appeared in The New York Times; "Scorn Not the Proscenium, Critic," in Theatre Arts; "The Men-Taming Women of William Inge" and a longer version of "Repertory Fever," in Harper's; the Foreword, in The New York Review of Books; and all the remaining articles and reviews, in The New Republic.

For my sons, Phillip and Daniel

ACKNOWLEDGMENTS

■ The author wishes to thank all those who helped with the preparation of this book, whether such help took the form of active assistance, moral encouragement, or (not least to be valued) editorial tact and permissiveness: Robert Evett, F. R. Ruskin, and Gilbert Harrison at The New Republic; Robert Gottlieb at Simon and Schuster; Albert Goldman, Stanley Kauffmann, and Luciano Rebay at large; Norma Brustein at home.

CONTENTS

FROM ABROAD

COMPANIES

GENERAL

FOREWORD:
THEATRE RETROSPECTIVE
1959-65

The articles and reviews selected for inclusion in these pages were all written over a six-year period, and primarily for *The New Republic*. In the fall of 1959, when I first joined this magazine as its theatre critic, America was preparing to awaken from that long, drugged sleep called the Eisenhower age; in a few months, it would begin to rub away the accumulated rheum of those eight dismal years. The end of our national lethargy was signaled, in most cultural areas, by a rush of radical dissent and artistic ferment; but the theatre, traditionally retrograde, continued to doze in the center of blandness and mediocrity, impervious to experiment, immune to achievement, hostile to thought. Financed by timid producers, manufactured by pedestrian playmakers, and evaluated by conventional-minded reviewers, most American plays were exuding an ooze of squalid contentment which worked like a narcotic on an audience already stupefied by affluence. In this atmosphere, theatrical advance was blocked before it could even get under way, and an increasing number of spectators—the more discriminating ones—were turning their backs on the stage.

These conditions helped to fix me in an adversary posture. Coming to criticism from the university, where I shared with my students the excitement of the great plays, I was appalled at the absence of distinguished drama on the American stage, and astonished that the standards of our theatre were being arbitrated (often in less than two hours of hurried scribbling) by newspaper reporters, many of whom had prepared for dramatic criticism through stints in such departments as music, foreign

13

affairs, dining and dancing, and sports. I loved the drama above all other literary forms—loved it for its blending of language and action, its galloping immediacy, its economical means and structural beauty—and I loved the theatre when it gave body and substance to plays I admired, or improvised a rich, imaginative life of its own. Now this art was in the hands of spoilers and profiteers; one style dominated our stage, and one system of acting; plays had lost their relevance to the deeper realities of contemporary life; and the only debate the theatre was stimulating (this issue raged week after week in the Sunday *Times*) concerned the rude treatment of theatre-lovers at the hands of the box office.

Talented writers of integrity, who might have helped to revive this failing medium, had grown wholly indifferent to it; some were even beginning to question whether the dramatic form could support a serious work of art. And while theatrical values were still being preserved in a few weekly and monthly magazines, the ranks of the serious critics had been badly depleted by the retirement of Stark Young and Eric Bentley. Impatient with the tripe and treacle that constituted the hits of each Broadway season, and depressed by the uncomprehending antagonism that awaited any work aspiring above the commonplace, I edged cautiously into a reviewing career, curious to see if a declining theatre could still be subjected to the same rigorous tests that were currently being applied to literature, poetry, music, and painting. This rather foolhardy undertaking involved me in two distinguishable functions—one literary and analytical, the other cultural and polemical. My principal responsibility as a critic of the drama was to evaluate and elucidate works of interest, but since these were appearing—let us put it gently—rather infrequently, I was forced to develop a secondary purpose: identifying the various obstacles in the way of a genuine dramatic art. Because such obstacles were so numerous and so stubborn, my secondary purpose eventually threatened to become paramount. Broadway was capable of lodging pleasant entertainments in its showshops; many of these I enjoyed. But I was soon convinced that the commercial system would never encourage real dramatic adventure, indeed was preventing such adventure from taking place. And so I joined the ranks of those who had warred upon Broadway as a cultural institution, underlining its inadequacies, exposing its values, anatomizing its fakeries, and attacking its heroes and saints.

Much of my writing, in short, had become a form of destructive criticism. This was hardly an endearing occupation in that smiling age when the highest Broadway virtues were togetherness and good will, but since there were a sufficient number of reviewers, press agents, producers, directors, and show biz sweeties bestowing flattering kisses on one another, the theatre could certainly survive those disgruntled outsiders who refused to join in the general embraces. And then I believed such destructive activity to be a secret good. As Shaw wrote: "Construction cumbers the ground with institutions made by busybodies. Destruction clears it and gives us breathing space and liberty." It certainly gave me breathing space and liberty: there was something exhilarating about being able to record impressions without having to hedge or weasel.

This freedom I owed to the grace of *The New Republic*. Thanks to the unfailing support of my editors, I had complete control over what, when, and how often I published; thanks to the growing circulation of the magazine, I enjoyed the luxury of an authoritative platform without being shackled by the restrictions of power. Because of the high volume of American mass communications, my own voice never carried very far. But although I was speaking in sibilant stage whispers, and uncertain at first about my audibility, I grew increasingly confident that I would somehow be overheard. Then, too, my advantages were many. Most of my readers did not attend the theatre, so my adverse criticism was not likely to affect the run of a play. And since few theatre professionals were reading my column, I did not have to worry too much about wounding feelings. I wounded feelings anyway, of course, as well as outraging many who thought me too harsh, too bitter, or too sweeping in my condemnations, but I was too deeply engaged in battle to stop and count the casualties.

My strategy raised certain tactical difficulties. How do you continually confront the specious products of a debased theatre without falling into an impotent rage or, worse still, losing faith in the value of your calling? These were problems without a satisfactory solution; I have not yet solved them. At first, I tried to justify my discussions of trivial Broadway successes by using them as frameworks for essay-reviews on more general subjects; but after a while, I began to write less and less frequently. The great majority of plays I couldn't bring myself to review at all. If an anemic little comedy or drama—bloodless enough to be absorbed by all the daily reviewers—was analyzed accurately by one of my colleagues on the weekly and monthly magazines, I felt relieved of the responsibility to cover it. If the daily reviewers themselves correctly evaluated an inadequate play, I ignored it completely. As time went on, only three types of events aroused me to write: the significant new work or revival; the portentous overpraised fraud; the local or visiting company whose work illuminated some aspect of the theatre as a whole. I grew less and less interested in the common run of plays, and more and more concerned with the conditions under which these plays were being produced.

For a short time, such conditions were very auspicious Off Broadway. The first play I was to review in my new post, coincidentally, was Jack Gelber's *The Connection* at The Living Theatre—a production now renowned for having helped to alter opinion about the American stage. Briefly dismissed, bitterly attacked, or totally ignored by all the newspapers and glossier magazines (even the helpful *New Yorker* notice appeared long after the play was established), *The Connection*, nevertheless, managed to survive its initial reception, hanging on to life through the faith of its producers and the support of a handful of partisans. When the magazine reviews began to accumulate in its favor, it went on to become one of the longest-running productions ever staged Off Broadway. For the next Living Theatre offering, the newspapers sent their first-string reviewers. And while the hostility of these men to minority theatre never disappeared, it did become more guarded and uneasy. On the occasion of its first New York showing in 1956, Walter Kerr could confidently patronize *Waiting for Godot* as some kind of precious highbrow curiosity written by an author out of touch "with the minds and the hearts of the folk out front"; after 1959, he was never again to seem so certain he was writing for a consensus. In the minority theatre, at least, the centers of influence were shifting. Artists and intellectuals, for the first time, began to hope that some day they might have a theatre too.

The Off Broadway movement, of course, had been in existence all through the fifties, but it had always depended upon the bounty of the majority reviewers. With this dependence more doubtful, the movement—led by the fanatically independent Living Theatre—grew more courageous for a time, going on to stage some of the most important plays in the contemporary theatre. These works, though occasionally mauled by bad productions, provided some of my most interesting experiences as a reviewer; and since they represented the theatre at its most elevated, they also served to whet an almost blunted critical purpose. Off Broadway was responsible, too, for discovering such native talents as those of Edward Albee, Lewis John Carlino, Murray Schisgal, Arthur Kopit, Kenneth H. Brown, and Kenneth Koch, but my own attitude toward some of these writers was usually more ambiguous. I never relinquished an instinctive suspiciousness toward certain tendencies in the American avant-garde, particularly its fashion-mongering and cultural opportunism, but I was always grateful to Off Broadway for remaining open to freshness and experiment.

Alas, success proved no friend to this movement, and it eventually began to falter. As an increasing number of spectators began to notice the minority theatre, so did an increasing number of unions, and spiraling costs soon made all adventure risky. Apparently determined to prove that it was merely another creak in Broadway's arthritic joints, Off Broadway began to grind out a huge number of musicals and revues, as well as many of the straight plays that Broadway no longer welcomed. And when The Living Theatre collapsed after a collision with the Internal Revenue Service (an episode which ended in the imprisonment for contempt of court of Julian Beck and Judith Malina), the heart went out of the movement, and never really returned.

But Broadway also had the staggers, a development which

caught me rather by surprise. I had enlisted myself against a giant who seemed extremely strong and formidable; but after lowering my head and charging wildly in all directions, I looked up one day to find this brawny Goliath supine—kayoed not by any of its critics but rather by its own internal failures and disorders. Each season was being declared the worst in memory; the press was full of sour news for investors. A few musicals and light comedies were capable of surviving in this noxious climate, along with occasional Merrick-imported shows from abroad. But straight plays were appearing rarely, and usually failing when they did appear. The works of Edward Albee were exceptions, his particular brand of astringency having proved acceptable to uptown as well as downtown audiences. But Miller was still silent, Inge was no longer considered a serious contender, and Williams was repeating himself from year to year. The aesthetic crisis of our theatre was finally manifesting itself economically—that is, in a way understandable to all—and the Great White Way was blanketed in gloom. Broadway had taken on the look of an expensive funeral chapel, admitting new victims every week. There were hordes of mourners, to be sure, waiting to file by the biers and pay their respects to cadavers that showed the slightest sign of life (whim! bang! hit!) but the more inert stiffs (whoosh! bink! flop!) were being quickly hauled off to the boneyard, unattended by family or friends. It had become a dark unwholesome sanctuary, and a drama reviewer couldn't help but feel a little like Vergil among the shades.

As a result of this deterioration in the commercial theatre, hope began to collect around cultural centers and permanent companies: the Repertory Theatre of Lincoln Center came into being, presumably to relieve the theatre from degrading economic pressures and tawdry commercial fare. But it soon became clear, after Elia Kazan and Robert Whitehead were appointed directors of this company, that relief was not yet in sight. What should have been a total revolution proved only a diversionary tactic by the palace guard permitting the very people responsible for the theatre's collapse to regroup their forces.

Intensely disappointed with these nominations, I had doubts about Lincoln Center before it even produced a play; I could sense a ghastly repetition of the whole Broadway syndrome, this time under the dignified aegis of subsidized culture.

I was extremely hard on Arthur Miller, too, for much the same reasons. Having broken his eight-year silence with two plays in succession, he was assuming a role with this company that was virtually guaranteed, I thought, to set back theatrical clocks. It was not simply that *After the Fall* and *Incident at Vichy* seemed to me bad and pretentious plays, but that they seemed so moribund in their style, ideas, and language. This was the theatre that had dominated Broadway for over twenty years, the theatre that effectually banished poetry and imagination from the stage. Had it been discredited on the commercial stage only to be resurrected in this new form?

Once again, I had overestimated the strength and vigor of the theatre establishment: Lincoln Center soon proved not a resurrection of Broadway but merely another of its post-mortem spasms. Harassed by the press and harried by the Repertory Theatre Board, Kazan, Whitehead, and Miller submitted their resignations shortly more than a year after their first production. The social-psychological theatre they had championed was losing its appeal for younger playwrights and more sophisticated audiences awakened by the radical metaphysical drama from France; and when Lincoln Center finally produced a classical play—*The Changeling*—it proved to be the major disaster of the repertory, demonstrating how inadequate was the realistic acting of our stage.

This histrionic inadequacy was also being demonstrated by the Actors Studio Theatre, a producing unit formed out of rivalry with Lincoln Center; it soon proved to be another branch of the same rotting tree. Like the Kazan company, the Actors Studio quickly exposed the substantial limitations of its Method when applied to works of range and thrust; play after play was choked up in the self-conscious mannerisms of its more famous personnel. Performances of a similar flatness had once enraged the poet Yeats enough to write:

> But actors lacking music
> Do most excite my spleen,
> They say it is more human
> To shuffle, grunt and groan,
> Not knowing what unearthly stuff
> Rounds a mighty scene. . . .

And such performances were enraging many of us. Splenetic over the prosaic "reality" of Lee Strasberg's earthbound school, we impatiently awaited not only a more ample kind of acting, but also the unearthly music of some mighty scenes.

Both were to come, first in William Ball's original approach to Pirandello's *Six Characters* and then in Jonathan Miller's production of Robert Lowell's *The Old Glory*. These two events—each so poetic, atmospheric, and heavily charged—were to awaken for the first time in years a sense of real theatrical possibility. Robert Lowell's play, particularly, was exciting not only in itself but also for the promise it held that gifted writers from other literatures would soon begin to nourish the stage; Saul Bellow's *The Last Analysis*, though disfigured by a meretricious Broadway production, offered a similar promise. Around the same time, the Lincoln Center company was taken over by Herbert Blau and Jules Irving, both of whom had already demonstrated their selfless allegiance to the repertory ideal by building the San Francisco Actor's Workshop into an ensemble notable for intelligence, versatility, and adroitness. And in anticipation of a more hospitable professional climate for unconventional drama, many young writers were beginning work on experimental new plays.

Are these the tokens of that renewal we have awaited so long? The signs are scattered, but I am tempted to suppress a natural skepticism and say yes. The American theatre finally seems to be emerging, five years late, from the Eisenhower age—its roots torn, its complacency battered, its center displaced, but healthier, nevertheless, for all the confusion and uncertainty. Consistent achievement is yet to come, but one can begin to have hope at last that it will come: theatrical conditions, still pretty awful, are better than they were, if only because everyone is now aware of a crisis. Should this awareness engender some exciting new plays and venturesome production techniques, then the crisis will have been justified. And I, personally, may be able to lay down my arms, forsake polemics entirely, and return to the primary critical task of cool analysis. Such a promise is admittedly rash, the products of our stage being so erratic, and my own threshold of exasperation so low. But I am counting on the American theatre to keep a long-delayed promise to us all.

A note about the structure of the book. It is divided into five sections: Off Broadway, Broadway, From Abroad, Companies, and General. These are arbitrary and not always consistent divisions, since reviews are not originally conceived with categories in mind. A reader may therefore wonder why, for example, a notice of Caligula is placed in the Broadway section and an essay on The Deputy in the section From Abroad, when both are European plays in American productions. I can justify such inconsistencies only by drawing the reader's attention to the way the discussion is weighted. In the case of The Deputy, my review deals more with the political implications of the play than with its implications for Broadway; in the case of Caligula, I am primarily concerned with how the commercial theatre violates a play of ideas. Similarly, the Actors Studio Theatre calls itself a company: why not include it in that category? The answer is that whatever this group calls itself, it functions less as a repertory theatre than as a Broadway producer, adopting itself to the star system and the hit-flop mystique, and so I have chosen to deal with its actuality instead of its publicity. I hope I have done the same for all the other plays and players examined in the book.

OFF BROADWAY

■

■

■

JUNK AND JAZZ

THE CONNECTION *by Jack Gelber:*
The Living Theatre

■ When you enter the Off Broadway theatre where *The Connection* is playing in repertory, you have a few moments before the action begins to formulate your expectations. The curtain is drawn, and on the stage some excessively seedy characters are arranged in various attitudes of weariness and gloom. The setting is a tawdry tenement, the furniture is dilapidated, the quarters cramped and dirty. Painted on the wall upstage is a crudely executed pyramid, a revivalist motto, and a huge disembodied eye; hanging from the flies is a single green light bulb. The play, you have been informed, is about drug addiction. The subject is unpromising, and Lower Depths naturalism, it appears, is to be the inevitable treatment. Yet, something is not in place here—the imaginary fourth wall has not been constructed. The actors are aware of the audience, and even somewhat distressed at its presence. It is making them nervous, disturbing their peace.

Soon, two actors, claiming to be the writer and the producer

23

of the play, run down the aisle, and begin to speak to the spectators. Your expectations shift. Inductions, direct audience address, entrances through the house, these are the familiar, generally gratuitous techniques of experimental theatre (you may have seen them clumsily employed by the same company, just the evening before, in a pretentious and tiresome trifle by William Carlos Williams). Echoes of Brecht, Beckett, Pirandello, and O'Neill begin to resound, and your new expectations harden. The play is arty and derivative; the characters are dull; the dialogue is flat; the directorial pace is flagging; the acting is dreary. Nothing, in fact, is happening, and you wait for boredom to release you from the need to care.

It takes about ten minutes to realize that you are witnessing an extraordinary performance in which everything, including your initial response, has been planned with absolute precision. The acting and direction are so true that it would be some kind of violation to single out individuals for praise; and Jack Gelber's play, despite obvious literary derivations, soon emerges as highly original and unpredictable. Free from stylized Studio "reality," pumped-up Kazan theatrics, and Broadway contrivance, The Connection even avoids that over-intellectualization of human behavior which informs the work of Beckett, Ionesco, and Genet. Gelber has managed to assimilate, and sometimes to parody, his borrowed techniques without a trace of literary self-consciousness; and by the use of live jazz (superbly played) as a rhythmic contrast to the cool junkie daze of the dialogue, he has introduced an effective theatrical device all his own. The most striking thing about this work is its Spartan honesty. The only false note of the evening is struck by your own conventional expectation, conditioned by years of phony drama and sociological indoctrination.

The play is structured like a work by Pirandello. A group of addicts, waiting throughout the first act for the arrival of their connection, are assumed to be "real" characters, improvising their parts in exchange for a free fix. The "playwright," the "producer," and a couple of cameramen (photographing them in action for an avant-garde movie) hope they will reveal themselves in melodramatic or sensational attitudes; but the junkies, although provided with strong, distinct characters, nervously follow the truth of their own lives, exposing themselves only piecemeal, through pointless stories and unfinished confessions. When Cowboy, their connection, finally arrives, accompanied by a bewildered Salvation sister, the junkies file into the bathroom one by one for their fix; a series of loaded ironies follows; the "playwright" is turned on himself and gets a real look at his subject; a fastidious hipster named Leach takes an overdose and almost dies; the action and the music turn phantasmagoric; the junkies scatter; and the play ends with two characters swaying over a phonograph, listening to the lonely, almost religious ritual of jazz.

Because the characters refuse to participate in false climaxes for the sake of dramatic excitement, the play goes nowhere, and—except for the conclusion that addicts find salvation in junk and jazz—it makes no strong point. But implicit in every moment is the understanding that human existence can no more be explained by social, psychological, moral or aesthetic theories than human life can be confined within the limits of a dramatic action. Thus, although Gelber borrows some of Pirandello's techniques, he is never guilty of Pirandello's operatic plot construction, for melodrama would merely be another distortion of reality. The characters of The Connection maintain their integrity in an atmosphere of frightening authenticity; and the naturalism of this anti-play functions as a sardonic comment on anything which would falsify for impure ends the truth of things as they are.

Quite clearly, then, the most severe indictment of the evening is reserved for the audience, and, by extension, for society at large. The spectator may think he attends the theatre for a few hours of harmless diversion, but if the dramatic characters are "real," then his presence is a violation of their privacy, motivated by a voyeuristic interest in freak shows. Similarly, the spectator may hold pat social attitudes toward addiction which he expects the play to confirm, but he soon finds himself under attack for seeking "connections" in tranquilizers, vitamin pills, alcohol, and success. By providing his downbeat characters with more dignity and self-awareness than the characters of most

American drama, Gelber has managed to transcend the limitations of his subject. He has not only accurately stigmatized such bad drama as *A Hatful of Rain*, but opened out into a scathing criticism of the spectator's most cherished pieties.

Constantly tripping over the boundary between life and art, stripped of significant form, antagonistic to all theory or morality which does not accord with practice, *The Connection* is probably not a "good" play by any standard we now possess to judge such things; but it forms the basis for a brilliant theatrical occasion, and it lives in that pure, bright, thin air of reality which few of our "good" playwrights have ever dared to breathe. The first hipster drama to be seen in New York, it offers promise that the language of "cool" might soon become a pulsing stage rhetoric similar to Odets' language of the blues. It may not be the healthiest sign for our culture that the only recent American play of honesty and imagination has issued from such alienated precincts. But when our commercial dramas genuflect before the cant, hypocrisy, and prosperity of our society, we must take our truth from whatever quarter it comes.

(1959)

LISTENING TO THE PAST

KRAPP'S LAST TAPE *by Samuel Beckett and*
THE ZOO STORY *by Edward Albee*

■ *Krapp's Last Tape* is Samuel Beckett's latest, and very possibly his best, dramatic poem about the old age of the world. Still obsessed with the alienation, vacuity, and decay of life upon a planet devoid of God and hope, Beckett is finally able to sound those chords of compassion which have always vibrated quietly in his other work. Yet, what really strikes me as new is the extraordinary economy of the writing, the absolute flawlessness of the form. *Godot* and *Endgame*, for all their poetry and insight, were ultimately marred, I think, by their length. It is one thing to affirm that life is a string of aimless, inconsequential, and monotonous events; it is quite another to produce and reproduce these events upon the stage. Although Beckett's art, like Ionesco's, lends itself most readily to short statements, the burden of his plays—that one day is very much like another—has led him into labyrinths of *longueur* and repetition.

In *Krapp*, Beckett disposes of this problem with the aid of a simple mechanical device. Today and tomorrow are, through the use of a tape recorder, simultaneously revealed. Set in the future (I suspect all of Beckett's plays are), this brief and beautiful artwork revolves around a solitary character, the perfect realization of Beckett's idea of human isolation. Like so many of the author's creations, Krapp is incredibly ancient. He putters laboriously around his eremitic cell, myopically examining his keys, peering dimly into his books, testing his shrunken vocal organs on words which please him, pouring whiskey noisily down his throat, sucking toothlessly on a banana with the same relish and resignation that Estragon eats his carrot and Nagg his soda biscuit. Reduced to his most elementary appetites, Krapp has no purpose or occupation except to listen to his organs die and to feel his functions fail. He is, like Eliot's Gerontion, "an old man in a draughty house under a windy knob," but he is without even Gerontion's dream of rain.

Krapp is surrounded, almost buried, by his past—boxes upon boxes of magnetic tapes, the vocal diary of his entire life. The action of the play is the replaying of one spool, a mundane yesterday recorded thirty years before when Krapp was middle-aged and already rather juiceless. The droning, slightly pompous voice from the machine evokes a variety of responses from the aged Krapp; anger, interest, melancholy, contempt, despair. A memory of feeling returns to his withered hand during a description of the texture of a black rubber ball; after hearing the story of a girl in a tattered dress glimpsed on a railway platform, he hurriedly plays the section over; he turns the set off in disgust in the midst of a rabid, excited account of a eureka insight into the meaning of life; he collapses into ruins of longing during the indifferently intoned narrative of a sexual experience in a rocking boat. On the last tape, Krapp intends to record his present day's activities, but there is now nothing left in him, "not a squeak," nothing but memory, loss, and impotent desire, nothing to do but put on the old tape and eavesdrop on his past when he could still press his flesh against another human body. The curtain descends on Krapp stiffening in his rented room, his head laid miserably on the machine, his arms around it like a grotesque and wizened lover. It is a haunting and harrowing work, brilliantly directed by Alan Schneider and played by Donald Davis with just the right balance of pathos and absurdity.

Accompanying Beckett's play at the Provincetown is an underground work by Edward Albee called *The Zoo Story*, a colloquy between a well-dressed bench sitter and a psychotic hipster who accosts him in the park. Out of this dialogue—or, rather, monologue (for the hipster does most of the talking while the bench sitter responds with raised eyebrows)—comes a convoluted story about the hipster's inability to connect with human beings. A brief account of his sexual failures with both men and women leads to a longer account of his relationship with animals, particularly his landlady's dog, which he tried to poison because this "black monster of a beast" was always making vicious passes at his leg. The murder, despite elaborate preparations, does not come off ("I wanted the dog to live so that I could see what our relationship would come to"); instead, the hipster experiences a kind of religious conversion, based on the principles of Zen. Realizing that his attempt to kill, along with the dog's effort to bite, was really an expression of love, he begins to see God everywhere: in the Negro queen who lives above him, in his lecherous landlady, even in the pornographic playing cards he keeps in his room. And, undoubtedly to prove his love for the bench sitter, he expropriates his bench, punches him in the ribs, maligns his manhood—goads him, in other words, into holding a knife on which he gratefully impales himself. Having scared the poor bench sitter half out of his wits, the hipster tells him, "Now you know what you see on your TV," frees him from the charge of being a vegetable, commends himself to God, and dies.

I should report immediately that portions of this play are extremely well written. The bench sitter is less a character than an idea (Mr. Square, straw man of the Beat Generation), so The Zoo Story lacks a convincing antagonist; but the dialogue, suspense, and sheer narrative flow of the work indicate that Mr. Albee, who is no Broadway sibling, has a powerful dramatic talent. On the other hand, I am depressed by the uses to which this talent has been put. In its implicit assumption that the psychotic, the criminal, and the invert are closer to God than anyone else, The Zoo Story embodies the same kind of sexual-religious claptrap we are accustomed to from Allen Ginsberg. The tendency of Beat writers to invest the French Rebel tradition (de Sade-Rimbaud-Jean Genet) with a pseudo-religious flavor seems to me quite similar to the tendency of Broadway playwrights to identify romantic love with God; and although such ideas may endear these writers to the Luce publications, they signify a general flabbiness in American feeling and thought. I will not elaborate on the masochistic-homosexual perfume which hangs so heavily over The Zoo Story except to say that Mr. Albee's love-death, like Mr. Ginsberg's poetry, yields more readily to clinical than theological analysis. In short, Mr. Albee has successfully avoided Broadway stereotypes only to fall into Beat ideology, and Jack Gelber remains the only new American dramatist steering a clear path between the two.

(1960)

A LIVING AUDIENCE

TONIGHT WE IMPROVISE *by Luigi Pirandello:*
The Living Theatre

■ To judge by the printed text, *Tonight We Improvise* would seem to be unworkable, particularly on the American stage. Written just two years after *Six Characters in Search of an Author,* it is, first of all, merely a reworking of the same theme in a more diffuse and chaotic manner. Once again, the action is located in a theatre; once again, it embodies Pirandello's conviction that the artificialities of the stage are inadequate to the expression of authentic passions. To illustrate this, both plays feature an egocentric director more concerned with advancing his own personality and career than with the demands of a play. But if the director of *Six Characters* is in conflict with the author's characters, the director of *Tonight We Improvise* (a three-foot tyrant named Dr. Hinkfuss) is busy combatting his own acting company—not to mention the spectators who rag him mercilessly throughout the action. The result is an atmosphere of anarchy and rebellion—often funny, more often incoherent, ultimately fatal to Pirandello's central idea.

The revolt of the actors reveals the play's intrinsic flaw. While the director is more preoccupied with stage effects and abstruse theories, the actors—supposedly improvising their parts from a Pirandello short story—insist on following the truth of their feelings. After two acts of contention, the actors throw the director out of the theatre and settle down to an uninterrupted presentation of plot. Theatrically, this proves to be an unfortunate victory: the last act is composed less of authentic passion than of Sicilian melodrama, operatic monologues, and jealousy scenes in a passion-tearing vein. While Pirandello has successfully demonstrated the absurdity of his director's approach to the drama, his own alternative proves equally unconvincing and unsatisfying.

The revolt of the audience in *Tonight We Improvise* poses a more special problem, for it is almost unthinkable that sober American spectators would comment out loud on a performance or a play. The American spectator will applaud stage settings, entrances, exits, and curtain calls; but aside from these modest tokens of his presence, only a cough, a sneeze, and the occasional rustling of his coat ever break his traditional silence. Drugged and hypnotized by the magical tricks of illusionistic theatre, he sits politely on his padded chair, passively cast as Peeping Tom.

Nevertheless, The Living Theatre company has handled this play so deftly, and delivered such an effective assault on the audience's peace of mind, that the play suddenly becomes extremely plausible in all but its basic flaw. The company is not distinguished by the brilliance of its acting (which rarely rises above or falls below a kind of inspired amateurism), and the last act, with its greater technical demands, remains tedious—perhaps even more tedious than necessary. Yet, despite some of the trials of the evening, I found this an extraordinary performance, confirming my impression that The Living Theatre is the freshest group I have seen in years, that it possesses an authentic artistic identity, and that it more than makes up in intelligence, imagination, and sheer daring whatever it lacks in professional skill.

The director, Julian Beck, has reworked Pirandello's text not only to preserve the original spirit but to impose added meanings as well. The Reinhardtian director, Dr. Hinkfuss, has been transformed into an eccentric experimental theatre director named Julian Beck, whose melancholy egg-shaped head is crammed full of pretentious avant-garde theories, and who has a penchant for commenting on his own abstract stage décor ("It's all very beautiful, but what does it *mean?*"). Hinkfuss' Sicilian

religious procession, introduced for local color, has been converted into a short movie called *Sicily, Land of Passion*, in
which collages of overexposed color film blend with occasional
glimpses of an icon of the Virgin, all to the accompaniment of
groans and gargling sounds on the loudspeaker; and Pirandello's
disgruntled spectators have now become skeptical hipsters given
to guying all the shibboleths of avant-garde theatre. At the same
time, the audience is constantly being turned on—encouraged
to walk out of the theatre, badgered into speaking up about the
play, confronted in the lobby with a continuation of the action,
and loosened up by a series of outrageous practical jokes (at one
point, I found myself in the aisle, holding on foolishly to my
coat, while an actor enjoyed the show from my seat). The
company has used Pirandello's play not only to indict the
careerist director but also to satirize its own experimental techniques; in fact, the total effect is an attack on the solemnity and
portentousness of the entire theatrical occasion.

By using the dramas in their repertory as scenarios rather
than holy texts, in short, these actors are accomplishing the
astonishing feat of restoring a living relationship between the
spectator and the stage. An effort is being made to create new
responses in the spectator by shocking him out of his old ones—
to create, in effect, a new spectator—and once again, the audience seems as youthful, buoyant, and alive as the actors; once
again, the theatre gives off a relaxed and casual air. Certainly,
one of the major reasons for the pallid quality of recent commercial theatre has been the extraordinary pomposity of the
theatrical event coupled with the playwright's reluctance to agi-
tate the tranquilized stupor of the audience—even such "experimental" plays as *Our Town* actually comfort the spectator
by complacently affirming his most cherished assumptions. The
Living Theatre, on the other hand, endowed with a spirit of
joyous anarchy, is constantly breaking the hallowed theatrical
contract, constantly destroying the barriers between life and art.
The company's talents, I suspect, are not shaped for more literary works of drama; and while there are a number of suitable
European works, few American plays can be presented profit-

ably in such an irreverent manner. But The Living Theatre is creating an atmosphere in which such works will surely be written. In its unique understanding that there can be no living theatre without a living audience, this group is paving the road toward real advance.

(1959)

THE BROTHEL
AND THE WESTERN WORLD

THE BALCONY *by Jean Genet*

■ Jean Genet is at once the most brilliant, the most gifted, and the most depraved of the new French dramatists; and while *The Balcony* is probably the most subversive work of literature to be created since the writings of the famous Marquis, it is a major dramatic achievement. Fashioned by a genius of criminality and revolt, the play is absolutely stunning in its twists and turns of thought, and (despite occasional thefts from Betti, Cocteau, and the Surrealists) highly original in its use of the stage. In its interpretation of history, it is both provocative and scandalous; in its assault on what we take to be "the real," both inexorable and intolerable; in its violent demolition of established authority, both appealing and appalling. It is extremely difficult, in short, to speak of Genet without employing the *both . . . and* construction. If you consider yourself a good citizen concerned with preserving the social contract, you might feel inclined to stone the author and picket the Circle in the Square; but if you are curious to know what the theatre can be like when a perversely honest immoralist writes for it, empty your pockets of missiles and doff your picket boards, for *The Balcony* is one of the richest and most fascinating philosophical plays of the decade.

Genet's most important ideological influence, aside from de Sade, is the tradition of French pornography, and the opening scenes of *The Balcony* contain some ritual echoes of the Black Mass. A Bishop confesses and feels up a half-naked penitent; a Judge, aided by a whip-happy executioner, judges, condemns, and kisses the foot of a fleshly thief; a General is taken on an imaginary tour of his battlefield by a pulchritudinous horse—all as a prelude to sexual relations. For The Grand Balcony is a brothel—a house of illusions where ordinary men, by identifying with the Great Figures of the Christian state, may engage in blasphemous revels. These revels are stage-managed by Madame Irma, the severe proprietress of the establishment, who provides the "props of a display that they have to drag in the mud of the real and the commonplace": the studios in which the masquerade takes place, the ladies who perform the supporting roles, and the proper costumes and cothurni, padded to give the impersonators a sense of their historical importance.

But Genet is less interested in the titillations of pornography than in its philosophical implications; and the erotic scenes are merely a prologue to his sexual-theatrical vision of society, life, and history. For the various sacred offices are not only being desecrated in the brothel; they are also being *preserved* there, since to imitate these functions even blasphemously is to assume their authority. The real threat to the System lies not in whorehouse imposture but in a puritan rebellion that is being waged outside, dedicated to "reality" or the destruction of the whole artifice of Government, Clergy, Magistracy, and Army. The rebellion is successful in that individual functionaries, including the Queen, are killed, but a failure because the hieratic sanctions of two thousand years cannot be destroyed. Led by Madame Irma, who assumes the robes of Queen, the brothel Bishop, Judge, and General begin to play their imposture in earnest, and—exploiting the people's love of illusion and their need to worship images they can be unworthy of—immediately establish their authority. For Genet, in other words, all functions are the manufacture of fakery and sham, and the artifice of the brothel is identical with the make-believe of the world. If the whorehouse is a mirror of society, society, in turn, reflects the whorehouse.

Yet, the play goes even deeper than this mordant social comment, becoming at last a rebellious assault upon the very heavens. The agent of this revolt is the Chief of Police (Irma's failing lover and the leader of the Government forces). Although, having quelled the rebellion, he is hailed as the Hero and has a colossal mausoleum constructed in his honor, his real ambition is to be impersonated in the brothel and thus to become a part of the Nomenclature. In his longing after classical *gloire*, in his desire to be the "One and Only," in his lust for power even over God's functionaries, he actually aspires toward Godhead—and his Godhead finally is achieved. Simulated by an impersonator who castrates himself in the process (mutilation is the destiny of the Man-God, whether he be Dionysus, Osiris, or Christ), the Chief orders "grub for two thousand years" and descends into his tomb, while the rat-a-tat-tat of machine guns announces that a new rebellion is beginning outside. Religion, revolution, and the cycles of civilization have been completely redefined as purely erotic phenomena and The Grand Balcony has become, in the short course of the evening, society, the universe, and the entire stage of history, as conceived by a cunning and diabolical mind.

It is, in short, a house that flies, and the Circle in the Square production, after a somewhat earthbound beginning, generally takes off as well. David Hays has designed highly ingenious mobile set units which are raised and lowered from the ceiling for each scene, and Patricia Zipprodt's costumes have an almost organic function in the play. While the performance as a whole is not always integrated, some of the individual parts are superbly and definitively rendered: Nancy Marchand regal and sinister as the brothel madam; Roy Poole sadistic and bullish as the Chief of Police; Betty Miller feline and fatigued as Irma's favorite whore; Jock Livingston pudgy and enigmatic as the Queen's envoy; Salome Jens lyrical, shining, and luscious as the General's horse. I would quarrel with José Quintero's cutting, which leaves some of the work unnecessarily obscure (whole scenes have been excised instead of parts from each), but his direction is full of lucidity and authority, and of humor too, for the author is a comedian of the grotesque whose savagery quite often verges on farce. Jean Genet, who conceives of all life as theatre, is one of the most theatrical of the modern dramatists; and Circle in the Square, which has been wasting too much time lately in reviving Broadway's failures and successes, is once again fulfilling its experimental function with this ingenious, profound, and provoking play.

(1960)

A DIRECTOR'S THEATRE

MACHINAL by Sophie Treadwell

■ It is commonly assumed that the American theatre is a director's theatre; yet, Broadway, at present, can boast of only three or four directors who do consistently distinguished work, and even these are extremely limited in their range. For all the extravagant claims that are made for Elia Kazan, I don't think he can be seriously compared, as un homme de théâtre, with such contemporaries as Michel Saint-Denis, Jean Vilar, Jean-Louis Barrault, Giorgio Strehler, Bertolt Brecht, or the old Orson Welles. Let us pass by his well-known compulsion to inject hypodermics into everything he touches; Kazan simply has not directed a great enough variety of plays. Although he now possesses more freedom than anyone on Broadway, he has never progressed (unless you call J. B. progress) past the established American playwrights, and we have yet to learn how he would handle a great work of the past or a truly experimental avant-garde drama.

In consequence of this Broadway provincialism, neither he nor any other commercial director has had much opportunity to develop in scope or imagination. The dominant form of our theatre—psychological realism—is appropriate to depth performances, but it forces the director to function primarily as an actor's coach. For while a director should always be subordinate to the play, the demands of illusion suggest that he disappear altogether. (One admires Arthur Penn, for example, because he is able to evoke true, unified, and meticulously detailed performances without signaling his presence at every turn.) In actual practice, of course, such unobtrusiveness is extremely rare—most directors in the realistic tradition not only impress their personalities firmly on a play but even strongly influence the quality and purpose of the script. Nevertheless, Broadway realism prohibits any audacious experimenting with style and with patterns of movement and speech.

As a result, American directors are not very impressive when they finally turn to plays of a less illusionistic nature. Kazan, apparently chafing in the iron maiden of realism, has lately been groping toward a kind of Federal Theatre experimentalism without any particular distinction or originality; and Harold Clurman's intermittent collisions with French drama, when not downright disastrous, have seemed to me peculiarly vacuous, stagy, and static. It is no accident that when producers want a play produced with sweep and flamboyance they usually call on Tyrone Guthrie, or that our musicals—which employ non-illusionistic conventions of a debased kind—are coming more and more to be staged by choreographers. Of the three most imaginative productions of the past year—the Pro Musica's *Play of Daniel*, the City Center's *Seven Deadly Sins*, and the Piccolo Teatro di Milano's *Servant of Two Masters*—none could conceivably have been staged by a professional Broadway director.

Off Broadway, however, has lately been showing signs of discontent with the established directorial order. The Living Theatre's production of *The Connection*—more "real" than anything uptown—embodies, in effect, a new style, developed in opposition to conventional realistic techniques; José Quintero's production of *The Balcony* is an interesting attempt to find a theatrical stance for the new French drama; and now Gene Frankel's production of *Machinal* renders the familiarities of Expressionism in novel and striking form.

Let us dispense briefly with Sophie Treadwell's 1928 play, which is one of those banal tabloid stories, out of Georg Kaiser by Elmer Rice, about how a sensitive dish of cream is curdled in the age of the machine. The heroine, who can't seem to perform her duties with the robot efficiency of her office mates, marries her boss, a good-natured business type with the unfortunate habit of conversing in industrial maxims ("Haste Makes Waste"). Since he is rather gross and sensual, and prefers the blinds down when she likes them up, she becomes allergic to him, but, nevertheless, bears him a child. This traumatizes her even more, so after she meets a smooth Lothario with a romantic past (he kills bandits in Mexico), she conks her husband with a bottle filled with pebbles. She is tried, convicted, and executed by a rigid and unsympathetic society which demands the submission of the individual.

Out of this airy nothing, Frankel and his companions have created a compelling theatrical experience which is as well orchestrated as a symphony and as imaginatively designed as a ballet. Aided by a gifted choreographer (Sophie Maslow), Frankel has given the play movement, grace, and focus, pacing each of the episodes with varying antiphonal rhythms to communicate its proper mood. Four Scene Changers, wearing black clothes, red rubber gloves, and black painted masks, dance lithely through the action, acting as prop men, mute characters, and sinister Fates; actors pantomime activities like washing, filing, typing, drinking, phoning, and ironing with remarkable accuracy; and brief overheard scenes are pasted one upon the other, like a collage, to create in simple deft strokes the atmosphere of metropolis, office, café, courtroom, and execution chamber. Ballou, plastering the gun-metal proscenium with artfully arranged newspapers, has constructed a functional, geometric unit set, backed by a projection of a cold, metallic building; and H. Arthur Gilbert's special effects, along with Ezra Laderman's ominous brass music, give an eerie sense of the neurotic's heightened sensitivity to noise.

All this signifies a director who controls the performance as rigidly as an orchestra conductor, but most of the acting, nevertheless, is individual (while selective) and true: Dolores Sutton's birdlike, hysterical, vaguely catatonic heroine; Vincent Gardenia's slobbering, perpetually triumphant husband; Gerald O'Loughlin's slightly boorish, self-satisfied lover. With this production (as with his equally graceful, though more ineptly acted, production of Stefan Zweig's Volpone), Frankel shows signs of becoming a real force in the Off Broadway theatre, for he has developed a sense of style and stage movement which is both original and faithful to the play. One might only wish, now that he has perfected his choreographic technique, that he would apply it to works more worthy of his talents.

(1960)

A SATANIC MASTERPIECE

IN THE JUNGLE OF CITIES by Bertolt Brecht:
The Living Theatre

■ In the Jungle of Cities is an extremely enigmatic and perhaps ultimately elusive work, but it has a diabolical brilliance and hypnotic power which are quite overwhelming, and it leaves its mark on you like a wound. Brecht seems to have been goaded to write this early play by some frenzy in his unconscious, for he displays here that "prodigious and rational disordering of all the senses" which Rimbaud identified as the special attainment of the visionary poet. The result is a cruel phantasmagoria of life on our forsaken planet, illuminated if not warmed by a fierce poetic intensity. The plot moves in an episodic series of seemingly gratuitous incidents; the characters act on one another as in a dream, without any conventional cause-and-effect motivation; and the atmosphere is thick with that harsh oppressive glow one sees in a Van Gogh interior. Yet, although the play has the quality of a hallucination, and is therefore tortured and obscure, it possesses a strange consistency all its own like the inner logic of a nightmare.

Located in Brecht's mythical Chicago and wandering through a sordid Chinatown possibly inspired by Anna May Wong movies or Charlie Chan novels, the action features an "inexplicable wrestling match" between two men, fought without apparent motive and concluded only when one of them is dead. The first round begins when an aging Malayan lumber dealer named Shlink offers to buy an opinion of a book from a lending library salesman named George Garga. The offer has been carefully calculated to lead to combat. Searching for a worthy antagonist, Shlink has fastened on the salesman because Garga, bred in the prairies, still maintains a vestige of idealism in a city jungle where everything is for sale. When Garga takes the offer as an insult, Shlink makes him a victim of economic pressures, knowing that Garga will fight to retrieve his isolation and independence. The duel is on. But while Shlink fights only for the excitement of the encounter, Garga fights to kill, seeking his former freedom through Shlink's death.

Shlink accepts this passively, actually having hired Garga to kill him, and places his power, wealth, and fate at Garga's disposal. But Garga—sacrificing his family, his girl, and his personal ambitions for his revenge—uses these weapons to destroy Shlink indirectly, by making him his own executioner. Ordering the submissive Malayan to engage in a series of self-condemnatory activities, including the seduction of Garga's sister (who already loves Shlink without return), Garga also makes him contract a fraudulent business deal. When Shlink is caught, Garga voluntarily serves his jail sentence, but not before he has deposited a letter, to be opened upon his release, accusing Shlink of having "raped" his sister. Having thus kayoed Shlink with a "very blunt blow," Garga, like Judas, spends three last weeks with his victim, now on the run from a white lynch mob. Instead of concluding the business himself, he leaves Shlink to commit a ritual suicide, full of despair over the futility of the struggle. Liberated both from human and economic demands, Garga then returns gladly to the isolation he once enjoyed, with only a twinge of regret for the chaos which is past.

I have selected this line of development from an abundance of plot details in order to clarify the thematic content of the play, now a source of confusion to many commentators. For example, Brecht's brilliant biographer, Martin Esslin—ignoring the author's warning not to "wrack your brains over the motives of this fight"—has urged a homosexual interpretation, glancing at the relationship between Verlaine and Rimbaud. But while Rimbaud's influence is clear in the style of the play, such an explanation misplaces the emphasis, introducing a physical motive into an essentially metaphysical combat. I think this puzzling duel must be interpreted as a metaphor for man's effort to make contact in a world of terrible isolation. Garga, who merely wishes to survive, embraces this isolation for the sake of his spiritual freedom, but Shlink (like Strindberg who sought the "joy of life in its strong and cruel struggles") tries to transcend it through "enmity," the Romantic form of love. Shlink fails because in the jungle of cities man's skin has become so thick that he cannot even perish cleanly at the hands of an adversary. Unable to connect either through love or hate, armored from everything but his own suffering, the wild beast man walks alone in a prison of self, and "generation after generation looks coldly into the eyes of the next." In dramatizing the failure of the Romantic will-to-life, Brecht has descended into a nihilism so desperate that only his later commitment to Marxism is to save him from total despair.

The Living Theatre has conducted its own wrestling match with the work, and with a little more rehearsal time might have pinned its opponent conclusively. The production has a great number of felicities and virtues, but clarity is not often among them—the sum of the evening adds up to less than its individual parts. Gerhard Nellhaus' translation is partly to blame, for it is needlessly vague and verbose. Judith Malina's direction is thoughtful, imaginative, and relentless, and she has developed a tough jazzy cabaret style closer to Brecht's intention than anything I have seen in America, but her approach lacks focus and emphasis. And there is too much of Teijo Ito's eerie Oriental music which, chillingly effective in certain places, now tends to drown the dialogue.

On the other hand, Julian Beck's skeletal setting—a wrestling platform above which are suspended mobiles, Japanese lanterns, and various pieces of jetsam—is an artwork in itself. And though Garga is played too feebly to make the combat meaningful, many of the other performances are superb—notably Khigh Dhiegh who enacts Shlink with masterful inscrutability, great variety, and ritualistic grace; John A. Coe who makes his associate, Worm, an amiably sinister George Grosz cartoon in a bowler hat and cavalry mustache; and Marilyn Chris as Garga's boozy, pushover girl friend. The Living Theatre, in short, has very effectively evoked that weird gallery of gangsters, coolies, pimps, whores, sailors, and Salvationists which make up the grotesque population of this play, but the essence of the work has escaped them. But then perhaps the play is ultimately indefinable. Puzzling, provocative, and painful, it remains a tantalizing satanic masterpiece, its meaning barely visible at the bottom of a vast abyss.

(1961)

OFF BROADWAY'S TRIAL AND TRIUMPH

THE KING OF THE DARK CHAMBER
by Rabindranath Tagore

■ For over a decade now, the Off Broadway movement has been the major source of nourishment for the devitalized American stage, but lately even its robust arteries are showing signs of hardening. Accompanying its heightened prestige—and only crustaceans like Jule Styne (who finds the minority theatre anti-

American and anti-religious!) will still deny its importance—has come a growing reluctance to take bold chances. For like all successful revolutions, Off Broadway is turning into a conservative institution, developing along the way severe institutional problems. The rise in ticket prices and production costs, the employment of high-salaried actors from the commercial stage, the burgeoning of new high-rent theatres, the marked increase in press-agentry and advertising—all these tokens, along with a general decline in the quality of Off Broadway fare, suggest that powerful economic pressures are putting the squeeze on Off Broadway's aesthetic freedom. Significantly, a counter-movement has already been organized in the cabarets (off Off Broadway) where ambitious young groups operating on low budgets are trying to revivify the minority theatre's flagging revolutionary ideals.

The erosion of these ideals has certainly been accelerated over the past two seasons. In the past, Off Broadway devoted itself almost exclusively to three types of plays: 1) great works of the past, 2) important, neglected works of the modern theatre, and 3) experimental works by avant-garde writers. Since all of these categories are usually shunned by the commercial stage, Off Broadway was originally established as an alternative theatre for serious works of art. To some extent, it still serves that function today, though with a good deal less ferocity and zeal. This season, for example, we have been able to see superior productions of works by Brecht, Pirandello, and Denis Johnston. On the other hand, many of the modern masters have been so mauled, mangled, and mishandled (Ibsen, Shaw, O'Casey, and—especially—Strindberg are the year's most conspicuous victims) that their revival seems a dubious advantage; and the classic drama, Shakespeare excepted, is now hardly ever played at all. What is worse, a growing proportion of Off Broadway plays look like Broadway rejects. The accumulation of musicals in the minority theatre is a depressing sign of commercial accommodation; and so is the emphasis on such doubtful ex-Broadway commodities as *Camino Real*, *Clearing in the Woods*, *Montserrat*, and *Our Town*. As for new works, many of these now find their way into the minority theatre not because they are too good for Broadway but because they are not good enough. I cite, as an illustration, *Call Me by My Rightful Name*, a "sensitive" hothouse problem play, studded with unnecessary violence, about a Negro and a white fingering each other's souls in their search for "love" and "communication." This one is not only impertinent to both races ("The soul," said D. H. Lawrence, "is a dark forest") but aesthetically trying as well, featuring a climax from the movie version of *Home of the Brave*, dialogue from the *Late Late Show*, and even an alternate (happy) ending in case some Broadway producer should decide to take an option.

By contrast, the current production of Rabindranath Tagore's *King of the Dark Chamber* more than compensates for Off Broadway's recent failures, for it fulfills the highest function of the minority theatre. This twentieth-century Indian masterpiece, with its allegorical fairy-tale atmosphere and its highly charged poetic intensity, is a stunning theatrical work, stunningly interpreted by its director, Krishna Shah. Clearly an inspired dramatic artist, Tagore manages to exploit all the various resources of the stage—music, mime, chorus, lyrical speech, song, declamation, gesture, make-up, costume—in a completely original manner. For in his hands, the conventions of Eastern theatre are liberating devices rather than restrictions, freeing his imagination to an extent almost unequalled in the modern Western tradition. Tagore's dramatic world is so multivarious that elements of broad farcical humor, sinister melodrama, and metaphysical soul-drama can jostle one another with no apparent friction; and his dramatic action is so multileveled that it becomes fairy tale, metaphor, and philosophy all at once. Tagore achieves dramatic unity primarily through the simplicity and directness of his vision. In his suggestive narrative of a Queen who gradually grows in love with a King so ugly his features cannot be exposed to the light, his characters have been totally stripped of their superficial sophistication to reveal instead a charming and childlike naïveté. It is this ceremony of innocence that Yeats (in his *Plays for Dancers*) and Brecht (in his *Caucasian Chalk Circle*) tried to restore to the Western theatre as a necessary antidote to the clichés of an exhausted realism, for it was only by freeing the stage from sterile inhibitions that its limitless possibilities could be fully explored.

Krishna Shah's production manages to enhance the beauties of this work through a superb recreation of the techniques of Indian theatre. The action is bursting with graceful mime and amusing horseplay; the stage is always gorgeously dressed, whether in movement or in repose; the work with the chorus (which acts as trees, lights, fire, and doors) is extraordinarily inventive; and the presentational style he has adopted is hypnotic, ceremonious, and stately. Astonishingly enough, he has achieved his effects with a predominantly American cast, though he has been aided immeasurably by the presence of an exquisite Indian actress, Surya Kumari, as the Queen. Watching Miss Kumari is not only a directly sensuous pleasure (her face has a kind of joyous limpidity which has long since faded from the features of American women) but a histrionic triumph as well: her performance is full of breathless, yearning, delicate grace. As for the Americans, they have managed to transcend their psychological conditioning to achieve a rather primitive middle style, halfway between rhetoric and sing-song, but it is a pleasant surprise to see them move so fluidly and, instead of shoving their hands in their costumes, manipulating them in the ritualistic gestures of the mudras. A complimentary word should be said for all of Shah's collaborators, but I would especially like to commend Bhaskar for his effectively conceived and sinuously executed dances: they are a welcome relief from the pseudo-folksy calisthenics of Western choreography. The King of the Dark Chamber exposes you to a rare and beautiful experience which works on your spine like long, cool, tapered fingers. It is with such works, infrequent as they have become, that Off Broadway redeems its almost forgotten pledge.

(1961)

FRAGMENTS FROM A CULTURAL EXPLOSION

THE AMERICAN DREAM and THE DEATH OF
BESSIE SMITH by *Edward Albee and*
ROOTS by *Arnold Wesker*

■ It is often taken as a sign of progress and maturity that our formerly Philistine fatherland has now begun to consume artistic objects with an appetite fully as ravenous as that once reserved for comic books. The phrase for this awesome phenomenon, I believe, is "cultural explosion"—but out of this explosion have come only scattered shell fragments which we vainly try to shore against our ruins. For despite increasing activity and interest, our culture is in a state of severe impoverishment. While everyone, including monkeys and IBM computers, is busy "creating," almost nobody is creating well, and the appetite for genuine works of art remains dreadfully undernourished by the native approximations. This fact is dimly, though indirectly, reflected in the various organs devoted to initiating cultural fashions. America's fascination with artists has always been much greater than its interest in art, but you can't have one without the other; and *Life, Esquire,* the women's magazines, and the newspapers are all revealing a measure of desperation in trying to unearth "exciting new personalities" to feed to an insatiable public. Years ago—and this may explain the comparative honesty of his early work—Tennessee Williams completed over fifteen plays before anyone took the slightest notice of him. Today, a Lorraine Hansberry or an Archibald MacLeish need produce only a single salable commodity before their "dramatic genius" is proclaimed in every middle-brow publication in the land.

Edward Albee was first promoted into an "exciting new personality" on the basis of one short play (*The Zoo Story*), but now that he has added a couple more one-acters to the canon, the press is fairly bursting with enthusiastic epithets. In the last few weeks, he has been tintyped by *Time*, interviewed by *Theatre Arts*, produced by *Omnibus*, and fluttered over by all the reviewers, with the result that we now know every detail of his life and his opinion on every conceivable theatrical subject. The irony of this situation is only surpassed by its essential sadness. To be so easily gobbled up by the media would be a forbidding omen even in a playwright who has already proven his ability. But since Mr. Albee's talent is still in a rather immature stage of development, his premature fame may prove very damaging to his creative growth.

The American Dream and *The Death of Bessie Smith* are further evidence that Albee's talent has not yet found its way out of chrysalis. Both plays are inferior to *The Zoo Story*, but all three embody the same vital defect: the absence of any compelling theme, commitment, or sense of life which might pull them into focus. Lacking this larger vision, Albee's plays—while beginning auspiciously, with a pyrotechnic display of arch, brittle irony—always collapse at the finish, either into whimpering melodrama (*Bessie Smith*) or into embarrassing self-exposure (*American Dream*). The consequence, reflected in both productions (which also end feebly after promising beginnings), is an abrupt switch in tone, and sometimes a sense of bewildering irrelevance—as in *Bessie Smith* where a Gothic report of the blues singer's death in an auto accident is forcibly superimposed on the main story of a malignant Southern nurse (out of Williams) and an idealistic intern who unaccountably pursues her.

The disunity of *The American Dream* is more damaging, since it mars a better work. The play begins as a scorching satire on upper-middle-class family life (aggressive Mommy and castrated Daddy tormenting sweet-crusty Grandma), in which the fatuities of daily conversation are brutally excoriated through the use of clichés, small talk, and illogical non sequiturs. Albee, who has not yet developed his own style, borrows Ionesco's techniques here, and he manipulates them well in a febrile, somewhat bitchy manner. But while *The Bald Soprano* opened out on to all vacuous families, Albee closes in on one (and an odd one, too); and with strong suggestions of personal bitterness, the play shifts into a story of adoption. This shift is signified by the entrance of the "Dream," a fully grown Adonis in regulation theatre garb (blue jeans, tee shirt, cowboy boots) who proceeds to pour out toneless pathological confessions about his inability to feel, love, connect, be whole, etc. When Mommy, who has already dismembered his twin, adopts him, the curtain descends, while Grandma (now "dead") poignantly comments on the repetition from the wings. Thus, like *The Zoo Story*, this play begins as a sardonic comedy and ends as a whining letter to the chaplain, compromised by the author's inability to objectify or transcend the wounded Self.

To judge by *Roots*, Arnold Wesker would seem to be another dramatist who has been praised too quickly; compared with Albee, in fact, he looks like a theatrical primitive. For while *The American Dream* is a high-fidelity playback of the latest avant-garde tunes, *Roots* is written as if the author had just stumbled on John Galsworthy. The exacting naturalism of this rural kitchen drama, even more labored than necessary in the current tortoise-like production, is extremely oppressive: one is exhausted by the never-ending housework and heartburned by full-course meals. For the first two acts, absolutely nothing happens, except for a careful documentation of the dialect and habits of some English Jukes and Kallikaks, and, in the third, when the theme emerges, it is so naïve one blushes for the author. The play concerns a simple Norfolk girl who, influenced by her absent Jewish-Socialist lover, tries to convince her uncomprehending family of the joys of art, thought, politics, and life. Beginning as a ventriloquist's dummy for her lover's opinions, she discovers—after he has abandoned her—that she has developed her own soul. And the curtain falls on her ecstatic cry: "I'm beginning."

Clearly, Wesker wants art, and it is easy to dismiss this piece as boring and banal. But it is written with such overwhelming sincerity that one is somehow prevented from a final judgment. Actually, *Roots*—gagged as it is by mindless characters—is the weakest play in the *Chicken Soup* trilogy. In the other two works, Wesker has more complexity about both politics and human nature, and proves if not more artful than Albee, then certainly less self-indulgent. There, his theme is not the ennobling of the masses, but their brutalization by mass culture; and, like John Osborne and Doris Lessing, he dramatizes the dilemma of the powerless intellectual, hungry for a social faith, but disillusioned by the failures of the preceding generation. Thus, while the American dramatist responds to the confusions of his time by withdrawing into himself and fixing on his own career, the English playwright still keeps an eye cocked on that anxious, frightened world beyond. Needless to say, it is in England, not here, that the juices of the drama are beginning to flow.

(1961)

GENET'S CALL
TO THE COLORS

THE BLACKS *by Jean Genet*

■ Considering the fact that *The Blacks* is a ritual of murder, violence, and crime, enacted by Negro supremacists, and culminating in the ceremonial slaughter of the entire white race, its thunderous success here is really rather astonishing. One would hardly be surprised if Genet's celebration of race hatred found favor with an audience of Black Muslims; but the play is now being praised by the same liberal community which so heartily applauded *Raisin in the Sun* for its benevolence, charity, and racial togetherness. It could be, of course, that *The Blacks* has simply been misunderstood—after all, the *Times* reviewer seemed to interpret the work as a plea for interracial harmony. Then, again, perhaps the insularity of our stage is so complete that nobody cares what a play says as long as it fulfills the aesthetic requirements of "sheer theatre." I am inclined to favor, hopefully, a third possibility: namely, that audiences have become so surfeited with the liberalistic pieties, platitudes, and exhortations always mouthed in American plays about Negroes that they are finally open to a more radical treatment of race, one closer to the uncensored stuff of dreams than to the official doctrines of the N.A.A.C.P. Whatever the explanation, *The Blacks* is a depth charge of evil which sinks the spectator well below the placid surface of social benevolence to the dark sea floor of the unconscious, leaving him totally submerged beneath a torrent of primitive impulses, sado-masochistic hallucinations, and myths of danger. As such, the play may do a great deal of harm to the cause of inter-race relations, but it is cut to order for that alchemical theatre of cruelty envisioned by Artaud where the spectator's "taste for crime, his erotic obsessions, his savagery, his chimeras . . . even his cannibalism" would be vicariously indulged, and, thereby, momentarily purged.

Genet's genius for cruel myth-making is evident from the opening moments of the play when eight Negroes and Negresses, dressed in the height of flouncy elegance, begin dancing a stately minuet around a catafalque supposedly containing the corpse of a white woman, freshly killed for the performance. These are the props and actors in a ritual rehearsal of an earlier murder, to be re-enacted by the murderer, Deodatus Village, and judged by a White Court consisting of the Great Figures of European colonialism: Queen, Queen's valet, Judge, Missionary, and Governor. The entire affair, however (including the corpse which later proves to be nonexistent), is a fake—a masquerade performed by ritual celebrants who keep their true identity carefully concealed. For the actors (all of them Europeanized Negroes in middle-class professions) are determined to expose not their individual lives but their collective racial identity: the Blacks by "negrifying" themselves "to the point of madness in what they're condemned to be," and the Whites (Negroes in masks) by satirically celebrating, through hyper-cultured postures and inflections, the various triumphs of European civilization. Consistent with these roles, the Blacks labor to caricature or suppress all "White" ideas like love and tenderness, intensifying their atavistic poetry, savagery, and cannibalism, and finding their meaning solely through acts of hatred and revenge, while the Whites preside over the events from a raised platform, contemplating their failing racial authority ("Have courage, Madame, God is White"), exploiting Africa's resources and manpower, and covertly admiring Negro sexuality, spontaneity, and beauty.

Behind this stage ceremony, however, a series of real events—periodically and cryptically reported by a messenger—is taking place off stage: first the trial and execution of a Negro traitor, and then the emergence of a new Black Hero to carry on the battle against White supremacy. The theatrical ritual, in short, exists only to mask secret preparations for a Negro uprising. But at the same time that it draws attention from these preparations, it predicts their outcome. For Village's murder of an anonymous Woman (played by a sad Negro curate in blond curls and a pasty mask) symbolizes the massacre of Europe by African hordes, the Woman being nothing less than the Mother of the White Race (before she is disemboweled, she gives birth to dolls representing all the Great Figures). Proceeding into the jungle to avenge this archetypal crime, the Great Figures are themselves exterminated, as a crowing cock signals the beginning of a new era. But Genet's theory of history is cyclical, and, as inevitably as night gives way to day, the Whites will return again in ten thousand years to renew the conflict. The play ends with a repetition of the minuet around the catafalque—this time without the Whites, the Black prophecy having become a fait accompli and the ritualistic vision a mythic rite of a past historic event.

The Blacks no doubt sounds impossibly complicated, and perhaps the play is ultimately too dense and opaque to be a totally successful work of art. Genet has a Pirandellian obsession with the idea that human identity is defined by play-acting; and The Blacks, like The Balcony (which it resembles in so

many other ways), examines the artificiality of human behavior
in a world of rigid definitions. But whereas this philosophical
probing enriched the vision of sham in *The Balcony*, it merely
muddies the ritualistic line of *The Blacks*, and sometimes even
produces puzzling contradictions (for example, at times the
Negroes are enacting their own definition of Black, at other
times that of the White audience). Because of Genet's failure
to integrate his conscious preoccupations with his unconscious
fantasies, *The Blacks* remains an elusive enigma. But while it
fails as a philosophical drama, it stands triumphant as a cruel
purgative myth, enlivened by a fierce imagination, a rich theatrical sense, and some of the most superb poetic imagery in all
modern drama.

It is the fantastic, ritualistic element of the work that is best
realized in Gene Frankel's production. Working with a scimitar-
shaped ramp which leads from an open stage to a raised platform, Frankel has staged the play with an uncanny eye for
handsome physical effects, and paced the scenes with a kind of
voodoo frenzy to the accompaniment of jungle sounds, African
chants, and native dances. Obviously, Mr. Frankel's stage technique is now impeccable, but his theatricalist emphasis does not
help to clarify Genet's thematic line, and his actors—except for
Roscoe Lee Browne and James Earl Jones—are not always very
strong, or penetrating, or even well cast. On the other hand,
this is surely the best production of a Genet work yet seen in
New York—superior to Quintero's interpretation of *The Balcony* in that it is highly imaginative *without* sacrificing the text.
As for this text, whatever its failings, it clearly displays the mind
of a genius; and whatever the evil implications of the play, it is
a welcome tonic for a theatre where the Negro lacks any substantiality at all, being either transparent—which is to say, dis-
cernible only as an object of White guilt, prejudice, and benevolence—or totally invisible—which is to say, exactly the
same as everyone else. In restoring to the Negro his high visi-
bility, Genet inadvertently halts, if only for a moment, that
inexorable process of mass assimilation which is draining the
color from us all.

(1961)

DÉJÀ VU

HAPPY DAYS *by Samuel Beckett and*
PLAY *by Samuel Beckett*

■ *Happy Days* opens, to the accompaniment of a clanging alarm bell and a blinding flash of white light, on a woman buried up to her breasts in a barren mound of earth. "Another heavenly day," she murmurs—stretches—and quickly intones a few snatches of half-forgotten prayer. Fumbling in the large handbag which contains all the essentials of her sorry existence, she proceeds to extract and examine, with laborious attention, the various articles of her toilet, as well as a parasol, a revolver, a nail file, and a bottle of patent medicine. Having momentarily satisfied her pointless curiosity by finally deciphering the maker's guarantee on the handle of her toothbrush, she stops to affirm the wonder of life and the happiness of her days.

The name of this hopeful futilitarian is Winnie, and for the balance of this brief two-act work she chatters incessantly over such trifles, pitiably determined to invest that penal servitude which is her life with some semblance of interest—quoting fragments of "unforgettable lines" by English poets, peering into the audience to see if anyone is there, reflecting nostalgically on trivial events of the past, and, above all, trying to communicate with her uncommunicable husband, Willie, an ancient who passes the time sleeping in a hole behind her mound when he is not by her side (but just beyond her vision) mumbling over the want ads and obituaries in his yellowing newspaper. Willie and Winnie exist in a totally vacant world without diurnal distinctions—even to speak of "the end of the day" is to speak "in the old style"—where time seems both to have stopped and to be rushing madly forward, and where progress is measured only by the tedious-rapid advance toward dissolution, decay, and death. Thus, while Winnie is trying to kill time, time is more successfully killing her: by the beginning of the second act, the earth has risen to her neck, rendering her completely paralyzed. In this condition, she half-cheerfully, half-desperately, awaits total interment, still attempting to amuse herself with memories and to bless even her most harrowing perceptions. Finally, Willie appears from behind the mound, crawling on all fours and dressed for a funeral, arthritically groping toward the revolver which lies up the mound by his wife's right ear. Failing in his efforts, he slips painfully down the mound, whimpering Winnie's name, while she—mistaking this attempt at murder as an act of affection—affirms, with a kind of hideous ecstasy, that "this is a happy day. This will have been another happy day." They remain immobilized, as the bells begin to ring with ominous frequency, and the curtain descends.

Happy Days is Samuel Beckett's latest dramatic comment on the irony, pathos, and chronic hopelessness of the human condition; and like all his work it is triumphantly *sui generis*. Yet, it strikes me, despite certain obvious felicities in the writing, as the least of his dramatic efforts. The language is flat and prosaic, enjoying none of that poetic intensity which so ennobled *Krapp* and *Godot*, the symbols are almost nude in their unambiguousness, and those repetitions of which Beckett is so fond (successfully avoided only in *Krapp's Last Tape*) have finally become rather boring. Worst of all, Beckett has fallen into self-imitation, which is almost as serious as imitating others. His dramatic techniques, though they owe something to Maeterlinck, have always been extraordinarily compelling, but in *Happy Days*, these same techniques—by which I mean the abandonment of all anecdote, the manipulation of Bergsonian time, the static dream atmosphere, the use of two parallel days laid side by side, and the employment of a visual metaphor to convey a spiritual feeling—are used almost mechanically, possessing neither variety nor intensity. Even the most striking thing in the play—the image of Winnie claimed by the earth (signifying how death is constantly claiming us all)—is only a visualization of that beautiful perception in Godot: "They give birth astride a grave, the light gleams an instant, then it's night once more. . . . The gravedigger puts on the forceps." In short—and this is admittedly an odd complaint to lodge against a dramatist once thought to be the apostle of mystery, murk, and meaninglessness—Happy Days is too predictable; so obvious, in fact, that I experienced the uncomfortable sensation, before the evening was five minutes old, that I had written the play myself, and was none too pleased with my handiwork.

Alan Schneider's production is a perfectly competent rendering of the play—no more, no less. His interpretation is based on strict fidelity to Beckett's intention, but (though we must not underrate the directorial problems explicit in a play where the central character is literally rooted to the ground) it never transcends the basic requirements of the text to achieve an imaginative integrity of its own. Ruth White, as Winnie, has the stage practically to herself, and she never abuses her monopoly. She is a splendid actress, with a truly enviable range; but while she manages to sharpen all the tortuous twists of Winnie's shifting moods, I found her a little too much the pleasant Connecticut clubwoman to capture the timelessness and the placenessness of the role. Her cries of despair ("My arms. My breasts. What arms? What breasts? Willie. What Willie?") are nevertheless heart-rending, and so is her Pollyanna cheeriness.

What of Beckett? He is obviously in a dilemma. Like Ionesco, he has a single, all-encompassing vision of existence which leads him to seek not new themes but new metaphors with which to dramatize the same theme. But, again like Ionesco, he has so successfully persuaded us of the validity, coherence, and theatrical relevance of this vision that we are impatient when he repeats the lesson. Ionesco's recent work has exposed his severe limitations, and I doubt if he will ever be much more than a stunning secondary dramatist. But Beckett, with his superior power, beauty, and intelligence, has the capacity for greatness; and it is saddening to see him coast along on what he already knows. It remains to be seen whether Beckett will remain in the ditch or will develop in an entirely new direction. But whatever the future holds, his place in the drama is secure. In a world of the tenth-rate, even the minor work of this man is like an Orient pearl.

(1961)

■ ■

Beckett's new work, *Play*, is subtitled *An Act*—it is more like a spasm, since it comes and goes in an instant. Still, for all its brevity, it is a strangely compelling experience; and although Beckett is again using a rather familiar stage image, the piece is something of a new departure. Immobilized in three gigantic urns, above which only their tilted heads are visible, a man and two women stare blankly into the middle distance, unable to budge, unconscious of one another's presence. They represent a wife, her husband, and his sometime mistress, and now they seem to be imprisoned in one of the lower circles of hell, damned to ruminate eternally on their petty lives and vices. What they recite, in abrupt and discontinuous phrases, is a litany of adultery, punctuated by the man's dyspepsia, the woman's screams, and the wife's laughter, and conducted by a cold finger of light which picks at their heads with cruel indifference to pain. Guided by a malicious unseen will, this diabolical beam sets the rhythm and the tone of their damnation— regular and irregular, swift and lazy, stern and humorous. When the spotlight is switched off for a moment, the trio is left mumbling together in a ghastly mummified glow, a hellish triptych in a bourgeois inferno. Mr. Beckett takes about twelve minutes to complete this eerie tableau, thus proving what a deft poet he is; and he is deftly served by Alan Schneider's precise direction, and the flat, droning performances of Frances Sternhagen, Marian Reardon, and Michael Lipton.

(1964)

ON FINDING A CURE
FOR SYPHILIS

GHOSTS *by Henrik Ibsen*

■ When *Ghosts* was first performed in the English-speaking world, it was greeted by one reviewer as "an open drain; a loathsome sore unbandaged; a dirty act done publicly; a lazar-house with all its doors and windows open," while his colleagues rallied to his support with a barrage of disease images so unwholesome that they could have formed the basis for a *Glossary of Fetid Terms* by Eric Partridge. One of the main reasons for all this delicious vituperation, I suppose, was Oswald's syphilis, a then unmentionable subject since it was unconditionally guaranteed to bring a blush to the cheek of the young person. Today, when the blush is obsolete and the journalistic vocabulary of abuse has dwindled to a few gray monosyllables, we must be satisfied with less colorful, though more patronizing, techniques for keeping Ibsen at a safe distance. For a glimpse into these, I refer you to the reviews of the current production of *Ghosts*, where, amidst the inevitable arguments over the pros and cons of "naturalism," you will find three general types of evaluation: 1) since syphilis is curable, the play is dated, 2) though syphilis is curable, the play is not altogether dated, and 3) because syphilis is curable, the play should never have been written in the first place. Still fixed on Oswald's unfortunate malady, a contemporary review can nevertheless be confidently expected to consist less of discussions of the play than of unsolicited testimonials to Sir Alexander Fleming and his discovery of penicillin. Now that a knowledge of syphilology is

essential equipment for every reviewer of *Ghosts*, I wish to
display my own credentials with the following clinical observation: Oswald's congenital disease is *not* curable, even by modern methods, because it is first detected only in an advanced
stage when his brain cells have already been damaged.

I relieve myself of this information in the vain hope that we
may at last put this dreary debate to bed, and turn our attention
from the latest medical advances to what Ibsen actually wrote.
For, considering the broken lines of communication between
the theatre and dramatic scholarship, it is obviously necessary to
repeat what even the most casual student of Ibsen already
knows: that *Ghosts* is not dated, is not naturalistic, is not about
Oswald, and is concerned with hereditary syphilis only as a
metaphor for Fate or Destiny. What Ibsen attempted here was
a modern tragedy constructed on a Sophoclean pattern, beginning just before the catastrophe and proceeding, by a process of
exhuming past events, to a terrible, though needlessly equivocal
conclusion. The theme of the work is that the ghosts of the
dead inhabit the bodies of the living, or, put another way, that
the mistakes of the past control the events of the present. It is
true that the title refers also to the phantoms of dead beliefs,
the persistence of which Ibsen dedicates substantial energies to
combating; and it is also true that some of the author's arguments, suffering the fate he prophesied for all ideas, have become a little ghostly themselves. But the validity of the work is
preserved because, on its deepest level, the drama of ideas is
always kept subordinate to a pattern of tragic action. The central character, Mrs. Alving, is not simply a *raisonneuse*, mouth-
ing the author's opinions, but also a tragic protagonist whose
suffering demonstrates the hollowness of even the most emancipated opinions when not backed with radical acts. Mrs. Alving
believes that she will be able to repudiate the dreadful Alving
inheritance if only she can interpret events correctly, and that
merely revealing to Oswald the truth about his father will be
enough to save him from destruction. But when the sun of
enlightenment comes up, permitting Oswald to "see your home
properly," he very fittingly goes mad. Mrs. Alving—pressed to
an act of euthanasia at the end, and screaming with character-

istic indecision—has learned, like Oedipus, that the past is un-redeemable, for her early decision to remain with her profligate husband after she had stifled his emotional life was, like Oedi-pus' killing of Laius at the crossroads, an initial error which started inexorable destructive engines in motion. Ghosts, in short, is about tragic Necessity, and with all due respect to Dr. Fleming, I don't think he has yet perfected a cure for that.

Considering the Pavlovian response that was to be expected from the reviewers, David Ross should probably be decorated for attempting the play at all; but I have a sneaking suspicion that he thinks Ghosts is about syphilis too. At all events, his production is hopelessly superficial. Some of the difficulties, ad-mittedly, can be attributed less to Mr. Ross than to Mr. Ross's theatre: to stage Ghosts in the three-quarters is to sacrifice three-quarters of its illustrative power. The symbolic garden, for ex-ample, associated with the sensuality and fertility of Regina and her mother, has been reduced to a few floral decorations on the side of the stage; and we have, therefore, lost our view, through the conservatory windows, of the fjord, so essential as a con-trasting image of the wild, natural life outside (in an ideal production, the fjord would be the last thing seen by the spec-tator, the cliffs around it looming up in rebuke). The limita-tions of the theatre, however, do not explain why Mr. Ross has chosen to ignore Ibsen's careful instructions about the lighting: why the stage is flooded with brightness when the author insists on gloom and drizzle, and why Mrs. Alving has been separated from her symbolic "enlightening" lamp. Nor can I understand why Oswald recalls the most nauseating experience of his child-hood (when his father made him smoke a pipe) as if he were remembering an afternoon of cake and candy; why Regina de-clares her Viking amorality and independence at the end in a tone of slobbering self-pity; why all indications have been muted that Engstrand's Sailor's Home is actually a brothel; why the company is so consistently miscast; or why the staging is so consistently awkward. I must break off my longer list of "whys" here, adding only a question about the text. The play was adapted by Carmel Ross from a translation of R. Farquharson Sharpe's, and between them they have managed to produce a version which sounds remarkably like William Archer's. I have no objection to this, since I believe Archer's translations to be unfairly maligned, but why—when the play is already short and every sentence is essential—must it have been so remorselessly cut?

(1961)

THE ABSURD
AND THE RIDICULOUS

THE THEATRE OF THE ABSURD by Martin
Esslin and THE THEATRE OF THE ABSURD at
the Cherry Lane Theatre; 3 × 3; OH DAD,
POOR DAD, MAMMA'S HUNG YOU IN THE
CLOSET AND I'M FEELIN' SO SAD by Arthur Kopit

■ That the faddists and the fashionmongers have now begun to exploit the avant-garde drama is hardly the fault of Martin Esslin—but his recent book, The Theatre of the Absurd, has partly determined the shape and content of this exploitation. Mr. Esslin's study of the modern experimental dramatists is undoubtedly an authentic contribution to knowledge. Informative, exhaustively researched, and bulging with useful facts, it has real value as an encyclopedic aid to scholars working in the field. Its influence on aspiring playwrights, playgoers, and cocktail party conversationalists, however, is bound to be less salutary. Though on one occasion (an analysis of Beckett) the book performs a genuine critical act, its critical judgments are often faulty, inflated, or misleading: Mr. Esslin praises Ionesco's worst work, overvalues Adamov, elaborates on an unending host of insignificant imitators, and tries to make Genet an important part of a tradition to which he does not belong. Furthermore, the disorganization of the book suggests that, if it was researched at leisure, it was written in haste; and much of the work is so mechanical that it seems to have been produced by a thinking machine. Mr. Esslin repeatedly refers to concepts like "the absurdity of the human condition" without ever convincing you that these concepts bear any relation to feelings; and his relentless catalogue of biographies, synopses, themes, and principles eventually creates the illusion in the reader's mind that every playwright is really the same person. Having theorized at length about this anti-theoretical drama, Mr. Esslin inadvertently reduces it to a formula—a manual of avant-garde dramaturgy, subject to imitation by every opportunistic scribbler. And though he frequently cautions us to regard each playwright as an inspired individual rather than just a figure in a movement, the effect of his exertions is to make us overwhelmingly conscious of the fashion—and a good deal less aware of the art.

The repertory program at the Cherry Lane, also called The Theatre of the Absurd, is an attempt to capitalize both on the fashion and on Esslin's book, the faults of which it shares. Also produced in too great a hurry, it too lumps the major and the minor together without enough discrimination, while making bedfellows of dramatists who would not particularly enjoy one another's company. I suppose, if we must concern ourselves with movements, that Beckett's drama of the fallout shelter, Endgame, and Ionesco's assault on the planned society, The Killer, might be forced into the same program, though the latter is a tedious work; and Edward Albee's The American Dream is an accurate enough imitation of The Bald Soprano (with additional characters and dialogue by T. Williams) to belong as well. But Genet's Deathwatch is totally sui generis; Albee's The Zoo Story is a compound of Genet, Williams, and Ginsberg; Richardson's Gallows Humor is descended from the French and German philosophical drama; and Arrabal's Picnic on the Battlefield, though it qualifies as an Absurdist play, does not qualify as art. Furthermore, most of the productions are warmed-over soup, having been offered by the same producers in the recent past; and though I did not return to all the shows

I had already seen, the ones I did see were largely unsatisfactory. Alan Schneider's version of *Endgame* has been revived, suffering a little from *rigor mortis* and from Ben Piazza, who plays Clov with a Southwestern drawl and a Method shuffle (Vincent Gardenia's Hamm, however, while unfinished, is a moving performance); and Donald Davis' production of *Deathwatch*—also scuttled by Piazza who enacts Green Eyes like the juvenile lead in a TV series—is self-conscious, arty, awkward, and quite inferior to the version of a few seasons back.

To me, the most original American play on the program was also the most modest: a series of blackout sketches called *Bertha*, by Kenneth Koch. Mr. Koch—also represented by *George Washington Crossing the Delaware* in *3 X 3*, another (short-lived) program of experimental plays—has discovered an inexhaustible vein of dramatic material: the corpus of Western myth, historical anecdote, and fairy tale, all of which he mocks gently in the anachronistic accents of romantic verse drama. In *Bertha*, amusingly directed by Nicola Cernovich and played with cranky affection by Sudie Bond, he follows the wacky adventures of a mad Norwegian Queen, redolent of every heroic Queen in fact and fiction, as she overcomes the Barbarians, decapitates her Counselor ("Let Higher Learning be dis-rein-stated!"), conquers Scotland, forbids (like Elizabeth I) lovers' garden meetings, and permits the Barbarians to triumph again so that she can reconquer them. In *George Washington*, he recreates, with the help of his director, Arthur Storch, a grammar-school pageant—replete with tableaux, blank verse, and cardboard props. Cornwallis and his redcoats praise the manly bearing of the American commander ("his shoes have a high polish"); Washington's soldiers advance in whispers while offering each other tobacco in the tones of cigarette commercials; and, in a dream sequence, Washington conjures up six-year-old Georgie ("the little squint") chopping down the cherry tree and running like hell from his malevolent father: "I cannot tell a lie. But I can run. I can flee from injustice." With this ingenious scalpel, Koch not only cuts through the absurdities of a stiff American legend, but slices into the degenerative tissue of a corrupt society which still pays homage, mechanically, to heroes it has become unworthy of.

With Arthur Kopit's *Oh Dad, Poor Dad*, the avant-garde fashion turns chi-chi. Jerome Robbins has obviously poured a fortune into his production, possibly to hide the thinness and immaturity of the play. But though the cash tinkles too loudly sometimes, let us be grateful for the things that money can buy. While Jo Van Fleet struggles to be flamboyant in a part (Madame Rosepettle) that is a little too rich for her naturalistic blood, Barbara Harris as a lecherous Betty Boop and Austin Pendleton as a stammering Mamma's boy are excellent acquisitions; and Mr. Robbins' imaginative use of props (spitting piranhas, collapsing furniture, animated flytraps) and of graphics (each scene is preceded by an elaborate movie credit, composed of surrealist montages) provide enough amusement to be worth the expense. As for the play—which Robbins has correctly directed like a cartoon—the final scene has a grisly humor, revolving as it does around a corpse which keeps falling on a laconic girl while she is trying to make love; but the rest of the work is inadequate and derivative. Mr. Kopit shares with Broadway psychological playwrights an abiding distaste for mothers and potential mothers, expressed by displaying females in possessive, smothering, and emasculating attitudes. With Tennessee Williams, he evokes a predatory world populated by man-eating fish, man-eating plants, and man-eating women. And with a growing number of aspiring young dramatists, he has a tendency to ape the techniques of avant-garde without adding anything original of his own. It is this desire to join a parade rather than to communicate a unique vision that tends to reduce the Absurd to the ridiculous. And though it offers excellent copy for journalists, it threatens to make the American Absurdist movement as arid a cultural phenomenon as the late, unlamented Generation of the Beats.

(1962)

THE SHADOW
OF A NOBLE SHADOW

ROSMERSHOLM *by Henrik Ibsen*

■ I often envy my colleague on the movie page his pleasant occupation. He follows a medium pulsing with youthful energy, while the theatre puffs and gasps like an exhausted sprinter stumbling toward the last post. But though his job is more consistently enjoyable than mine, I need only remember the masterpieces of recent dramatic literature (not to mention those of the Greeks and Elizabethans) to come to myself again: I would not trade one for a storage-house of films. The movies inspire one with a sense of promise, the theatre with a sense of fulfillment; the one is all future, the other all past. Yet, Antonioni, Bergman, Kurosawa, and the other gifted film-makers of our time, seem no more than interesting neophytes beside such figures as Ibsen, Strindberg, Chekhov, Brecht; and while a modest Hollywood picture provides more true amusement than the most portentous Broadway play, nothing has yet hit celluloid to match the power and complexity of real dramatic art. The theatre may be dead, but it is certainly haunted by an illustrious army of shadows; and though these shadows mock our present endeavors, they can still invoke in us a sense of awe and possibility.

Having thus cheered myself up, I must gloomily admit that the American theatre is rarely visited by more than a shadow of a shadow: its infrequent revivals are almost invariably botched. True professionalism, perhaps scenting the end, has begun to abandon our stage; and true interpretive intelligence has never been there. The best we have is good intentions, paving the way to an artistic vacuum. Fearing that the well-intentioned fumblers will soon chase great plays from our stage forever (thus robbing me of my critical *raison d'être*), I am just about ready to swear out writs of injunction—the first one going to David Ross, enjoining him to stay away from Ibsen. Like his two previous assaults on Ibsen's drama, Ross's production of *Rosmersholm* is just finished enough to persuade the reviewers that the play—and not the players—is the source of the evening's aridities; but the fact is it takes a heap of bungling to make Ibsen's house a tomb. Examined in the study, *Rosmersholm* is thick and juicy, devious and profound, fleshed with ambiguity and mystery; at the Fourth Street Theatre, it is thin, starchy, windy, obvious, and superficial—a collection of advanced Victorian opinions so watered down that the *Times* reviewer was stimulated to observe that "we" (*we!*) have grown more "tough-minded" than Ibsen!

If the "tough-minded" journalists are right, and the play is mainly the author's defense of outmoded opinions about emancipated women, free love, and freethinking, then Mr. Ross's production, for all its inadequacies, is probably justified. For he has directed the play like a stilted melodrama of ideas in which the representative of Conservatism and Evil (Professor Kroll, played by Patrick Waddington in sibilant whispers and archaic stances) combats the representative of Liberalism and Good (Pastor Rosmer, played by Donald Woods like an Ethical Culturist dieting on homogenized milk) against a love story background out of Daphne Du Maurier's *Rebecca*. Except for Nancy Wickwire, who, in other circumstances, might have made a strong and willful Rebecca West, nobody even dents the surface of his role; and even Miss Wickwire's emotional power tends to evaporate in the general blandness of the atmosphere where all wildness has been suppressed and all complexity stifled in the embarrassed gestures of the players.

A cursory glance at the text, however, should convince us that Ibsen is less interested here in ideas than in the people who hold them: in their blindness, conditioning, and guilty secrets. This work he has structured not as an ideological melodrama (like *Enemy of the People*) but as a detective story (like *Ghosts*); and there are enough supernatural hints (e.g., the

White Horses) to suggest the atmosphere of a ghost story as well. *Rosmersholm*, in short, is not only political, but profoundly psychological, even metaphysical. It is less a drama of broad daylight than of half-lights and shadows—less a brush along the surface than a journey into the hidden soul.

Consider the action. Johannes Rosmer, scion of an influential line of clerics and statesmen, has decided to break with the traditional conservatism and morality of his house. Though vaguely guilty over the suicide of his first wife, Beata, he has fallen under the influence of her emancipated companion, Rebecca West. And having repudiated his religious beliefs, he now wishes to devote himself to the ennoblement of mankind. For separate reasons, this brings him in conflict both with the Liberals and the Conservatives; and when he discovers the opportunism and maliciousness of his enemies, his convictions about man's instinctually moral nature are shaken. He loses faith in his ideals altogether when Rebecca confesses that she caused Beata's death—motivated by sexual passion for Rosmer, and exploiting Beata's lesbian passion for her. Declaring that the Rosmer way of life has ennobled her, Rebecca agrees to restore Rosmer's ideals by committing suicide herself, and Rosmer joins her in the millrace. The White Horses appear because the dead have claimed them—not only Beata but Rosmer's ancestors. He has returned, at the end, to their traditional morality—to the concepts of sin and atonement, even without God.

The motives of Rebecca, however, are complicated enough to have inspired speculation by Sigmund Freud, who examines her curious refusal to accept Rosmer's earlier marriage proposal, her uncharacteristic confession of guilt, and her sudden acquisition of conscience. Finding the key in the third-act revelation that Rebecca had, unknowingly, been the mistress of her own father, Freud concludes that Rebecca admits to a lesser crime (murder) in order to conceal the greater (incest), and turns down Rosmer to avoid repeating this offense. The typical fantasy of the governess, a projection of the Oedipus complex, is to get rid of the mistress and take her place with the master. Rebecca has acted out this fantasy, partly, with Dr. West, and is about to realize it fully with Rosmer; but the incestuous implications of the deed infect her will. As for her transformed nature, this, indeed, is the result of her association with Rosmer—just as her Viking amorality stemmed from her association with the free-thinking Dr. West—for rather than being an emancipated woman, she merely takes on the quality of her paternal influence. Incest, lesbianism, murder—these are the crimes which lie concealed beneath the humdrum surface of everyday life, coiled like some prehistoric reptile ready to strike at our illusions of progress, emancipation, and enlightenment. For despite the literal reality of Ibsen's world, he deals in primeval myths; and like the archetypal detective stories (*Oedipus*) and ghost stories (*Hamlet*), *Rosmersholm* has the power of a probing, tragic work.

Neither this nor anything else of substance is suggested on the Fourth Street stage, but I am still not quite prepared to switch my loyalties to the movies. For whatever the actuality, the ideal theatre still compels us; and despite the pleasing surface of the films, it is in the depths of the drama that the human soul continues to be revealed.

(1962)

OFF BROADWAY TRIO

Brecht on Brecht arranged by George Tabori,
Desire Under the Elms by Eugene O'Neill;
Six Characters in Search of an Author
by Luigi Pirandello

■ *Brecht on Brecht* is a selection of the German playwright's writings, carefully edited to cast a warm glow. In Tabori's program, Brecht emerges as a liberal, anti-Nazi humanitarian, discomforted only by the plight of the poor, the dispossessed, and the persecuted—a kind of Barry Gray with talent. To use

Brecht's own phrase, he has been made "nice instead of bold"
—all the danger has been removed from his works—and even
when the author's voice scratchily comments on his life and
plays, there is nobody to tell us that these remarks were recorded at a Congressional investigation into his politics. For
Tabori's Brecht apparently *has* no politics—neither the simple
Stalinism with which he is sometimes mistakenly credited nor
the ambiguous Marxism he actually held—and without a politics of indignation, Brecht is almost indistinguishable from
Thornton Wilder. The production, too, under Gene Frankel's
surprisingly ersatz direction, is a model of unctuous geniality.
The actors, in this staged reading, wink, smile, and twinkle at
one another so much that I wanted to throw my coat at them.
And when they are not nodding sanctimoniously over the old
philosopher's sage apothegms, they are undermining Brecht
through their interpretations of his works: one throwing fits of
hysterics in *The Jewish Wife*, another turning Galileo into a
sentimental dullard, still another dripping molasses over an un-
born child in a scene from *The Good Woman*. Only Lotte
Lenya—cold, metallic, seemingly detached from the proceedings—conveys some of the steel and ice that were in Brecht.
But even her presence fails to authenticate this factitious attempt to make Brecht fashionable.

(1962)

■   ■

Desire Under the Elms, I suspect, has achieved its reputation
by default. Compared with such sluggish behemoths as *Strange
Interlude*, *Mourning Becomes Electra*, and *Lazarus Laughed*, it
is a miracle of control and understatement; and even its grunt-
ing, monosyllabic dialogue, where "purty" and "ay-eh" are re-
peated until your brain clogs, is something of a relief after
O'Neill's more windy verbalizing in this period. On the other
hand, the play contains the same painful self-consciousness as
all of O'Neill's middle dramas—the tragic posturing, the phony
elementalism, the dreadful plotting, the omnipresent incest—
and next to the terrifying honesty of his last works, it seems very

hollow indeed. Still, it is a better play than one would guess from the production at Circle in the Square, where it looks like Our Town as written by somebody in the middle of a hysterical seizure. José Quintero is indebted to Thornton Wilder for his techniques of dressing a scene, but he is a true child of Kazan in his passion for meaningless frenzy: yelps and yowls render much of the evening incomprehensible. Rip Torn and George C. Scott contribute generously to the general incoherence, both demonstrating that acting has long since left the neurasthenic stage, and entered the pathological. Torn, playing Eben like a refugee from a Texas lunatic asylum, giggles when he is in despair, stares blankly when he is happy, and spits when he is undecided. And Scott, playing Ephraim like an aging Richard III—shuffling, hoarse, stiff-necked, his eyes bouncing with mad evil—is beginning to use the stage not for purposes of communication but rather for violence and aggression. I am grateful to Colleen Dewhurst for enacting a role and not a psychotic episode; but I did not think she was particularly well cast as Abbie, which she played like a beefy Earth Mother, all smiles, teeth, hairbun, and bosom.

(1963)

■　■

Ever since the time, eight years ago, when that old whip-master, Tyrone Guthrie, transformed Pirandello's tragi-comedy of the theatre into an animal circus with magical acts, Six Characters in Search of an Author has been in search of a director; in William Ball, it has found one to redeem that other ill-conceived event. Ball's current revival of Six Characters is the most splendid directorial work of the season, and if this seems like faint praise, let me add that it restores one's belief in a meticulous theatre artistry. Ball brings to his work the flamboyant theatricality of the young Orson Welles, along with values that Welles often lacked—exquisite taste, and abiding respect for an author's intention. From the initial appearance of the six, bathed in an eerie luminous halo and undulating like black waves of mourning, until the moment when the panic-stricken director scurries out of the house, leaving a bridge of spots swaying ominously over an empty stage, an atmosphere is sustained so brilliantly that one cannot even pause to admire the precision of the workmanship or the imaginativeness of the approach. Yet, precision and imagination are abundantly displayed, accompanied by a firm, controlling intelligence taking infinite pains.

This rare intelligence is clear enough in the production scheme, which solves a vexing theatrical problem. Pirandello's satire on stage illusion, paradoxically, demands an illusionistic stage; the spectators must be persuaded that an actual rehearsal is in progress at which they themselves are not present. Because of this, and because Pirandello wrote for a uniquely Italian theatre, the play has never been satisfactorily adapted to American stage conditions. But in Paul Avila Mayer's very sensible translation, the action has been removed to an Off Broadway theatre, where a group of experimental actors, dominated by a fussy, intellectualistic director in pipe pants, are rehearsing a stylized avant-garde drama before an invited audience of college students. Furthermore, when the six characters arrive, the actors are permitted to have human reactions to them; and, unlike the hammy matinee idols of Guthrie's production, they try to enact the characters' roles with some conviction, employing the fashionable techniques of "sense memory" and "emotional recall." Thus, the histrionic reality is not simply a burlesque of actual reality; it is just inadequate to it. And if the actor-character relationship is less comic than it might be, it is much more real.

This reality is further amplified by the characters themselves, who, in this version, make even the rather tedious first-act background exposition the occasion for dramatic tension. The family's memories, for example, are no longer narrated but enacted —even the Stepdaughter's appeals to the "Author" (represented on stage by an empty white chair) are fully represented. As for the two scenes the "Author" actually wrote—the one in Madame Pace's dress shop, the other in the garden— these mount to a feverish climactic excitement, as the Father, entering with the bedside manner of a well-paid physician, comes to seduce the Stepdaughter, and, later, the Boy shoots himself, falling off a ladder after a hair-raising chase. The lighting designer, Jules Fisher, is a master of his craft, and the entire cast is superb. But I do wish the director had persuaded the actors to forgo the curtain calls. To reintroduce the conventions of the stage after such reality is to let the audience wriggle away when it was firmly in your grasp.

(1963)

BRECHT ON THE RAMPAGE

MAN IS MAN by Bertolt Brecht, translated by Gerhard Nellhaus: Living Theatre; A MAN's A MAN by Bertolt Brecht, adapted by Eric Bentley

■ At the conclusion of Shaw's St. Joan, when the Maid—long martyred and newly canonized—offers to return to earth as a living woman, all her worshipers blench. "What?" she asks. "Must I burn again? Are none of you ready to receive me?" Cauchon replies: "The heretic is always better dead. And mortal eyes cannot distinguish the saint from the heretic." Mortal eyes have had a similar difficulty, lately, with Bertolt Brecht. A heretic recently sanctified by Pope Fashion, Brecht is still totally unacceptable as a living being. For the past year, the dramatist's remains have been on display in a crypt called Brecht on Brecht, where a few trifling pieces of his anatomy—raised eyebrows, wrinkled nose, twinkling eyes—have become objects of veneration by a relic-hungry public. But when the living Brecht, a compound of spleen, horns, and genitalia, rampages like a maddened bull down our tame, "sophisticated" stage, the audiences, and the reviewers, begin to scatter in terror. Instead of a genial Socratic humanitarian with some neat theatrical tricks up his sleeve, an ugly, brutal, dangerous artist confronts them; and Brecht must burn again.

Unfleshed, repetitive, and sometimes a little tedious, Mann

ist Mann is a minor work of its author, but since this makes it a major work of any New York season, one suspects the offense lies in its heresy: it is a savage clown show which uses the devices of farce, vaudeville, Expressionism, and cabaret theatre to demonstrate the total insignificance of the individual personality in the modern world. Located in a fantastic, Kipling-esque India, complete with Imperial British soldiers, an Oriental bonze, an all-girl orchestra, and the ubiquitous Widow Begbick (she appears again in that superb Brecht-Weill masterpiece, *Mahagonny*), the play follows the metamorphosis of the meek laborer, Galy Gay, into the "human fighting machine," Jeriah Jip. The real Jip, the fourth member of a machine-gun unit, has been incapacitated while drunkenly helping to plunder a Chinese pagoda; his three comrades need someone to conceal their own part in this hilariously funny crime; and Gay, "a man who can't say no," looks like the ideal fall guy. The soldiers, however, have to impress upon Gay the dangers of insisting on one's name; and they do so in a series of fast circus numbers, during which Gay is apprehended for selling a phony elephant—tried, convicted, shot (with blanks), and forced to read a funeral oration over his own corpse. These tactics of terror are partially effective, but what really transforms Gay into Jip is the fate of the sadistic sergeant, Bloody Five. An army-manual martinet when the sun shines, Bloody Five cannot control his gargantuan lust when it rains; and in order to remain "myself," he is ultimately forced to shoot away his manhood. Gay, witnessing the violent consequences of being a "great personality," is finally convinced of the importance of being a cipher, for acquiescence means safety and survival. Wolfing down the rations of his three tormentors, he proceeds to blow up, single-handedly, a Tibetan fortress. Gay equals Jip. Man equals Man. One man's the same as another.

"As has been demonstrated"—so ends a later version of the play—and reviewers have been inclined to criticize the Q.E.D. simplicity of the plot line. But the simplicity lies in them—the play is exceedingly devious, its complexity rooted in the author's ambiguous feelings toward his own demonstration. For Brecht is saying both that the human will is weak and malleable, and that it is savage, brutal, and uncontrollable—that man is forced to conform by a cruel, oppressive society, and that he must conform in order to suppress the murder in his heart. Brecht's horrified awareness of external and internal anarchy accounts for his rejection of Romantic individualism, and it is the subject of all his early, semi-autobiographical work. In *Baal*, for example, he follows the career of a ruthless, bisexual poet who satisfies his instincts without conscience, and finally dies amidst offal and urine, declaring that the world is merely "the excrement of God"; in *In the Jungle of Cities*, he shows the awful consequences of maintaining personal opinions, concluding when his rebellious hero repudiates his idealism in order to escape with his "naked life"; and in *Mann ist Mann*, he rejects altogether the chaos of personal identity, beginning to insist on the complete extinction of the personality. From this, it is only one step either to Communism or to Buddhism; and, as a matter of fact, Brecht commits himself to Communism like a submissive Buddhist monk, trying to lose himself in a process which will satisfy both his impulse to revolt, and his desire to discipline his terrifying aggressive impulses. But no matter how "rational," "scientific," and ideological the surfaces of his plays become, the depths are always rumbling with poetic intensity and Neo-Romantic horror, and those savage aggressions which Brecht could never quite subdue.

The two versions now on view at the Masque and The Living Theatre represent two stages in Brecht's continual revisions of the play. Eric Bentley's free adaptation of an earlier text emphasizes its comic-anarchistic elements, Gerhard Nellhaus' translation of a later variant, its more serious Marxist implications. Those interested in the development of Brecht's thinking will profit from both, for both are excellent. Both productions should also be seen, though for opposite reasons. Neither is excellent; and only between them can one begin to collate a satisfactory interpretation. John Hancock's production at the Masque has the advantage of a strong external concept, aided by Bentley's interpolated additions (including a wicked parody of "Gunga Din"). An amusing prologue and ironic legends introduce the action; the high button shoes, fringed dresses, and ratty fur pieces of the women evoke the smoky decadence of the Berlin cabarets; and the clever use of make-up illustrates first the contrast, then the union, between Gay and the others, as he gradually assumes the pasty white mask that everyone wears.

But the acting at the Masque is too casual and relaxed, not sufficiently ironic or styled. John Heffernan as Gay—too much the corn-fed innocent throughout most of the evening—creates a fine surrealistic concluding scene in which he roars about the stage like a tank stripping its gears, and Clifton James occasionally suggests some of the bloated menace that should be in the soldiers. But the rest of the military seems to have been recruited from the Harvard R.O.T.C. (Bloody Five from the U.S. Marines), and the whores tend to mince like Wellesley girls. At The Living Theatre, the acting is also indifferent; but at least it is not middle-class. Some of the performances are amateurish; some, like Joseph Chaikin's Galy Gay, too screechingly intense. Still, three characters leap from the stage with astonishing life: Warren Finnerty's fierce cockney Bloody Five; William Shari's reptilian Uriah; Benjamin Hayeem's Mr. Wang, a nasal, whining, toothy, obsequious Oriental cartoon. And though Julian Beck's functional bamboo and canvas setting is more impressive than his direction, he does manage to get a harsh, macabre, dirty quality into the play which sometimes startles you into discomforted attention.

Mann ist Mann shows Brecht thumbing his nose at nineteenth-century ideals, which is to say, at the ideals held by most of the twentieth-century West: freedom, heroism, liberalism, and the sanctity of "personal opinions." "An easygoing man can really have two or three different opinions at the same time," notes one cynical character—(if you doubt the truth of this, read a review by Howard Taubman)—and Brecht's agonized perception of the insignificance of the individual in a Copernican universe forms the basis both of his politics and of his art. Mass wars and mass states prove his contention; but his art belies it. For in writings like Brecht's the complicated opinions of a highly gifted individual still find their expression, transformed into an enduring testament of unremitting revolt.

(1962)

TONIGHT WE TRY
TO IMPROVISE

THE PREMISE at The Premise; To THE
WATER TOWER at The Second City

■ Since the war, advanced creative activity in America has come to rely increasingly upon improvisation, a technique which aims to add spontaneity, personality, and chance to the more rigid components of traditional art forms. From its beginnings in jazz, American-type improvisation has had a radically Romantic coloration—emotionally charged, unconsciously stimulated, and, above all, intensely personal. In the most extreme improvisational art, Action painting, the improvising artist even suppresses line and theme entirely, recording instead his mystical emotional state at the moment of composition. Literature is by nature less accidental, self-indulgent, and subliminal, since words are less emotive than colors, but whenever a writer tries to improvise, the subjective element in his work, nevertheless, becomes very prominent. Salinger's "Seymour," for example, despite its characteristic winks and literary blushes, is a relatively honest attempt to convey the author's feelings toward his material in the act of writing it; and it would have been better understood if critics had stopped arguing over whether or not Seymour is a saint, and explored the technical innovations of the story, which is an account of the actual process of literary composition, improvised out of anguish and frustration. American-type improvisation, then, emphasizes the process of the subjective artist as well as the content of his objectified art—through improvising, the creator becomes a performer.

Theatrical improvisation, on the other hand, is the work of those who are already performers; and since it usually occurs amidst the humming conviviality of the cabarets, it is a much less solitary activity. For this reason, it is sometimes compared to jazz, but only Lenny Bruce, among the cabaret comedians, has made improvisational bits the basis for a personal and creative expression in the manner of the best jazz musicians—or the manner, to use Albert Goldman's suggestive comparison, of the primitive shaman, exorcising the demons of the tribe. Most of the other theatrical improvisers are more akin to court jesters, for they are less concerned with liberating the unconscious than with entertaining the audience. Thus, the Self is suppressed through the assumption of a character mask, and the audience is even permitted to suggest the scene to be improvised. This extemporizing from an assumed character and a given scenario, though traceable to the interpolations of Elizabethan clowns and the improvisations of *commedia dell' arte*, is directly influenced by Stanislavsky, who developed it as a rehearsal technique to examine the possibilities of a scene or to loosen up an actor's inhibitions. And it is even more immediately influenced by those Method directors and actors who brought Stanislavsky's techniques to the creation of such plays as *A Hatful of Rain* and such movies as *On the Waterfront*.

Although designed as a rehearsal technique, on-the-spot improvisation is now taking place before cabaret audiences; and I have yet to see it really click. Even in the capable hands of Nichols and May—who wisely used it sparingly after the completion of their prepared program—it never seemed more than ingenious. Watching a scene originate before your eyes can be interesting but not convincing. One is too aware of the performer's self-conscious efforts; character and situation rarely merge; and too seldom do the actors make connection. Still, encouraged by overly indulgent audiences, on-the-spot improvisations are becoming more and more important to cabaret troupes like The Premise and The Second City, both of which recently opened new shows. At The Premise, Theodore Flicker warns the audience to expect "a great theatrical moment or a gigantic aesthetic disaster"—only one of these promises is kept.

Among the improvisations, some brief blackout sketches on topics of the day are competent though rather bland, but, at best, The Premise contributes only a mildly interesting charade. At worst, however, the group makes one tingle with acute embarrassment. This occurs fairly frequently, and is a far more uncomfortable feeling than one gets seeing an actor forget his lines. To go up in a play is to reveal a faulty memory; to goof on an improvisation is to expose a faulty imagination. Pirandello, who wrote plays around improvising actors, was always careful to write out the "improvisations" in advance; and The Premise demonstrates why. A creative artist may be able to perform, but a performing artist is not often capable of sustained creativeness.

The instant theatre at The Second City also caused me more pain than pleasure—out of the twelve improvisations I witnessed, ten were duds. Still, the group is more talented than The Premise company, and its approach more iconoclastic. And an improviser like Anthony Holland begins to suggest some of the possibilities of the method when the performer has a wild imagination, an interesting mind, and complete confidence in his abilities. Holland's persona is that of a shrill, redheaded Jewish sissy—overpampered, overeducated, physically fragile, and given to unmotivated hysterical outbursts. When he is improvising the dialogue, situations, and conventions of an O'Neill play, the character he creates is very funny indeed—delivering moody soliloquies, getting girls confused with Mom, and yelling "Cripes" at his seagoing (and seasick) brother. Even this, however, was only the germ of a good idea that needed development, expansion, completion.

I would suggest, then, that the real value of histrionic improvisation is to provide inspiration for a scene which rehearsals can form and finish. And like The Premise, The Second City is most professional in rehearsed material. These sketches are often distilled from newspaper events—both groups disprove an earlier contention of mine that American satire is rarely political—but the better ones are usually sociological. Like Lenny Bruce, who has total recall about the culture of his childhood, The Second City sometimes engages in satirical nostalgia; and one prepared episode finds Anthony Holland as a sensitive camper in a progressive camp upsetting his counselor by painting representational pictures (the subject being Mr. Bardot and Miss Kreisberg in the bushes). A mimed sequence depicts Bob Dishy, a creature with an elastic face and electrified hair, being tortured by his dentist—the character and the situation might have been created by a cartoonist for *Mad* magazine. The most impressive sequence of the evening constitutes the entire second act, a production number about a couple of businessmen seeking "action" in an after-hours bistro. Using the visual devices of *The Establishment* and the visionary fantasies of Jean Genet's *The Balcony*, the proprietor caters to his customers' hidden sexual demands by projecting an appropriate setting on a screen: Nazi sadism and *Our Town* wholesomeness; a First Lady Room ("Why not? We're all equal!"); a Cuban invasion of Florida's Fontainebleau; and finally, a moment with a beautiful girl in a swing, against a background of green-minty trees, which turns out to be a commercial for Salem cigarettes.

These sketches were probably stimulated by improvisations, but they also show a controlling intelligence guiding the group collaboration, and it is doubtful if they were ever suggested by an audience. It remains an open question how radical improvisation should be in the theatre, and I won't presume to prophesy its future. Everything depends on the gifts of the individual performer, since only he has the capacity to transform improvisation from crude and infantile exhibitionism into a spontaneous and thrilling event.

(1963)

A HARROWING NIGHT
IN THE BRIG

THE BRIG by *Kenneth H. Brown:*
The Living Theatre

■ Instead of a curtain, there is a stretch of barbed wire; behind this, a yard; beyond the yard, a compound filled with sleeping prisoners; around the compound, a narrow corridor, divided by four white lines. It is 4:30 A.M. in the Marine Corps Brig at Fuji, Japan. The guards are talking softly while the men snore. Suddenly, one guard enters the compound, and drags a newly arrived "maggot" to his feet; he stands at attention by the turnkey's desk, and after being humiliated, threatened, and pounded in the belly, is sent back to bed. Time for reveille. A garbage can cover clatters on the deck, and the overhead lights go on. The men scurry to their feet and sound off by the numbers (they have no names). The Warden addresses them, fondling his billy: "Good morning, kiddies, this will be another glorious day in the history of the United States Marine Corps." The prisoners shout their reply: "YES, SIR."

They put on their fatigues and make their beds at top speed, looking neither up nor down: if their heads bob, they are punched in the stomach. To move from the compound, or anywhere within the confines of the brig, they must loudly request permission to cross the white line; if they touch the line, or speak too softly, they are punched in the stomach. Walking or lounging is prohibited—prisoners must stand at attention, and when ordered to move, run everywhere at a dog-trot, or take a punch in the stomach. They must never speak except in reply to the guards, giving standard answers to all commands. They must never touch the person of the guards; they must submit to search when returning to the compound; they must stand at attention reading the Marine Corps Manual upon completion of every task—any infraction of the rules, however slight, brings a punch in the stomach, and sometimes the blows come for no reason at all. As the day proceeds, and the routine grows more frenzied, the action turns into a brutal ballet danced by terrorized men under the direction of particularly sadistic dancing masters, their guards.

The Brig, which now holds the stage at The Living Theatre, is not a play but a punishment; and I don't suppose I will ever spend a more disagreeable evening in the theatre. Instead of organizing a dramatic work, Kenneth H. Brown, the nominal author, has chosen to function as an absolutely mute witness to a typical day in the infernal regions, the only departure from this terrible realism being his compression of time. Similar representations of penal servitude—Dostoevski's *House of the Dead*, Solzhenitsyn's *Ivan Denisovich*, or (to take an American example) the stockade sequence in *From Here to Eternity*—have contained dramatic incidents: *The Brig* has none whatever. Since communication among the prisoners is forbidden, the dialogue is limited to barked commands and bellowed requests to cross the white line; and since all individual action is prohibited, the only conflict in this relentless documentary comes when a prisoner cracks up and is carried out in a strait jacket. Visually, there is plenty of excitement in the way Judith Malina has drilled her company into a stolid automatism vibrating in rhythms of pain; but aside from this, there is nothing to break the awful monotony of the proceedings, where even brutality and violence soon grow dull and routinized. One leaves the theatre with a headache and jangling nerves, having shared all the agonies of the prisoners except their physical torments.

Still, if you can take it, *The Brig* will supply you with direct experience of American totalitarianism, and first-hand knowledge of concentration camp techniques: the universal terror, the gratuitous violence, the performance of meaningless tasks, the deadening of instinct. *The Brig* will show you, too, the essential totalitarian conversion: how, through the theft of personal identity, a human personality is transformed into a mindless machine. The men have become numbers, and are treated like things: they are "maggots" and "insects" with less significance than a swab or a shovel. They move like robots through a series of mechanical rituals, and even after they have been bludgeoned to the ground, they must rise to attention wearing the same expressionless mask. Dehumanized by fear, depersonalized by cruelty, their only escape is into nullity, the hope of being zero. "My name's not six—it's James Turner," screams the man who cracks up; but only he has the temerity to assert his true identity, for only a lunatic can claim to be human in this mad and frightful world.

The Brig, then, is an activist play, designed—through the use of documentary realism—to arouse responsibility, shock, and indignation over human distress; and to measure the work by standards of "good theatre" is to lapse into a kind of inhumanity oneself. Yet, inevitably, this is precisely the way The Brig has been treated by the daily reviewers. It is true that Howard Taubman has called for a Presidential investigation, while adding this interesting gloss on penal torture: "Unless [the prisoners] are guilty of murder or treason, their punishment is in outrageous excess of the crime" (that unless has a lovely humanitarian ring). But Taubman is worried less about the prisoners than about the performers ("think how tough a way this is for an actor to earn a living"), and notes that The Brig is "a far cry from drama." So is Auschwitz a far cry from Broadway.

As for Walter Kerr, he has a more sophisticated method of turning away his face: "It has clearly been 'author' Kenneth H. Brown's intention, as it has certainly been director Judith Malina's achievement, to harass, bedevil, irritate, numb, and appall an audience with exactly those things that harass, bedevil, etc. those who have been unlucky enough to land themselves in this sort of hoosegow,"—thus Kerr proceeds to draw the reader's sympathy from the victims to the audience. Harass and bedevil indeed—and bewitch, bother, and bewilder to boot. If Kerr were less concerned with entertaining his readership, and protecting the sensibilities of his musical-going audience, he might have had a less facetious response to this play ("hoosegow" in this context is particularly insensitive). Still, I come more and more to believe that we are all in the brig, our instincts deadened, our identities shattered, by the way we write, think, and talk about human misery.

Hannah Arendt has illustrated, in her brilliant book on Eichmann, how a nation is inured to totalitarianism through the corruption of language: euphemisms come between the thinking mind and the heartless horror; the phrase softens the implications of the act. With this ruthless documentary, The Living Theatre confronts you with the thing itself, trying to break through that crust of indifference which Americans have developed in the face of evil; and the mere staging of the work becomes an act of conscience, decency, and moral revolt in the midst of apathy and mass inertia. Whether the revelation of those conditions will affect that bureaucratic mechanism which creates them, I cannot say. But if you can bring yourself to spend a night in The Brig, you may start a jailbreak of your own.

(1963)

BROADWAY

■

■

■

THE MEN-TAMING WOMEN
OF WILLIAM INGE

The Dark at the Top of the Stairs

■ *The Dark at the Top of the Stairs* is William Inge's fourth play to be produced in New York. It is being extravagantly hailed both by critics and the public as another major achievement in the substantial canon of a developing playwright, keeping Inge's star firmly fixed in the small pantheon of Broadway's top dramatists. Unlike the other members of Broadway's triumvirate, Tennessee Williams and Arthur Miller, Inge has never had a critical or box-office failure, and the three movies made from his earlier drama—*Come Back, Little Sheba, Picnic* and *Bus Stop*—have ranked high among the top grossers of all time. Considering the modesty—one is tempted to say the mediocrity—of his work, it is clear that the excitement over Inge has been inspired by something other than the intrinsic value of his plays.

One explanation may be that Inge is regarded as Broadway's

first authentic Midwestern playwright. The theatre up till now, treating the Midwest as a large mass of unidentified land west of Sardi's and east of Schwab's drugstore, has been content to celebrate only the wholesomeness of the area, usually in song and dance. New England has denoted incestuous family life and the Puritan conscience; the South, tortured libidos and crumbling institutions; New York City, the glitter of witty high life and the social unrest of idiomatic low life. But the Midwest has always, in its Broadway stylizations, remained free from the complexity and suffering of those areas. Rodgers and Hammerstein exalted it, in *Oklahoma!*, as a joyous zone of calico gowns, scrubbed blue jeans and homogenized souls, while Meredith Willson recently identified it, in *The Music Man*, with big brass bands, "Ioway stubbornness," and ingratiating con men.

Inge, on the other hand, seems to have restored to Midwesterners their privilege to be as traumatized by life as any other Americans represented on Broadway. His characters, suffering in a purgatory of low-pressured "realism," adamantly refuse to twirl their skirts, burst into song or ripple with good feeling. A closer look at his work, however, reveals that beneath the naturalistic dirt and cobwebs lies a view of man as blandly nerveless as that held by Rodgers and Hammerstein—and more sinister since it robs the individual of his aspiration, his heroism, and even his manhood.

Wandering aimlessly in a number of directions, *Dark at the Top of the Stairs* chronicles the fortunes of the Floods, a middle-class family living in an Oklahoma boom town in the early twenties. Concerned primarily with the crises of daily life, the play is conscientiously unheroic. The only climax it can boast hinges on an improbable turn of plot, the suicide of a Jewish boy who has been insulted at a country-club dance; the only plot concerns the breakup and reconciliation of the mother and father after a spat over the cost of a dress. There is practically no action; the crucial scenes all occur off stage (Inge uses the Messenger device as extensively as Euripides). The play moves, if at all, by a series of character revelations, and the dialogue, in keeping with the unheroic line of the play, is dry, repetitive, and monotonously folksy.

Over the placid lake of this play, Elia Kazan hurls thunder-bolts. His production is in a state of carefully controlled frenzy. Pat Hingle as the father shouts his lines so vigorously that one expects him to be answered from the house across the way; Eileen Heckart, though vastly amusing, is miscast as the aunt and bawls her part in the brash, busy accents of musical comedy; the daughter's flapper friend sibilates her hissing con-sonants, exposes her bloomers to her date and lifts her leg into her skirt on gag lines as if she were playing the soubrette in *The Boy Friend*. Where Inge indicates a tight bond between mother and son, Kazan slams home all the incestuous implications; where Inge indicates plainness in the daughter, Kazan casts a conventional stage adolescent with the face of Corliss Archer and the look-at-me-I'm-radiant speech of Julie Harris. Inge pro-poses calm and lassitude, Kazan imposes theatrical high jinks. What with all the nut-cracking, chicken-eating, behind-patting, jewelry-fingering, shoe-shining, sewing, crying, stuttering and yawning that goes on, his characters are rarely empty-handed or empty-mouthed—and in a play almost devoid of climaxes we are served a climax every five minutes. The period set and the period costumes seem strangely alien elements amidst these tempestuous goings-on. Only Teresa Wright as the mother, quiet-voiced, tiredly pretty, lined with anxiety, seems to belong among the faded daguerreotypes of this old house.

Kazan's treatment of the play shows his understandable im-patience and bafflement with it. *Dark at the Top of the Stairs* drones on like a Midwestern cricket, making no powerful state-ment, displaying no moving action, uttering no memorable dia-logue. Although Inge had previously gestured toward Kazan's brand of high-pitched drama, with a naturalistic play about re-ality and illusion (*Come Back, Little Sheba*), a satyr play glori-fying the phallic male (*Picnic*) and a vulgar folk vaudeville with night-club acts and dirty jokes (*Bus Stop*), here he has created a nostalgic tribute to his childhood in that most tenuous of Broadway forms, the mood-memory play.

The play is dedicated to Tennessee Williams but it is the first of Inge's works not to be largely dominated by Williams' per-sonality. In fact, *Dark at the Top of the Stairs* yields little personality at all. Inge is becoming so detached from his works that he does not even contribute a style to them. Here he carefully distills his facts and memories until they acquire a vagueness which robs them of anything personal or immediate except the author's sympathy. The effect is that of affectionate reminiscence. We are meant to be shielded from the world's glare, not blinded by it; we are to be cradled in the bittersweet security of family life. Seen through the eyes of the ten-year-old protagonist, the world of trouble loses its threat—the most dire events have a happy resolution and even our most intense fears (our fear, for example, of darkness near the door of our room) are dispelled when we can ascend the stairs on Mama's arm. How could the director of *Death of a Salesman* and *Streetcar Named Desire*, the anatomizer of psychological turbulence, see this work other than as something he must "keep going" and make recognizable to the audience which views it?

Despite the smoke screen sent up by the production, one can agree with the critics that this is Inge's best play. He has finally acknowledged that he is dealing with a quiet family theme (his genre is domestic romance) and thus can partly dispense with the souped-up vitalism, the artificial melodramatics, the seedy naturalism and the ambiguous symbolism that marred his other more theatrical work. But if *Dark* is better than his other drama this is because it is more honest, not more original. The play reinforces my opinion that Inge is a dramatist of considerable limitations with a very small gallery of characters, situations, and themes.

Inge follows Williams in writing she-dramas, in giving to women if not the leading then certainly the pivotal (and most insightfully created) role in his work. Inge, however, concentrates more on the pathos of the woman's suffering and, unlike Williams, permits this suffering to issue in triumph. Although the central conflict is a struggle between man and woman, the woman's victory does not necessarily posit the man's defeat. Rather he capitulates, giving himself up to the woman's power to comfort and provide his life with affirmative meaning. Thus Inge's plays end—like most romances—in marriage or reconciliation.

Specifically, Inge's basic plot line revolves around a heroine threatened either with violence or sexual aggression by a rambunctious male. Both terrified and attracted by him, she tries to escape his influence until she learns that, despite his apparent confidence, he is riddled with doubts, loneliness, and need. Once he has confessed this, he loses his ogre quality and the woman is able to domesticate him without difficulty. In *Come Back, Little Sheba*, the plaintive good-natured frump, Lola, is threatened with a hatchet by her alcoholic husband. Though she tries to leave, she is reconciled to him when, returning from the hospital, he indicates his helpless need of her:

> Doc: (*Tears in his eyes, he all but lunges at her, drilling his head into her bosom.*) Honey, don't ever leave me. *Please* don't ever leave me. . . . Please forgive me. . . . And I'll try to make everything up.
>
> LOLA: (*There is surprise on her face and new contentment. She becomes almost angelic in demeanor. Tenderly she places a soft hand on his head.*) Daddy! Why, of course I'll never leave you. . . .

Picnic, Bus Stop and *Dark at the Top of the Stairs* present the situation of the helpless child-man and the comforting mother-woman in progressively disguised form. In *Dark*, Rubin Flood and his wife Cora dispute over his reluctance to assume the responsibilities of married life. She accuses him of infidelity, drinking and indifference toward the children while he charges her with trying to inhibit his freedom. After slapping her and leaving the house in a fury, Rubin later returns to apologize and to confess his fears of the future. Heartened to learn that a self-possessed man like Rubin could fear, Cora encourages him to bring his problems to her and the play ends on a note of mutual compromise. The dark which has always enveloped the top of the stairs, a source of fear not only to their little son but a symbol of the family's fears, is dispelled by a shaft of light on the naked feet of Rubin Flood, waiting for his wife to ascend into his arms.

From this it can be seen that Inge's purpose in writing drama is not political, moral, aesthetic or social, but rather psychological or, more accurately, homiletic. The pervasive surface theme of his work is that people find salvation from fear, need and insecurity only through the fulfillment of domestic love. For the men, however, this fulfillment is always accompanied by a sacrifice of a very curious order. Some idea both of the men and their sacrifice is suggested by the following anecdote related in *Picnic:* "Last year . . . some of the [women] teachers made such a fuss about a statue in the library. It was a gladiator and all he had on was a shield on his arm. Those teachers kept hollering about that statue, they said it was an insult to them every time they walked into the library. Finally they made the principal—I don't know how to say it, but one of the janitors got busy with a chisel and then they weren't insulted any more." Most of Inge's heroes have the physical and cultural characteristics of this gladiator, and all of them have a hidden fear of sharing, through their contact with women, his emasculation.

Inge's hero, like Williams' after whom he is modeled, is a member of a new theatrical type that Herbert Gold has called the "male impersonator." Dressed in a conventional uniform of blue jeans, cowboy boots and tee-shirt (which the hero invariably has an opportunity to remove), he is equipped with bulging biceps and enormous sexual potency. He proclaims his manhood in much the same way that Jayne Mansfield proclaims her womanhood, not by evidence of maturity, intelligence or control but by exaggerated physical characteristics.

Inge emphasizes this further by fitting his hero with some special prowess, usually athletic, which might attract from the American mass audience the same kind of admiration that gladiators enjoyed in Roman circuses. Sometimes, as in the case of the "sated Bacchus" Turk in *Come Back, Little Sheba,* the male's athletic gifts and sexual power are combined in the same symbol. Turk is a champion javelin thrower but the javelin is described in unmistakably phallic terms ("It's a big, long lance.

You hold it like this, erect—then you let it go and . . . it sticks in the ground, quivering like an arrow"). For the man who stakes all his claims to masculinity on his muscles, castration fears can be, of course, very powerful. The castration motif is underlined when Doc, in Lola's final dream, takes over from Turk and makes the javelin and all it stands for disappear completely from their lives ("You picked the javelin up real careful, like it was awful heavy. But you threw it, Daddy, clear, clear up into the sky. And it never came down again"). After this threat has been removed, Lola, who has up till now been letting her husband fix the breakfast, starts about the business of making his eggs. Significantly enough, she reverts to the wifely role, not like Molly Bloom through her husband's assertiveness, but rather through his declaration of dependence on her.

Hal of *Picnic*, Bo Decker of *Bus Stop*, and Rubin Flood of *Dark at the Top of the Stairs* all combine Turk's athletic and erotic prowess with Doc's dependent fate. Hal, a potential All-American back, is described in the familiar imagery of the phallic fraternity as a boy "stud" and "King Kong." Before the heroine can freely give herself to him, he must sacrifice his sexual and muscular bravado and admit he is only a liar and a "bum." This sacrifice is symbolized by the loss of his boots, introduced earlier as a sign of his militant masculinity. Bo Decker, a rodeo champion, after violently trying to abduct Cherie, cries, apologizes before the company, and indicates his tamed domesticity by solicitously putting his leather jacket around her shoulders. An older man than Inge's usual hero, Rubin Flood was in his youth an Oklahoma pioneer who fought Indians and buffalo. First seen by his wife "riding down the street on a shiny black horse like a picture of Sin," he had such appeal that he impregnated her before they were married. Like all of Inge's males, however, his rambunctious masculinity hides a need for solace and comfort. Rubin, however, is less reluctant than the others to admit why he has to suppress this need: "It's hard for a man t'admit his fears, even to hisself. . . . He's always afraid of endin' up like . . . your brother-in-law Morris." With Morris already characterized as a man henpecked by his wife into "wrecked virility," it becomes clear that

Rubin is expressing his fears of symbolic castration. That his fears are groundless is indicated by the ending of the play. Rubin has surrendered his cowboy boots also (he leaves them outside the door for fear of muddying Cora's carpet) but awaits his wife in bare feet for the sweet fulfillment of conjugal love.

Thus underneath Inge's paean to domestic love lies a psychological sub-statement to the effect that marriage demands, in return for its emotional consolations, a sacrifice of the hero's image (which is the American folk image) of maleness. He must give up his aggressiveness, his promiscuity, his bravado, his contempt for soft virtues and his narcissistic pride in his body and attainments, and admit that he is lost in the world and needs help. The woman's job is to convert these rebels into domestic animals. If this requires (as it always does in Inge) going to bed with the hero before marriage she will endure it; and although she may accuse her husband (as do Lola and Cora Flood) of marrying her because she was pregnant, she nevertheless has managed to establish the hero's dependence on her and thus insured that he will remain to provide for the family. The hero has been made to conform, not to his own image of maleness but to the maternal woman's. Each of Inge's plays reads a little like The Taming of the Shrew in reverse.

Now it would be hard to quarrel with this if it were simply an objective and categorical description of relations between a certain kind of people. The man who hides fundamental insecurities behind an exaggerated show of maleness is a familiar figure in American culture (clearly Inge sees Stanley Kowalski with more psychological depth than Williams) and it is very likely that he will end up in a filial, dependent relationship with his wife. What is suspect is the persistence with which Inge presents the same situation. Depicting this limited brand of healthiness as fanatically as Williams depicts his limited brand of sickness, Inge seems to ignore all other possibilities for happy family life. A quick glance at his minor characters will show that almost everyone in his plays is characterized by their willingness or unwillingness to sacrifice their individual selves to love. The plain self-pitying daughter in Dark astonishingly turns out to be the indirect cause of the Jewish cadet's suicide because, feeling sorry for herself, she wasn't around to help him when he needed comfort ("The only time anyone wanted me, or needed me in my entire life. And I wasn't there"), while the poetry-spouting professor in Bus Stop owes his unhappiness and his perversity (he molests young girls) to his inability to subordinate himself to love ("I never had the generosity to love, to give my own private self to another, for I was weak. I thought the gift would somehow lessen me"). Inge has been accused of giving a sexual construction to every action, but although he will exploit sex (and circuses) for theatrical effect he is certainly more interested in the redemptive power of conjugal or romantic love. Inge visualizes the world as a mass of outstretched arms, blindly groping for each other, with every problem resolved in the marriage bed.

Compare Inge's with even the most outlandish enactment of sexual relations (such as Shaw's: "I love you. The Life Force enchants me; I have the whole world in my arms when I clasp you. But I am fighting for my freedom, for my honor, for my self, one and indivisible") and you will see where his most serious limitations lie. John Tanner of Man and Superman fights to keep inviolable a self which Shaw has shown us in action, writing pamphlets, arguing socialism, speaking wittily and incisively about the lifeless conventionality of his time; the Inge hero, if he struggles at all, fights to maintain an idea of self which is wrong from the start. In marrying, Tanner gives up his individual freedom, not his genius; Inge's hero gives up his one distinguishing characteristic, phony though it may be, the sexual dynamism with which he has caught the attention of the spectator. Thus Shaw's vision opens out onto political and moral horizons; Inge's vision closes in on the family and holds us trapped there within the four walls of the home.

The limited boundaries of Inge's moral and social perspectives are dictated both by his subject matter and his characters. With evil equated with lovelessness, evil by some strange process disappears as soon as its character is explained. Inge needs villains but they never appear on his stage (the anti-Semitic woman of Dark is merely spoken about) while whoever on stage has the capacity to cause serious trouble grows harmless as soon as we learn that they too are sad, lonely and frustrated. Concentrating on motives and causes rather than actions and results, Inge avoids confronting any serious moral issues. Although Inge, by his use of the indirect method in *Dark*, tries to make us think of Chekhov, the differences between the two dramatists are vast. Chekhov always emphasized that sympathetic people can cause evil too, that the harm they do is not palliated but rather all the more terrible for understanding it. Inge's characters labor to become as "well-adjusted" as the audience; Chekhov's characters are the audience and reflect its sins and faults ("Have a look at yourselves and see how bad and dreary your lives are"). Thus while Chekhov's impersonality reveals his moral passion, Inge's conceals his secret flattery of the spectator.

Inge lacks Chekhov's social passion as well. The social world for Inge is merely a dim image of outside practically invisible to the family eye. *Dark at the Top of the Stairs* purports to say something about the Midwest's transition from a frontier to a money culture but all it really says is that some people (never shown) got bigoted (they weren't before?) and rode around ostentatiously in expensive cars. Inge eventually escapes the entire issue in the helpless incomprehension of Rubin Flood ("I dunno what to think of things now, Cora. I'm a stranger in the very land I was born in").[1]

This is life without heroism, wit, intelligence or even true energy, akin in its lack of hard virtues to life as despairingly visualized by Beckett and Ionesco. Inge's mood, however, re-

---

[1] Inge's handling of the Jewish cadet also reveals his tendency to evade social issues. Sammy Goldenbaum is too pathetically sweet to be believed. His impeccable manners, his great concern for people's feelings, and his soft stammering speech make everyone else in the play look boorish and, although he is unwanted by his mother (a Gentile movie star—obviously Jews are incapable of behaving badly), he thinks of her with great love and generosity. Inge describes him in exotic terms as a "darkly beautiful man of seventeen" with "something a little foreign about him. . . . He could be a Persian prince strayed from his native kingdom"—Sammy is certainly more Persian prince than Jew. Inge's treatment of anti-Semitism seems very unreal when his subject is neither human nor Jewish.

mains steadfastly optimistic, for with serious problems, other than finding a proper adjustment to love, never threatening, optimism comes easy. It would be unfair to compare this world with the heroic universe of Shakespeare (can you imagine Hamlet, Lear or Macbeth each solving his dilemma by laying his head on a woman's breast?)—simply try to apply Inge's panacea to the domestic difficulties of Ibsen's Nora, O'Neill's Hickey, or even Miller's Willy Loman. No, Inge can maintain his affirmations only by a simplistic view of life and a careful selection of characters. *Dark at the Top of the Stairs* is Inge's most acceptable play because, seen frankly through the eyes of a child, it makes less pretense at being adult; it is, after all, a child's world where social and moral issues assume no importance and where whatever is dark and evil can be expunged by the comfort of a woman. Although the play has depth, however, it has no width. By Inge's own choice, it wallows in commonplaces. Its most significant statements are like a series of homilies out of the *Farmers' Almanac:* "The people we love aren't perfect. . . . But if we love them, we have to take them as they are"; "Bad people you don't hate. You're only sorry they have to be."

Thus Inge's Midwest, despite its occasional psychological intensity, is not really different from the Midwest of Rodgers and Hammerstein, a land where the gift of milky happiness is obtained when some obstacle ("pore Jud" or resistance to love) is removed. Despite its flirtation with the "dangerous" subjects of modern American drama (sex and violence), Inge's drama is in the end ameliorative, and this fact accounts for his present-day popularity. Inge can hardly be called a "developing playwright" because he merely changes his forms rather than his content. But he does represent a new phenomenon on our stage—he is the first spokesman for a matriarchal America. Inge's family plays constitute a kind of aesthetic isolationism upon which the world of outside—the world of moral choice, decision and social pressure—never impinges. Although he has endowed the commonplace with some depth, it is not enough to engage serious attention. William Inge is yet another example of Broadway's reluctance or inability to deal intelligently with the American world at large.

DR. CHAYEFSKY'S PANACEA

THE TENTH MAN *by Paddy Chayefsky*

■ Since most of Paddy Chayefsky's previous writings give the impression of having been pieced together out of conversations overheard on an IRT subway platform, *The Tenth Man* is something of a new departure for this author. The characters have more flavor and *élan*, the plot is constructed around a sturdier scaffolding than the trivial incidents of soap opera, and, for the first time, the dialogue seems to have been written rather than tape-recorded. Chayefsky's identifying characteristic has always been his morbid preoccupation with the mediocre and the banal, but in *The Tenth Man*—set in a tumble-down Long Island synagogue and revolving around a Jewish maiden possessed by an evil spirit—he is flirting with the outlandish and the strange. While his passion for minutiae remains constant, it is no longer centered on the sordid details of soiled linen and wrinkled beds but rather on the atmospheric intricacies of cabalistic rituals. The bard of butchers, bobby-soxers, and bachelor parties has experienced an unexpected metamorphosis into a blithe spinner of exotic fantasies.

The Tenth Man is Chayefsky's first work to be written expressly for the stage (*Middle of the Night* was a converted TV script), and so this metamorphosis may have been partly dictated by the new medium. Television audiences, as we know, are addicted to the commonplace, but the Broadway spectator has more of an appetite for the exotic, providing it conforms to conventional expectations. In *The Tenth Man*, Chayefsky is exploiting the local color of the Orthodox Jew in the same manner that Joshua Logan last season exploited the Oriental. The stage is populated by bearded worshipers in prayer shawls and phylacteries—disheveled, argumentative, superstitious, charming, goodhearted types—who are given to commenting at length, in studied upward inflections, on ungrateful children, cemetery plots, rabbis, and the Old Country. Tyrone Guthrie—when he is not grouping the characters in the attitudes of a Chagall painting—gives the show away by directing it like a cartoon, and the performers (with the exception of Arnold Marle in a powerful characterization) are concerned less with acting in depth than with ingratiating themselves with the audience. The result is an amiable cast of characters possessing humor but no essential reality—Orthodox Jews who pray in English and scrupulously refrain from using Yiddish phrases. One reviewer has called them "universal," which is one way of saying that they never break through the rigid conventions of dialect comedy by displaying anything unique, individual, or true.

This is not to say that dialect jokes cannot be immensely amusing; and when this garrulous coterie holds the stage, things are very lively indeed. Chayefsky makes a comic juxtaposition between Old World simplicity and New World complexity, and most of his jokes stem from the bewildering effect of a bustling New York civilization on these cloistered, hermitic creatures. Quite often, this humor is strikingly successful: the play's most effective moment is an extended vaudeville about two Jews who have never before left Mineola trying to find the right train to Williamsburg. Sometimes, especially in the hands of the director, it is rather forced: Guthrie has one *alte kocher* enter the synagogue, take off his coat, and reveal a red football sweater underneath. But aside from the success of the jokes, they seem to me fundamentally unJewish in character. Yiddish humor is traditionally based on a contrast between the Jew's practical sense of reality and the lofty ideals of the more refined society outside, but Chayefsky has made the Jews the impractical ones. In this play, simplicity, superstition, and mystical awe are supreme virtues, and one remains pure in heart by turning one's back on the Enlightenment.

In the main plot, this latter-day obscurantism results in spurious theatrics. *The Tenth Man* is the story of a disturbed girl who has been spirited from an asylum by her grandfather.

To the muddled outside world she seems insane, but when she begins speaking in the accents of a whore from Kiev, the Jews conclude that her soul has been inhabited by a dybbuk and begin searching for a Chassidic rabbi to exorcise the demon. A young man enters, defeated, cynical, and suicidal—an unbeliever under analysis who has concluded that life is meaningless. In his presence, the girl's distemper takes a different form (she thinks she is a De Mille movie star), and so he foolishly assumes that she is psychotic. In more lucid moments, she decides she loves him, but when he speaks of the impracticality of such a marriage, she asserts that he too is possessed by a dybbuk which will not permit him to love. A dialectic ensues between the boy and a renegade rabbi named Hirschman who tries to convert him to mysticism ("It is better to believe in dybbuks than in nothing at all"), but he stands fast in his scientific explanation of behavior. The exorcism rite proves him wrong. It is the boy's demon which is banished; permitted now to love, he prepares to cure the girl with the strength of his feeling. As the happy couple leave hand in hand, and the codgers line up to wave them out of the door, Hirschman reads the moral: "He still doesn't believe in God—he just wants to love—and when you think of it, gentlemen, is there any difference?"

Perhaps this ending might have seemed less sentimental, flabby, and evasive had the play remained within the confines of a fairy tale, but Chayefsky's object is to comment on the modern, particularly the Freudian, view of objective reality. Now Freudianism is open to criticism on many scores, but it can hardly be confuted by demonstrating that it is incompatible with a world which exists only in an author's fantasy. One might have guessed—from his exaggerated obsession in previous works with naturalistic dirt and cobwebs—that Chayefsky disliked reality, but the extent of this distaste was never clear till now, and one may hazard that his quarrel is less with Freud than with the Reality Principle. Like the Catholic Graham Greene and the mystic Carl Dreyer, Chayefsky has used the dramatic form to create a world more consonant with his hopes, and, like them, he has not hesitated to invent a few miracles to prove this wish-world is the true one.

As for Hirschman's moral, the curtain unfortunately descends before anyone can shout, Yes, there is a difference between religion and romantic sentiment, and a profound one too. But the Broadway audience seems perfectly satisfied with such soft-headed conclusions. *The Tenth Man* is Chayefsky's most entertaining dramatic work but it openly betrays that omnipresent molasses which seeps under the flinty exterior of all his writings. Unlike Greene and Dreyer, Chayefsky holds to no traditional religious doctrine; instead, he melts down all doctrines into the gluey ooze of Love.

In this, he is one with almost every American playwright writing for the commercial theatre. At the end of the Elizabethan period, in a time of conspicuous animalism and depravity, most dramatists adopted a philosophy of defeat called Stoicism with which to confront the hypocrisy of the social world and the indifference of the universe. In the American age, when decay, hypocrisy, and corruption are equally conspicuous, most dramatists have adopted a philosophy of defeat called Love with which to obscure unpleasant, difficult truths under a haze of romantic abstraction. Hiding their lights beneath a bushel of facile sentiment, they have thus become less the conscience of society than another symptom of its ills.

(1959)

NO LOSS

A LOSS OF ROSES by *William Inge* and
NATURAL AFFECTION by *William Inge*

■ Acting on somebody's suspicion that William Inge's new play would inspire me to something less than ecstatic encomiums, the press agent withheld my tickets, leaving me no recourse except to the box office. I grant that this attempt to prejudge my response is probably deplorable, but I can't seem to work up much indignation over it. I once wrote that all of Inge's plays are wrinkles on the same quite uninteresting theme, namely the relationship between the weak male and the comforting mother-woman. Since *A Loss of Roses* turns out to be another repetition, I find myself filled less with anger than with sneaking admiration for that cautious gentleman who, knowing this beforehand, so accurately anticipated my reaction.

I am not the only pariah in the pack. Two radio reviewers—"unnecessarily cruel," according to a Shubert spokesman, in their comments on "personalities who are the foundation of our theatre"—have been crossed from the opening night lists. A time may come when everyone will be declared *non grata* who does not join in general rejoicing over the high artistic state of Broadway. Yet, in my present state of forgiveness, I can view even this gloomy eventuality with tolerance and understanding. As anyone will attest who watches *Open End* (where theatre people practically fall off their chairs in their efforts not to disagree), Broadway flourishes today through mutual accord, back-slapping, and self-congratulation. This "totalitarianism of the totally pleasant personality" (Norman Mailer's phrase) is undoubtedly a result of economics—one chink in the solid wall of unanimity and the whole financial edifice might collapse. The motto above Shubert Alley might be: "We must applaud one another or die."

Another justification for barring the dissenting critic has to do with protecting the playwright's peace of mind. American dramatists have always been more sensitive to criticism than any other breed of writer, not just for money reasons (movie sales often guarantee even the most horrendous flop) but because their very sense of themselves may sometimes be dependent on good notices. Inge, for example, was recently quoted in an interview as saying: "Until the New York opening, you don't know who you really are, you don't know how good or bad your play is. . . . It's the New York first-night audience that gives you your definition of yourself." Granted that a writer so insecure about his own identity is not going to write very cogently about the identity of others—granted also that one so hungry for approval might be tempted to take the easiest road to success—this still puts a heavy burden on the critics who are responsible now not only for judging the play but for the emotional stability of the playwright. To avoid this, I would suggest that we all be crossed from the lists.

On the other hand, it is only fair to confess that strange things happen to a critic forced to pay for his seat. I found myself, for example, rating Inge's play more as a commodity than as a work of the imagination, and suddenly developed a wild, irresistible impulse to evaluate it in dollars and cents. After careful calculation, I can announce with a precision I will justify later that A Loss of Roses is worth exactly thirty-six cents—and you can save your money altogether if you have already seen The Dark at the Top of the Stairs.

For the situation is the same. At the end of The Dark at the Top of the Stairs, the mother was arguing that her ten-year-old son was getting too old to sleep in the same bed with her; in A Loss of Roses, eleven years have passed and the argument is still going on. Since Kenny is now twenty-one, this promises an incest story, and the one thing that held my interest was how this somewhat dangerous issue would eventually be dropped. The answer came in the shape of a battered tent-show actress named Lila who, because she used to kiss Kenny good night when he was a child, is characterized as his "substitute mother." When she begins cooking for him, sympathizing with him, and tucking him in bed at night, he starts shooting her hot glances; and, in the play's only action, he finally seduces her. This has an immediate therapeutic effect on Kenny ("It's like I wanted something my whole life and all of a sudden I don't want it any more"), and presumably results in a cure—not, I hope, recommended for every family. Leaving Mom to perform her less arduous duties, Kenny goes off to Wichita, while the actress departs to make pornographic movies in Kansas City, where, as Rodgers and Hammerstein have already informed us, "they've gone about as fur as they can go."

This abbreviated one-act skit has been stretched, squeezed, and pulled until it lasts exactly one hour and fifteen minutes (six cents a minute when you buy a $6.90 ticket), but I calculate there is enough material here for only six minutes' playing time. For the rest, Inge gives us a dollar's worth of argument about who is going to sleep on the sofa when the guest arrives; eighty cents is devoted to a group of itinerant actors who say such things as "It's most nobly generous of you to receive we actors"; over a period amounting to sixty cents a young man resembling Alfred E. Neumann makes leering remarks about seduction; and ninety cents of time is spent describing characters like Kenny's father ("He gave his life saving somebody else") and Lila's first husband ("Ed was sweet to me—but he was weak"), who never appear on stage.

The rest of the admission, amounting to $3.24, is expended by Daniel Mann, the director, who is given to five-cent significant glances, ten-cent reactions, and fifteen-cent pauses. The work has been directed in a plodding realistic style which Mann has already made familiar to us through the less expensive medium of the movies (I looked in vain for Anthony Quinn), and you will recognize those scenes, more costly here, where two characters get together over a kitchen table and deliver the exposition during mouthfuls. As for the acting, it owes more to imitation than to nature: Betty Field plays Teresa Wright, Carol Haney plays Shirley Booth, and Warren Beatty comes through with still another imitation of James Dean.

Boris Aronson, one of the better scenic artists in our theatre, has modestly suppressed his talents to create a pair of tasteless rooms complete with flowered wallpaper and overstuffed sofas. For some inexplicable reason, the set is mounted on a revolving stage which gives us three different views of precisely the same area. Since this is Inge's fifth (and let us hope final) version of the same situation, I took this as some sort of underground comment on the play.

(1959)

■ ■

After the first act, I stopped thinking *Natural Affection* a perfectly wretched realistic play, and began regarding it as a monstrous chimera proceeding from a heat-oppressed brain.

William Inge, formerly the sweetheart of the old ladies in the mezzanine, has climaxed his story of adultery, homosexuality, alcoholism, incest, nymphomania, and juvenile delinquency with a scene in which a boy stabs a woman he believes to be his mother, has intercourse with the corpse, and then drinks a carton of milk. How do you like them there apples? The scene has the same evil fascination as the climax of 'Tis Pity She's a Whore, where Giovanni enters with his sister's heart on his dagger. It is theatre of cruelty with a vengeance, the only disturbing thing being that Inge obviously believes it to be a credible psychological study.

(1963)

SETTLING FOR HALF

The Fighting Cock by Jean Anouilh

■ I used to wonder, in more innocent days, just what in heaven prevented the audience at a really agonizing play from rising en masse before the work was over, marching ominously down the aisle, and letting fly at the stage with every object in sight, including hats, minks, pocketbooks, chesterfield coats, programs, and back copies of Cue magazine. After half a season of regular playgoing, I think I've found the answer: nobody has the strength. Current Broadway drama functions like a powerful infernal machine which systematically pumps the blood out of everyone's veins.

Consider my case. I am, I think, in perfect health. Yet over the past four months I have been growing steadily more enfeebled until now my thin and pallid fingers can hardly depress the keys of the typewriter. After Dore Schary's The Highest Tree, my heartbeat became weak and irregular; William Inge's last contribution drained all the blood from my head; and coming out of Robert Anderson's *Silent Night, Lonely Night,* I found my toes had turned cold. It is not simply that these plays were not well written. My resistance to the virus of clumsy playwriting has always been abnormally high, and, anyway, it was *Five Finger Exercise,* engineered with metronomic precision, that nearly did me in (the effect was sneaky—I had expected a drama about the English drawing room and was given instead a mechanical psycho-sexual play about slander, incest, adultery, and homosexuality in a family I could swear was from Long Island). The present unhappy condition of my nervous system is the result of something much more intangible—namely, that most recent plays have been so deficient in vital juices they have begun to dry up my own.

I would not even have the strength to tap this out had I not just received a half-pint of plasma from Jean Anouilh. *The Fighting Cock,* as his play is called here (the original title, *L'Hurluberlu,* means a reckless idiot), is full of flaws, and perhaps we'd better get to these immediately. Structurally, it's a mess. As a play, in fact, it has yet to be written. What emerges instead is a series of character sketches strung together with transitional dialogue. Certain scenes—like an ancient vaudeville wheeze about an ugly old maid who asserts, hopefully, that she has been compromised—seem to have wandered into the play by mistake; and whole speeches, characters, and theatrical devices have been lifted, without alteration or improvement, from the author's previous works. In *The Fighting Cock,* Anouilh lunges abortively like a fencer who can't make up his mind among a choice of opponents, and there is very little that is unified about the play other than a theme, a sentiment, and a mood. In our present state of artistic parch, however, I am almost willing to settle for these, especially when the theme is pertinent, the sentiment deeply felt, and the mood so bittersweet.

Recalling General St. Pé in *Waltz of the Toreadors,* Anouilh's hero is once again an aging authoritarian in love with the past, defeated by the present, heroic and foolish in his refusal to accommodate to modern life. A great hero of a republic he despises, the General of The Fighting Cock has organized a futile, farcical movement designed to "rid the world of maggots" (the comfort-loving, mindless, greedy insects that populate modern society), and to restore to the country the virtues of "austerity, discipline, and hard work"—he cannot accept a France from which all the old absolutes have disappeared. Sometimes, the General merely functions to express Anouilh's own prejudices—we are treated to a violent attack on the techniques of Beckett, Adamov, and Ionesco through an "antidrama" parody called Bing-Bong, consisting entirely of "an utter and engulfing silence." More often, his discontent extends to more general aspects of democratic life—egalitarianism, progress, and (as represented by a cold-blooded tricheur named Tarquin Edward Mendigales) the moral collapse of the young. But since this tide is inexorable, the General's movement flops weakly; his wife (telling him that "France and I continue to change") prepares to leave him; and he is left alone on stage with his tiny son to ruminate on the sadness and absurdity of life.

Clearly, there is not much substance here. But one must be grateful for a play animated by observation of life rather than by clinical theory, and for a playwright who is an artist rather than a psychological adjustment broker. The Fighting Cock is valid if only for the strength and vigor of its intelligent dissent, and, happily, some of this intelligence and vitality has been preserved in the production. Rolf Gerard's transparent, watercolorish settings are the work of an unusually bold yet delicate imagination, and Peter Brook's direction, while somewhat precious (his besetting sin), is generally competent for the occasion. Natasha Parry is that rare thing, an ingénue not girlish but womanly, and she gives a soft, glowing performance as the General's wife, while Gerald Hiken contributes an extremely funny caricature as an idiotic but loyal petty bourgeois craftsman. Rex Harrison looks wonderfully like an Asiatic warlord, his eyes narrowed, his hair a close-cropped gray; and, aside from a maddening habit of not listening when others are speaking, he performs wonderfully too. But I think he is rather miscast. The General, because he knows next to nothing about modern life, is constantly being deflated and surprised, while Harrison is an actor who looks as if he had nothing more to learn. He is hip, the General is square. Were he quite a bit younger, he would be more properly cast as the sophisticated Tarquin Edward Mendigales—a character who, in the hands of Roddy McDowall, now seems too brash and callow.

Anouilh first came to attention in America falsely labeled as a playwright of the French Resistance; he has lately become a playwright resisting modern France. Always disposed toward traditionalism in his forms and techniques, Anouilh is now trying to dramatize the anachronistic quality of his own position. His recent plays are about the conflict between the past and the present, and the importance and futility of maintaining traditional values in a world which no longer cares. He is evolving into a stringent critic of contemporary life; yet he remains a popular Boulevard dramatist, proving that, in France at least, commercial drama does not have to scrape before the public's values any more than it has to express the public's failure of nerve. Thus, even when Anouilh's work is shoddy, his sap still flows free.

(1959)

NIHILISM ON BROADWAY

CALIGULA by Albert Camus

■ In a world of surprises, Broadway still remains predictable. Once you are able to swallow the jawbreaking news that Albert Camus' *Caligula* will be performed on the main street, everything that follows—from the half-respectful, half-hostile bafflement of the daily press to the stupefying opulence of the production—becomes as inevitable as the digestive process. Unable to soften down this dangerous play of ideas, Sidney Lumet, the director, has chosen to drown it out, imposing over the pop-pop of explosive thought a recurrent din of more familiar Broadway sounds: resounding gongs, breaking mirrors, mournful string arpeggios, clashing cymbals, stamping feet, and vibrating drums. And just in case some meaning should still find its way through the thunder, he has introduced visual distractions as well: languorous, mute courtesans lolling diaphanously on the floor; armies of half-clad, powdered male torsos marching militarily through the action; running Olympic leaps performed up, down, and over a precarious group of stairs; and murky battles fought in the gloom with sword and fire. As for the acting, while it is mixed (patricians from the classical theatre, plebeians from the Studio), it is rarely blessed. Colleen Dewhurst contributes some sturdy, matronly moments as Caligula's mistress and Sorrell Booke is amusingly loathsome as the emperor's comic foil; but, as Caligula, Kenneth Haigh alternates too abruptly between grim irony, which he controls, and temper tantrums, which he doesn't, while stumbling floppily around the stage like an Eton schoolboy dizzy on his first cigarette. Meanwhile, the entire spectacle—periodically bathed in a frenzy of colored lights exceeding even Stanley Kowalski's orgiastic imagination—is spread over a gray raked apron which is thrust into the orchestra like the launching platform of an aircraft carrier. Designed to be performed in cool, classical quiet, Caligula in its current production is instead a credit to the memory of Cecil B. De Mille, and might even bring a gleam of envy to the imperturbable features of Tyrone Guthrie.

But let us (reversing the usual Broadway procedure) dispense with the production and examine the play. For, while hardly a model of dramatic art, it contains, in Justin O'Brien's lucid translation, some of Camus' most provocative ideas. Written when the author was only twenty-five, Caligula is a study in total refusal. Camus characterizes the Roman emperor as an early nihilist with an artist's craving for clarity and order in a world without meaning. Brought, through the death of his sister, to the realization that life is absurd and imperfect ("Men die, and they are not happy"), Caligula determines to work out the inexorable consequences of this conclusion. Rebelling against the very conditions of life, he exercises complete freedom from moral, spiritual, or canon law. "If God is dead," observed Dostoevski, "then everything is permitted"—Caligula's absolutism is an attempt to achieve the impossible (symbolized by the "gentle, weightless, and naked" moon), to impose on life a form and purity which it does not possess.

Elsewhere, Camus once predicted that "the rebel, who at first denies God, finally aspires to replace him," and Caligula's crimes soon become his aspiration toward divinity. Observing that "there is only one way of equaling the gods—all that's needed is to become as cruel as they," Caligula conducts his reign according to the same heartless justice he sees operative in the universe. What results is a reign of dispassionate terror. Patricians are ordered to disinherit their sons and leave all to the state ("Governing amounts to robbery. . . . As for me, I shall rob openly"); wives are ravished, sons tortured, and fathers murdered out of sheer whim. Everyone is guilty—not of any particular crime, but because they are subjects of Caligula, because they are alive under a merciless god. After Caligula makes his divinity physically manifest as Caligula-Venus rising from a seashell (homosexuality is merely another expression of his license and revolt), his personal suffering begins to overwhelm him. He has achieved that solitariness necessary to the Promethean rebel, his contempt for mankind has reached its zenith, and he is ready to die. But he soon realizes, just before he is assassinated, that he too is guilty. Though liberated from memory, illusion, happiness, and the desire for security, he has recognized no limits, and his own fear of death signifies that his freedom has not been pure. Camus' final position goes beyond nihilism: man must refuse the divinity he has inherited from a dead God in order to share in the "struggles and destiny" of suffering humanity.

Caligula, obviously, is not a work which Americans will understand readily or accept with any enthusiasm when they have understood it. Camus eventually works his way through to a liberal-humanist position, but he arrives there the hard way, without sentiment, moralizing, or didacticism, having come through the tenebrous forest of nihilism. While we in America have left unexplored even the borders of this forest, Camus recognized that nihilism was the central position against which he had to define his own, since it was the inevitable culminating point of nineteenth-century thought. It is still a powerful force in Europe, partly accounting for the excesses of Hitler and Stalin (in its most monstrous shape), and (in more harmless form) for the vacillating anarchy and authoritarianism of French government.

But the impact of nihilism on France has also resulted in some of the most original drama written in the last decade, a drama which—in the direction of its thought—would be almost inconceivable in America. For while we are trying to come to terms with human conditioning, the French are trying to pass the boundaries of human limitation; while we are seeking security, ease, and happiness within the social unit, the French are seeking metaphysical freedom outside of human institutions; while our key words are *adjustment* and *affirmation*, the key words in France are *alienation* and *negation*. In consequence, our plays—with their official tone, their pious pronouncements, and their social-psychological orientation—seem to be the work of a collective, embodying the collective's distrust of freedom, heroism, and individual salvation. In this early play of Camus, on the other hand, as in so much French drama, the individual's relationship to his universe is once again being fully explored.

(1960)

POLITICS AND THE HIGHER GOSSIP

THE BEST MAN by Gore Vidal

■ When I was a student in drama school, I once attended a comedy by a particularly insecure student-playwright who had invited a few producers and agents to see his work. The play was not funny and the audience was unresponsive, so the playwright decided to help things along by sitting in a different part of the orchestra during each act and guffawing loudly at his own lines. I have never forgotten the terrible quality of that laughter. It had the desperate raucousness of an ego striving not only to justify itself but to survive, and was, in fact, so far removed from genuine merriment that it sounded inhuman, like the mechanical braying of a klaxon.

I have been spared the sound of that laughter for ten years, but I heard it again the other night, rising in great honks from inside the Morosco Theatre. It was as if the author of *The Best Man* were sitting everywhere in the house, cachinnating at his own conceits and zealously cheering his own achievement when the curtain fell. And, in a sense, this was true. The nominal author, Gore Vidal, has manipulated the action and calculated the effects, but the play's material, I suspect, was provided by an Audience Survey Tabulator and a frighteningly efficient Univac machine. For *The Best Man* is less an original drama than an uncannily precise recording of the Broadway spectator's most simplistic notions of politics and politicians, as gleaned from the tabloid liberalism of the New York *Post*, the insider anecdotes of Leonard Lyons, the intimate hinting items of Walter Winchell, and the Higher Gossip which circulates in bars, night clubs, and living rooms.

The result is a work which appears to offer controversial material but which really thrives on unanimity of audience opinion (imagine the shock in the house when one unhip spectator booed a slighting reference to J. Edgar Hoover). Inevitably, therefore, *The Best Man* takes the form of melodrama, tailored with a smart sophistication appropriate to the times. While the incumbent, Hockstader (a peppery, laconic, practical politician in the style of Harry Truman), looks amusedly on, two men contend for the Party's Presidential nomination: the Angel of Light, a former Secretary of State named William Russell (dedicated to "Man" and "human decency"), and the Angel of Darkness, a Senator named Joe Cantwell (who will "lie, cheat, and destroy reputations to get elected"). Since Cantwell worships expediency, he depends on the smear technique, passing around to the convention delegates reports that Russell is estranged from his wife and that an earlier nervous breakdown was really an attack of lunacy. For Russell, on the other hand, intelligence, integrity, and honesty are the prime political virtues. When he receives information that Cantwell had homosexual experiences in the service, he refuses to use it, despite the urging of Hockstader and the prompting of his own ambition. In consequence, he loses the nomination, though he regains the love and admiration of his wife.

In skeleton, this is a conventional enough situation, and it embodies a reasonably accurate, though oversimplified, liberal diagnosis of the political scene. But while outwardly flattering to the political opinions of the spectator, *The Best Man* is secretly destructive of all intelligent politics: complex ideas harden into ideology, and liberalism itself is tainted with the demagoguery it professes to abhor. It is worth observing that while we are encouraged to sympathize with the upright Russell (a composite of Stevenson and Acheson, played with humor and charm by Melvyn Douglas) in his uncompromising concern with issues rather than personalities, there is not a single political issue of any consequence discussed in the play. And at the same time that we are hooting Joe Cantwell's low-road penchant for malicious scandal, we are giggling at gossipy wisecracks about the sex life, drinking habits, and personal idiosyncrasies of prominent political figures and their wives. That these politicians are presented in composite serves not to disguise them so much as to multiply the scandals in their public and private lives.

Take the character of Joe Cantwell. As played with unblinking directness by Frank Lovejoy, he is the image of Richard Nixon: beetle-browed, smooth, unctuous, pugnacious, and unscrupulous, his only reading matter the latest Gallup poll. But, as if this were not enough, Cantwell is given some of McCarthy's characteristics too. It was McCarthy, remember, who was rumored to have had a homosexual past, and it is McCarthy's technique of self-advertisement which Cantwell exploits in the play. As Hockstader tells us, Cantwell rose to prominence by charging that "the United States was secretly governed by the Mafia" (!). After announcing that "there was no such thing—you just cooked it up," Hockstader goes on to contradict himself, adding that Cantwell only prosecuted the small rascals because the big ones contributed to his campaign fund. I have neither the patience nor the stomach to document how—when you lump together political personalities, and confuse, in consequence, such enormously complicated issues as the Hiss case, Communism in government, and the admission of Red China to the UN—political thinking has a tendency to stop altogether. But I will say that it was ritualistic liberalism of just this kind that accounted, in part, for the rise of such demagogues as McCarthy and such opportunists as Nixon in the first place.

In short, *The Best Man* demonstrates that expediency can be operative in playwriting as well as in politics, and that there is not such a wide gulf between our commercial drama and our national life as one might imagine. Since one can hear an author's true voice speaking in only one of his lines, it is difficult to say how committed Mr. Vidal is to the flaccid attitudes he grinds out in his play. "As a playwright," he once wrote in an article, "I am a sport, whose only serious interest is the subversion of a society which bores and appalls me." Whether wittingly or not, he is certainly realizing his objective with this cynical and mechanical work.

(1960)

COMEDIANS OF THE UNDERGROUND

An Evening with Mike Nichols and Elaine May

▪ Because of its harsh and critical spirit, and because it aims at the brain rather than the gut, satire has never exactly been a popular form on Broadway, but over the past fifteen years it has been disappearing from our stage (not to mention our literature and movies) at an alarming rate. There are obvious economic reasons for this. In the media that depend on mass support, any art as subtle as satire is inevitably a poor financial risk unless offered in comparatively small doses. There are cultural reasons, too, though these are more debatable. James Thurber used to blame the decline of legitimate satire on the fears and tensions of the McCarthy era, but I must confess I never found this argument completely persuasive. While McCarthyism may have discouraged political satires, it was not a McCarthyite who complained recently that a parody of Japanese movies by Sid Caesar was an insult to the Oriental people: it was the liberal-minded TV reviewer for the New York Times.

Much of our legitimate culture is manipulated and supported by just such progressive, well-meaning, and soupy-headed citizens, and this may explain why the stage still shuns satire years after McCarthy descended to his reward. Ever since Plato, it has been obvious that if your major concern is with the community (either as a Legion patriot or a Liberal defender of minority groups), you will not feel very sympathetic to genuine art unless it supports your social convictions—which art, being highly individualistic, very rarely does. On the other hand, while satire is more subversive of society than any other literary genre, it has, fortunately, not yet been completely banished from the Republic. The growing emphasis on community welfare in America has managed to destroy our farce comedy, forcing anarchists like Groucho Marx, Phil Silvers, and Bert Lahr into more socially acceptable pursuits, but so far it has merely diverted satire from the legitimate culture into more furtive channels without affecting its quality. America may not yet be able to boast of any satiric novels, films, or plays to equal *Lucky Jim*, *I'm All Right, Jack*, or *Expresso Bongo*,* but the political monologues of Mort Sahl, the confessional soliloquies of Lenny Bruce, and the relentless comic strips of Jules Feiffer make up an underground body of satiric expression enormously penetrating in its effect despite the unconventionality of its form.

Two leading members of this underground school are Mike Nichols and Elaine May, a cool couple who have hitherto confined their subversive activities to night clubs and brief TV appearances. They have now come up for air at the John Golden in a full evening of satiric entertainment. The more sudsy atmosphere of the commercial theatre does not seem to have rusted their barbs any, for they are currently contributing an enormously intelligent program of animated aggression.

More than those of their fellow satirists, the techniques of Nichols and May are eminently adaptable to the theatre, despite the intimate character of their work. The tradition they tap is Horatian rather than Juvenalian, which is to say they take their revenge on society merely by presenting it instead of by whipping it with rods and scourges. The result is a hilarious imitation of a social action, only slightly exaggerated. In the manner of their less sophisticated mentor, Sid Caesar, they employ extraordinary powers of observation to locate the clichés of conventional middle-class life, transforming them into precise vignettes stripped down to their essential absurdity, so that the action tends to criticize itself. Miss May, a superb actress, brings

---

* This, of course, was written before black humor invaded our literature with *Catch-22* and films with *Doctor Strangelove*; so fast does the cultural climate change.

enormous reality to a wide range of native female types, while Mr. Nichols, a superb comedian, provides the necessary grain of ironic comment without which the performance might seem too cruel or terrible. For Miss May is so accurate in her impersonations that she often threatens to break out of comedy altogether, a talent which is used with chilling effectiveness in a sketch called "Pirandello" (where both play upon the conditioned responses of the audience in a manner guaranteed to possess you with terror and excitement).

The rest of the evening is devoted to prepared sketches and an improvisation based on suggestions from the audience. The improvisation is the least impressive thing in the program, since it only suggests the remarkable ingenuity of this team; the sketches demonstrate they have brilliance, irreverence, and wit as well. A wicked satire on P.T.A. meetings introduces Miss May—equipped with black glasses, a formless dress, and a huge flower which keeps shedding its petals—to declare a week dedicated to Art ("perhaps one of the best mediums of self-expression we have") and to describe the tribulations of the French Impressionist painters ("You know, thank God for the Ford Foundation"), while Mr. Nichols, as a Southern playwright named Alabama Glass, shrilly outlines his latest play, a melodrama in which the heroine takes to "drink, prostitution, and putting on airs!" after her husband ("unjustly accused of not being a homosexual") has committed suicide. Along with these bitter buffooneries, we are treated to a skit on adultery in America, England, and France, burlesquing the sexual peculiarities of each country; a sketch about name dropping in show business ("Bert Russell is not pushy . . . personally, I think a pushy philosopher is always a drag"); a telephone colloquy between a possessive Jewish mother and her son, an eminent rocket scientist reduced to infancy in the course of five agonizing minutes; and assorted blasts at vacuous teen agers, conformist suburban couples, Midwestern matinee ladies, mindless movie stars, and vulgar TV interviewers, not to mention a sampling of the countless lunacies with which America is now so abundantly provided.

Nichols and May, in short, are the voice of the outraged

intelligence in a world given over to false piety, cloying sentiment, and institutionalized stupidity, and if this small voice can
still be heard above the racket being produced all around us,
then satire is still performing its traditional function: to relieve
that overwhelming sense of frustration, impotence, and isolation which afflicts the better spirits in our fatuous times.

(1960)

BROADWAY
NON-CONFORMISM

INVITATION TO A MARCH by *Arthur Laurents*

■ If you want to know why Broadway plays often bring out the
more venomous elements in my nature, I think I can provide an
answer: after two years at this work I have not only failed to
develop an adequate defense against the radioactive vapidity of
our stage but have even grown more vulnerable to it. A casual
spectator can always take shelter in a lead-lined box of sleep or
indifference, but since the duties of a reviewer rule out such
protective escapes, my pores are always wide open to lethal
doses of dramatic fallout. The effect is something like a physical
mutation: my eyeballs turn glassy, my brain freezes, my blood
runs cold—each night I am in mortal danger of turning to
stone. To avoid the granite-like condition of my older colleagues
(some of whom now clump into a theatre like the Commenda-
tore in *Don Giovanni*), I have learned to convert to the nearest
liquid state, which usually turns out to be molten lava.

I admit, then, that my poisonous feelings about Arthur Laurents' latest opus are probably in excess of the event. It is an
undernourished little romance, and were it performed under
more appropriate circumstances (say, at the annual dinner for
the female staff writers of *Modern True Love Stories*), I might

be able to summon up a less impassioned response (say, a muted sound from the depths of my internal organs). It is, however, a Moderate Broadway Hit, which means that it has achieved a certain sanction from the people who support our theatre. And since underneath all the frozen custard, confectionary sprinkles, and artificial fudge flavoring in the plot, there is a rotten cashew nut disguised as a "serious" idea, I am forced into the absurd position of treating *Invitation to a March* as if there were something weighty it was trying to say.

The fault is not entirely mine. It is the author who introduces such pretensions—though, to be sure, rather haphazardly. After declaiming in ringing Ibsenite tones that he is treating "the problem of individualism, of standing up against the forces that try to fashion men in one mold," he immediately goes on, in his preopening article, to offer a definition of dramatic art so frivolous it makes James M. Barrie look like a hardened nihilist: "The theatre should be a land of magic. When the curtain goes up the audience should be in fairyland." Out of this schizoid commitment comes a modern version of the Sleeping Beauty legend as seen through the eyes of the society columnist for the *Fire Island Times*: Mr. Laurents' stage fairies live on expensive vacation beaches, wear a variety of tasteless costumes ranging from purple toreador slacks to Chinese red sports coats, dye their hair blue, engage in atrocious witticisms, and throw confetti all over themselves in moments of ecstasy. As for the "forces that fashion," these turn out to be nothing but mothers—a whole stageful of mothers—all contending for the anemic little soul of a young debutante so bored with life she tends to fall asleep in the middle of cocktails: two evil mothers who want her to join the "march" of conventional existence ("martinis at seven, breakfast at eight, dinner at nine"), and a good one who offers her the "dance" of "doing what you want." There are also a couple of fairy princes, one stuffy, principled, and rich (dressed in evening clothes), the other carefree, illegitimate, and poor (dressed in a tee shirt, cowboy boots, and tight pants). I'll leave it to you to guess who wakes her up, to the accompaniment of string music and flying confetti.

As for Mr. Laurents' concept of "non-conformity," this is about as advanced as his plot. Watered down to soap bubbles, it is expressed through the character of the good mother who really responds to visual delights ("Look at that evening—God-damn nature!"), and who disturbs her neighbors with such audacious acts as calling herself Camilla Jablonski ("an un-American name"), swimming naked in the ocean ("it's nasty"), and fostering an illegitimate child ("a bitch mother breeds a bastard son"). This staggering assault on nonexistent conventions is apparently so winning that it inspires the heroine to wear an afternoon dress at an evening party and (in one climactic moment) to drink a martini at an improper hour in the day. Not content merely to shock the audience with such daring activities, Mr. Laurents (who considers himself a non-conformist playwright) introduces a "new," "different," and "disturbing" technical innovation into his work: "In my play the actors speak to the audience." And so they do. Of such stuff is Broadway non-conformism made.

Unfortunately, Mr. Laurents not only shares this "innova-tion" with eight or ten of his Broadway colleagues, but employs it for precisely the same effect: to keep the audience in a per-petual state of self-satisfied euphoria. As a playwright, Mr. Laurents has already flattered his spectators into thinking they too are unconventional; as a director, he busses them even more with the sly winks, ingratiating poses, and grinning asides of his performers. I suppose I should be grateful to Celeste Holm for sparing me the ordeal of Shelley Winters in the part of Camilla, but her performance is so soaked in flat-footed, open-eyed, sugar-voiced good fellowship that I found it almost impossible to watch: Jane Fonda, evoking the Beauty by languidly draping herself over a variety of beach furniture, is most impressive in absolute repose (i.e., when she is asleep); and Eileen Heckart and Madeleine Sherwood, as the malevolent mothers, labor un-successfully to preserve a little authenticity in an atmosphere alien to truth, art, or life. *Invitation to a March*, like so many Broadway plays which emasculate serious ideas, is merely an-other horrible chapter in that dismal chronicle of the American bourgeois mind which is every day being written on our com-mercial stage.

(1960)

DISPUTED AUTHORSHIP

PERIOD OF ADJUSTMENT by Tennessee Williams

■ *Period of Adjustment* is a bourgeois psycho-drama written to formula by a fledgling writer insufficiently schooled in his trade. The name of Tennessee Williams has been affixed to the title page, but the play is so tedious, aimless, repetitive, and imitative—so utterly lacking in style, grace, or imaginativeness—that I have a sneaking suspicion it is really the work of an impostor. Admittedly, familiar echoes can occasionally be heard (faintly) in the circumlocutory swing of its dialogue, while its Southern setting, weird place names, and gratuitous symbolism—not to mention its mechanically sexual interpretation of every human action—are sometimes suggestive of Williams' past writings. But beyond this, I can find little internal proof to support his claims for authorship. Whatever his literary failings, Williams never bored us like this before; and while his previous work may have been extravagant, exaggerated, and absurd, it was never derivative or banal.

Well, it is now, and this suggests an impostor about whose identity future researchers will undoubtedly quarrel. One school may plump for some disciple of Arthur Miller, since the play contains a few affirmations (such as "There is dignity in the agrarian, the pastoral, way of existence! A dignity too long lost out of the American dream") which might have been yanked from the larynx of Biff Loman. Another school will hold out for a ghost writer in the tradition of William Inge, and with more sufficient evidence. Firstly, the play is set in the suburbs, plumbs the cavernous depths of the suburban middle-class mind, and passes as a "warm and human comedy" of marriage.

Secondly, it features such Ingian characters as a delicate but strong-willed female who pleads for love and tenderness ("I am naturally gentle, I am gentle by nature"), a violent rambunctious male with the shakes who is really sensitive and frightened underneath ("Last night, you were scared of impotence with her? Was that the problem?"), and a suburban Miss Lonelyhearts out of Joyce Brothers by Rose N. Franzblau who boils down everyone's anxieties and errors into armchair analytical equations ("She let you down by having psychological problems that you brought on her. . . . You made her feel inferior all her life"). Finally, the play revolves around two estranged couples, all afflicted with some sexual malfunction which is endlessly discussed and eventually resolved in a pair of beds.

What this play indicates to me is that Williams, who now can write with conviction and power only about the conflicts in his own unconscious, has momentarily run out of usable autobiographical material, and is marking time by placating his most vociferous critics with a clumsy reproduction of current dramatic formulae. In his present occupation as a love broker, peddling adjustment, affirmation, and cheer at top Broadway prices, he may seem a long way from his former role as sexual revolutionary, "carrying the banner of Bohemianism into the enemy camp," but I suspect the move is only a temporary expediency. A few months ago, the "enemy camp" was after his scalp. Now Walter Kerr has already welcomed him back into the community, and Marya Mannes, David Susskind, and the editors of Time will probably soon follow suit. That Williams should be praised for "loving the human race" on the basis of anything as obviously manufactured as this artifact is merely added evidence that words like "compassion," "tenderness," and "love" have so lost their meaning in a culture which trades on them that their mere invocation works like bells summoning Pavlov's dogs.

As for Williams himself, his career remains an enigma. Balanced precariously between an aggressive apartness and a need to be accepted and supported by the very groups he assaults, his art has always been tinged with ersatz, his radicalism always tempered with elements of conformity. These elements seem now to have triumphed. Yet, while we may never get from him again the purity of The Glass Menagerie, he will not long remain in his present role. In the past, whenever I was tempted to be apocalyptic about Williams, I always remembered Edgar's cautious admonition in Lear: "The worst is not/ So long as we can say 'This is the worst.'" After seeing Period of Adjustment, however, I am going to ignore this Stoical admonition. This is the worst. From such a bedrock, his art can only rise.

(1960)

THE ENORMOUS
SUM OF ZERO

RHINOCEROS by Eugene Ionesco

■ In Molière's Le Bourgeois Gentilhomme, a Cartesian philosopher tries, by logical demonstration, to instruct his unlettered patron in the theory behind actions he has always performed by instinct. After praising that moral philosophy which teaches you to moderate your passions according to ancient scientific principles, the philosopher then loses his temper utterly, getting embroiled in a battle royal with three other narrow specialists who question the validity of his function. The moral is this: The unconditioned man is wiser than the learned philosopher, scientific theory falsifies human experience, and every systematic thinker harbors dangerous destructive impulses beneath his apparently ordered surface. Molière's twentieth-century disciple is Eugene Ionesco who—noting that "scientific" political movements like Nazism offered contemporary proof of his master's axioms—not only adapted Molière's short interlude in The Lesson but made its moral central to his entire work. In *Rhinoceros*, he has not varied his theme; he has merely found another form through which to express it.

The form he has selected here is social parable, whereby a simple idea is embodied in a complex poetic metaphor. As the central character (an alcoholic, unkempt anti-hero named Berrenger) watches in shocked horror, the inhabitants of a small provincial town are gradually turning into rhinos. First to go are those most fully committed to Society or System: Berrenger's conventional friend, John, who speaks perpetually of the need for will power and moral strength; a pedantic Logician who confronts all natural phenomena armed with the weapons of syllogistic logic (thus proving that Socrates was a cat); a Marxist-Unionist who presumably wishes to replace the existing social order with an even more rigid one; and sundry officials, lawyers, romantics, and government authorities. The rhino pack symbolizes "community spirit triumphing over anarchic impulses"—in other words, a kind of collective insanity, similar to the total conformity of Nazism, by which the mildest rationalists are transformed into raging, violent, thundering, trumpeting beasts. Only Berrenger remains immune to this metamorphosis, for he is a social misfit, committed to nothing but his own harmless pleasures. At the end, the whole world has gone over to the rhinos and he is left totally alone, musing on the sad fate of the non-conformist ("People who hang on to their individuality always come to a bad end"). Half inclined to join the pack but now unable to change, wavering between defiance and despair, he finally determines to "put up a fight against the whole lot of them," pitting his weak powers against an increasingly mad society.

Since *Rhinoceros* contains a number of delightful scenes, and dramatizes an idea which, with a little less paranoiac tenacity, I hold myself, I feel almost churlish in adding that there is not enough nourishment here for a full length play. In a short farce like *The Bald Soprano*, Ionesco could hold our attention with his deft annihilation of language, logic, and cliché, for he possesses a unique gift for manipulating the absurd which makes him an uncanny comedian. In his longer works, however, his farcical gifts are suppressed in favor of expanded intellectual allegories, designed for social commentary rather than comic invention. Ionesco obviously thinks a great deal, mostly about the futility of conceptual thought, but his intellect strikes me as the weakest of his faculties. I suspect he was once, like the old Groucho Marx, an instinctual anarchist; then read Antonin Artaud and the French Existentialists who converted him to the *philosophy* of the absurd, a far different thing. No longer content to be purely destructive, he is now defending this philosophy in more conventional (and tedious) dramatic form, and so runs the risk of becoming a bit of a Cartesian ideologist himself. For unlike Shaw—another dramatist who attacked System from a highly systematic position—Ionesco possesses neither sufficient complexity nor enough command of dialectic to write a play of ideas; and *Rhinoceros*, for all its intermittent power, finally suffers from a certain impoverishment of mind.

Joseph Anthony has chosen to slice great hunks of fatty abstrusity off this work and direct it as if it were a Marx Brothers romp. Ordinarily, I would feel compelled to defend the author's interests; here I can only applaud the director's wisdom and perspicacity. Anthony's production is distinguished by its swift pace and orchestrated style, and particularly by its generous supply of ingenious business, all of which might have been more impressive if executed properly—but few of the actors, alas, have mastered burlesque technique. The great exception is, of course, Zero Mostel as John, who justifies the entire evening by contributing another of his extraordinary histrionic creations. When he first enters Leo Kerz's pastel set, fastidiously wrapped in a bulging morning suit and double-breasted vest, his mustache elegantly waxed, his few strands of hair plastered forward on his head like seaweed, the lyric grossness of his physical presence is a marvelous sight gag; but he proceeds to demonstrate that he has a great dancer's control of movement, a great actor's control of voice, a great mime's control of facial expression as well. The gracefulness with which he executes a Chaplinesque back-kick; the ease with which he shifts his emotions from calm to fury to bafflement; and above all the rapidity with which he transforms himself into a rhino before your eyes, thickening his features, hoarsening his voice, chomping his leg impatiently on the floor—these are the moments that make you believe implicitly in the world of this play, for by some improbable magic, Mostel has filled its slender outlines and expanded it into art. Most of the others have not been so fortunate. After spending the first two acts playing straight man to Mostel, Eli Wallach finally turns Berrenger into a pathetic and appealing little idealist who has wandered into Ionesco's world by mistake; and Anne Jackson suspends his girl friend, Daisy, somewhere between caricature and reality, unable to make a hearty leap in either direction.

But the play also hangs in a state of suspense, too intellectually anti-intellectual to be completely persuasive. An inept performance of *The Killer* last season convinced me then that Ionesco did not have the artistic stamina to write an effective three-act play; *Rhinoceros* (its sequel) confirms me in this view, but I am much less dour about it now. For the play enables Zero Mostel to demonstrate once again that he is a very great actor; and if the sum of the work were only Zero, this alone would be an ample sum indeed.

(1961)

THE MAHOMET
OF MIDDLE SERIOUSNESS

GIDEON by Paddy Chayefsky

■ If Paddy Chayefsky had never existed, Broadway would surely have invented him. No playwright has ever been so perfectly made in the image of his audience or reflected more accurately its changing aspirations and pretensions. For while most other commercial dramatists are still engineering their wares for moribund types like the chittering Helen Hokinson lady and the Cleveland Rotarian, Chayefsky knows exactly who is in the theatre party out front, and writes for them as if he were privy to their inmost desires. (Even his recent conversion from a soap opera naturalist to a mystical fantasist shows his responsive awareness of the new spectator's more sophisticated demands.) It would not surprise me if Chayefsky, before writing Gideon, had made a sociological depth study of upward cultural mobility among the newly rich, the growing religiosity in the suburbs, and just how much rebellion an audience is willing to tolerate before running for the exits. In his new play, he has managed to unify all three columns of the questionnaire (Yes, No, and Undecided) by combining secular sentiments with religious pieties, vaudeville effects with Herman Wouk metaphysics, and the titillation of revolt with the security of conformity. Cannily measuring just how much intellectual gas will fill the commercial tank, he has even bothered to raise some questions about theology, humanism, the Copernican universe, and the relationship of man to God—before gingerly dropping the whole mess into the yawning cavern of Love. Can he do this, and cannot win a crown? Tut, were Broadway titles further off, he would pluck them down, for he now leads all rivals as the Koheleth of Kitsch, the Benefactor of the Benefit Crowd, the Mahomet of Middle Seriousness.

His secret is this: He simply selects a work of some literary distinction, squeezes it dry of all significance, power, and depth, and adapts it to the more conventional expectations of his audience—calling in Tyrone Guthrie to contribute false climaxes, burlesque routines, and sensational effects (belly dances from the Egyptian Gardens, Jewish rituals from the Fifth Avenue Synagogue, execution scenes from his old production of Tamburlaine) when his own imagination flags. In The Tenth Man, we saw Ansky's Dybbuk through the smiling tears of Molly Goldberg; in Gideon, a far more tedious work, we get a look at the Book of Judges as André Obey might have seen it, had he worn the minifying bifocals of Archibald MacLeish. For Chayefsky's Gideon—based on the great Israelite hero who, inspired by an Angel of the Lord, annihilated the Midianite host with a tiny force—has been reduced, like MacLeish's Job, to a lumpish mediocrity, capable neither of heroic deeds nor heroic suffering. In the pudgy, sluggish, ingratiatingly muddle-headed performance of Douglas Campbell, he looks like Marty in a cuirass and buckler—at his worst moments, the village idiot; at his best, a Jewish Falstaff as cowardly as any subaltern in his pusillanimous army (he spends the entire battle hiding out from the enemy). Even in his moments of command, he is merely a dummy manipulated by a celestial ventriloquist, following the Lord's directions with baffled incomprehension.

In French myth drama, the reduction of a heroic character to a commonplace nonentity is an ironic device to satirize the inadequacies of the spectator; in American plays of this type, the technique is employed to flatter the spectator's democratic averageness. But Chayefsky's eagerness to cajole his auditors makes him even condescend to God. As played by Frederic March, wrapped in a burnoose, his speech muffled by a ton of stylized hair, the Angel of the Lord is egotistical, vain, smug, envious, absent-minded, intellectually confused, and sentimental—in short, God has been thoroughly secularized for easy laughs. Even the "jealousy" of the Old Testament Deity has been given its familiar suburban equivalent. In Chayefsky's harrowing imagery, the relationship between Gideon and the Lord is that of man and wife—and the Lord is the female partner! Having won Gideon's love by feats of magic, He must hold it with constant vigilance; and when Gideon later rejects His advances ("I don't feel affectionate at the moment"), the Lord feels banished to the tent "like your other wives." God is characterized, in short, as a possessive woman, responsible for her husband's career and continually demanding credit for his success, who is jealous of all his adventures beyond the "home."

This incredible marital situation provides the soupy climax of the play. When Gideon, anxious to elevate himself, begins to explain his victory in rationalistic terms, the Angel equates this with the belief that the sun revolves around the earth; and when he disobeys the Lord's command to kill the Elders of Succoth, the Angel finds him guilty of marital infidelity. Gideon, however, is ready to declare a "divorce between us." He has discovered that he cannot love the Lord ("You're too vast a concept"), he can only fear Him; and His very existence robs Gideon's life of meaning. The kind of meaning he aspires to is suggested when Gideon, pleading for "at least some bogus value," hungrily eyes the golden ephod he has made for the Lord. As the Angel prepares to strike him down for this blasphemy, Gideon, putting on the garment, begs, "If you love me, God," while the Angel, weeping like a self-sacrificing wife, cries, "I—love—you—Gideon"—and lets him wear it. Following this Second Avenue theatre epiphany, the Lord begins to disappear from the earth altogether, as Gideon—strutting in his rich raiment—exits, discussing the "socio-economic, historico-cultural-psychological" basis for his victory.

It should be perfectly obvious that Chayefsky, like his character in *The Tenth Man*, "doesn't believe in God. He simply wants to love." And for his outrageous tendency to swallow up both belief and unbelief in a molasses mixture of false sentiment, one can find plenty of precedents (*J. B.* is one) in Broadway plays. I have had my say about Broadway Love (Emerson said it better: "The doctrine of hatred must be preached, as the counteraction of the doctrine of love, when that pules and whines"). Let us talk about Broadway Rebellion. In one fell swoop, Chayefsky has neatly reduced the whole great tradition of revolt since the Renaissance to an American bourgeois vision of worldly ambition and material gain, thus robbing it of all its spiritual, moral, and intellectual values. I have not the patience to compare Chayefsky's Gideon with such great rebels against God as Goethe's Faust, Ibsen's Emperor Julian, Brand, and Solness, Shaw's Don Juan, and Strindberg's Stranger; suffice it to say that, by providing his "rebel" hero with the soul of an American businessman, Chayefsky has once more struck a courageous stance right in the center of conformity. *Gideon* is a long-winded play, in which even Chayefsky's substantial comic inventiveness seems to have failed him; but its success was fore-ordained before the author wrote his opening scene. I have a vision of Chayefsky greedily turning his eyes on that golden ephod which lies down the glittering alleys of Times Square, while casting apprehensive glances toward the dead god who once demanded some fidelity to Truth. . . .

(1961)

A LITTLE NIGHT MUSIC

The Night of the Iguana *by* Tennessee
Williams; The Milk Train Doesn't Stop
Here Anymore *by* Tennessee Williams

■ In *The Night of the Iguana*, Tennessee Williams has composed a little nocturnal mood music for muted strings, beautifully performed by some superb instrumentalists, but much too
aimless, leisurely, and formless to satisfy the attentive ear. I
should add that I prefer these Lydian measures to the un-
melodious banalities of *Period of Adjustment* or the strident
masochistic dissonances of *Sweet Bird of Youth*, for his new
materials are handled with relative sincerity, the dialogue has a
wistful, graceful, humorous warmth, the characters are almost
recognizable as human beings, and the atmosphere is lush and
fruity without being outrageously unreal (no Venus flytraps
snapping at your fingers). With this play, Williams has returned once again to the primeval jungle, where—around a
ramshackle resort hotel near Acapulco—the steaming tropical
underbrush is meant to evoke the terrors of existence. But he
has explored this territory too many times before—the play
seems tired, unadventurous, and self-derivative. Furthermore,
the author's compulsion to express himself on the subjects of
fleshly corruption, time and old age, the malevolence of God,
and the maiming of the sensitive by life has now become so
strong that he no longer bothers to provide a substructure of
action to support his vision. *The Night of the Iguana* enjoys no
organizing principle whatsoever; and except for some perfunctory gestures toward the end, it is very short on plot, pattern, or
theme.

One trouble is that while Williams has fully imagined his personae, he has not sufficiently conceived them in relation to one another, so that the movement of the work is backward toward revelation of character rather than forward toward significant conflict. "The going to pieces of T. Lawrence Shannon," a phrase from the play, might be a more appropriate title, for it focuses mainly on the degradation and breakdown of its central character—a crapulous and slightly psychotic Episcopalian minister, very similar to the alcoholic Consul in Malcolm Lowry's *Under the Volcano*. Thrown out of his church for "fornication and heresy"—after having been seduced by a teen-age parishioner, he refused to offer prayers to a "senile delinquent"—Shannon now conducts guided tours in Mexico, sleeping with underage girls, coping with hysterical female Baptists, and finding evidence of God in thunder, in the vivisection of dogs, and in starving children, scrabbling among dungheaps in their search for food. Other characters brush by this broken heretic, but they hardly connect with him, except to uncover his psycho-sexual history and to expose their own: the Patrona of the hotel, a hearty lecherous widow with two Mexican consorts, out of *Sweet Bird of Youth*; Hannah Jelkes, a virgin spinster with a compassionate nature, out of *Summer and Smoke*; and Nonno, her father, a ninety-seven-year-old poet—deaf, cackling, and comatose—out of *Krapp's Last Tape*. The substance of the play is the exchange, by Hannah and Shannon, of mutual confidences about their sexual failures, while the Patrona shoots him hot glances and the poet labors to complete his last poem. When Shannon goes berserk, and is tied down in a hammock and harassed by some German tourists, the iguana is hastily introduced to give this action some larger symbolic relevance: the lizard has been tied under the house, to be fattened, eaten, and to have its eyes poked out by native boys. Persuaded by Hannah to be kinder than God, Shannon eventually frees the iguana, tying its rope around his own neck when he goes off, another Chance Wayne, to become one of the Patrona's lovers. But though Shannon is captured, Nonno is freed. Having completed his poem about "the earth's obscene corrupting love," he has finally found release from such corruptions in death.

The materials, while resolved without sensationalism or sentiment, are all perfectly familiar: the defeated perverse central
character, punished for his perversity; the Strindbergian identification of the human body with excrement and defilement; the
obsessively sexual determination of every character. But by
keeping his usual excesses to a minimum, Williams has provided the occasion for some striking performances. Margaret
Leighton, especially, has endowed the stainless Hannah with
extraordinary sensibility and tenderness, plumbing depths
which Williams himself has been unable to reach since his
earliest work. Bette Davis, playing the Patrona in flaming red
hair and blue jeans, bats her pendulous lids in her laugh lines
and is always on the surface of her part, but she is still a
strongly felt personality; Alan Webb's Nonno is humorously
senescent; and Patrick O'Neal plays Shannon with suppressed
hysteria and a nagging, relentless drive which sometimes remind
one of Frederic March. Always on hand to produce rain on the
stage, Oliver Smith has forcibly stifled his passion for opulence
in the setting, within which this gifted ensemble seems to find
its way without directorial eyes (Frank Corsaro's name is still
on the program, but I can detect his influence only in a couple
of Method Mexican extras).

For all its virtues, though, the play is decidedly a minor opus.
A rich atmosphere, a series of languid scenes, and some interesting character sketches are more than Williams has offered us in
some time, but they are still not enough to sustain our interest
through a full evening. Perhaps Williams, identifying with
Nonno, has decided to think of himself as only "a minor league
poet with a major league spirit," and there is enough fatigue in
the play to suggest that, again like Nonno, he feels like "the
oldest living and practicing poet in the world." But even a
minor poet fashions his work with more care and coherence
than this; even an aged eagle occasionally spreads its wings. I
am inclined to persist in my heresy that there is at least one
more genuine work of art left in Williams, which will emerge
when he has finally been able to objectify his personal problems
and to shape them into a suitable myth. Meanwhile, let us put

down *The Night of the Iguana* as another of his innumerable exercises in marking time.

(1962)

■ ■

Tennessee Williams has a new play, and this puts him, by purely subjective count, about four plays ahead of Lope de Vega, who wrote over 2,000. Insofar as it has an action, *The Milk Train Doesn't Stop Here Anymore* is Williams' 434th version of the encounter between a pure-corrupt young man and an ogrish, corrupting older woman in a lush and fruity setting (here, the Southern Italian coast). Perhaps aware that the material is rather familiar, Williams treats it in a very peremptory fashion, concentrating instead on a character study of his central figure—a raucous, rich ex-Follies girl, writing her memoirs, and finally accepting the death she is afraid to face through the ministrations of the young man, whom Williams, possibly with a glance at Albee's *Sandbox*, calls the Angel of Death. The female character is occasionally interesting, but the writing is soft, the theme banal, the action sketchy, the play unfinished—and since there is no drama, why should there be a review, especially when the directing, the décor, and the acting (except for a sharp portrait of a Capri witch by Mildred Dunnock) are as indifferent as the text? For more extended commentary, I shall wait until Mr. Williams' desire to form a finished work has caught up with his desire to have something annually produced.

(1963)

HIPSTER DRAMATISTS, SQUARE SPECTATORS

THE EGG by Felicien Marceau;
ROMULUS by Gore Vidal

■ The Broadway theatre has this much in common with American society: It is rapidly becoming an operation of hipsters for the bilking of squares. The hipster—if you are still unfamiliar with the term—is a sophisticated careerist who adapts himself to meretricious surroundings for the sake of advancement, concealing his derisive contempt for his customers while prospering on their gullibility, pretentiousness, and bad taste. He is identified, therefore, by the schizoid split that separates his public from his private personality: he wears a mask of charm and sincerity over a face of scorn. In the past, a person with hipster instincts was forced to become a confidence man (the personification, for Melville, of nineteenth-century American life). But today, the confidence man has emerged from underground to enter respectable institutions, functioning as an advertising executive, a fallout shelter contractor, a teacher of the Twist.

The smoothest of these legitimized con men is the cultural hipster. A product of the "cultural explosion" (which may turn out to be the biggest swindle since the South Sea Bubble), this type operates exclusively in the entertainment media, feeding the square's insatiable appetite for debased cultural objects. But though he manipulates the media behind the scenes, you will not often see his face in public. In TV, for example, where cameras can quickly expose the slightest insincerity, hipsters like David Susskind or Rod Serling have not achieved the eminence of squares like Jack Paar, Lawrence Welk, or Ed Sullivan, for while the square spectator is willing to embrace all varieties of mediocrity, he will not tolerate a hint of condescension. On the other hand, wherever the hipster can hide his face—say, in television programming, mass publications, or the Broadway theatre—his control is more secure. And as the fakery of our society continues to mount, he will probably take over the culture altogether.

The activities of the con man have fascinated dramatists from Ben Jonson (*The Alchemist*) to Bertolt Brecht (*The Three-penny Opera*). But until Felicien Marceau's *The Egg* recently opened, nobody had yet bothered to celebrate the progress of the hipster. If you want to know why, consider the reception of the play in New York. Though it enjoyed substantial runs in more sophisticated capitals like Paris and Jerusalem, *The Egg* was greeted here with unanimous hoots from the daily reviewers and expired within a week: official opinion cannot accept the existence of the hipster, even when he comes from France. With the evidence stored away in a scenery morgue, then, you will have to take my word for it that *The Egg*, except for an abrupt and inconclusive ending, was the most consistently amusing light entertainment of the year. Using a narrative style and vaudeville techniques, Marceau chronicled the picaresque adventures of an ambitious petit bourgeois, determined to make his way against an intransigent system. The image of this system is an egg—it is rotten inside, and in order to pierce its shell, our hero must become just as rotten himself. This he does with an engaging insouciance which grows gradually more ominous as he wends his way through seduction, adultery, theft, marriage, and finally murder (he shoots his wife and successfully pins the rap on her lover). Lacking poetic justice, the play was dismissed as lewd and cynical, probably because it confronted the facts of sex and society without blenching; but compared with such manufactured lubricities as *Shot in the Dark* and *Sunday in New York*, it was a work of unexampled moral idealism.

For once in an import from France, the production did not fail the play. Dick Shawn (a compound of Robert Preston and Eddie Albert that adds up to more than the sum of its parts) played the central character with energetic charm and cheerfulness; and Lamont Johnson, directing the action with an unerring eye for illustrative business, generously permitted some imaginative character actors complete freedom in creating a number of hilarious caricatures. The entertainment, in fact, lacked only one element to make it completely delightful—an appreciative audience. For the hipster that might have enjoyed this play has long since ceased to attend the commercial theatre.

Which does not mean that he has ceased to operate in it. Let me cite, as evidence of the hipster's flourishing influence, the recent adaptation of Duerrenmatt's *Romulus der Grosse*—or GORE VIDAL'S ROMULUS, as the program more shrewdly identifies it. I am certain that Mr. Vidal would have seen the point of *The Egg*, but he is much too clever to make Marceau's mistake: his dramatic writings, while superficially sophisticated, are carefully designed for squares. Confirming in spades his press agent's boast that "Vidal has done it again," he has even managed to make *Romulus* indistinguishable from his other two Broadway opiates, transforming Duerrenmatt's tough parable into an effeminate charade enacted by the theatrical smart set.

What Duerrenmatt wrote was a bitter comedy about the last Roman Emperor—an absolute idealist who permits Rome to be conquered by Germanic hordes as a judgment on its evil past. Vidal has preserved the shell of the original while hollowing out the center, adding a confectionery filling sprinkled with witless political jokes, irrelevant anachronisms, and open thefts from Wilde and Shaw ("Thank heaven," says one character; "No, don't thank heaven, dear, thank me," replies Romulus, a quip lifted from *Major Barbara*). In a pastel setting out of *House and Garden*—populated with Jeeves butlers, pansy courtiers, and, later, bearded Goths in boots, berets, capes, and Sam Browne belts—one hears references to "unRoman activities" and "coddling of subversives," "medical plans for the aged," "the struggle for men's minds," etc., as if Vidal had no other function as an adapter than to recapitulate the inside-dopesterism of *The Best Man*. (With the whole first act devoted to such badinage, the more serious second act seems like a complete change in tone.) As for the characters, these, too, might have walked out of *The Best Man:* the sinister Empress Julia, now endowed with Helena Rubenstein blue hair, has turned into a frivolous Washington hostess, while Romulus has become an effete epigrammatist concerned less with justice than with "style."

About Cyril Ritchard's performance I am of two minds. From the moment he enters the set, scratching his back against a fluted column and winging his lines like Lord Foppington, it is clear that he has been incredibly miscast. But though he destroys Duerrenmatt's Romulus, he almost salvages Vidal's, for he has the art to read the most exhausted witticisms as if they had just been freshly minted. The rest of the cast, however, is not so fortunate; and Joseph Anthony's direction merely compounds the vulgarities of the evening (the casting is particularly insensitive, and to make the Romans into homosexuals is simply in bad taste). *Romulus* is not Duerrenmatt's most stirring work; and it is a little absurd to defend the interests of an author who shows so little interest in defending himself. But in our theatre, no artist is safe from the cultural hipster—or, for that matter, from the square spectator, because despite their contrasted natures, both are the natural antagonists of genuine art.

(1962)

THE COMPOSITE
MUSICAL PLAY

No STRINGS, *Book by Samuel Taylor, Music and Lyrics by Richard Rodgers*

■ It may be that the products of the commercial imagination have now grown so debased that they are no longer suitable objects of satire. Instead of requiring detonation from outside, they are inclined—like Jean Tinguely's self-destroying machines—to blow themselves up with their own built-in explosives. Consider a recent experience of mine. About a week ago—casting around for some distraction during a typical dark night of the soul on Broadway—I began to imagine for myself a composite hit play. Bowing to all theatrical tastes and commercial possibilities, I instantly determined that the work would have to be a musical (Native American Art Form), with a Jewish flavor (Benefit Audience Appeal), and a "serious" theme (nod to the Cultural Explosion). While all the other elements fell nicely into place, the theme had me stymied for a while. Interracial love was good, but overworked; a musical on the subject of the Peace Corps was promising (two such projects have been announced for next year), but as yet untried. Taking note of plays like *Gift of Time* and *Isle of Children*, I finally concluded that the fashion this season was Death. I would make my hero the victim of a mortal disease upon which he could reflect courageously and melodiously (the idea struck me as especially happy since works of this type, emitting a long low whine, are inherently musical). Having hit upon a theme, I stumbled upon a title. The musical would be called *Milk and Cancer*, featuring such catchy tunes as "Tea for Tumor" and (for the coronary subplot) "Zing! Went the Strings of My Heart." Warming to the subject, I even decided to have a Carcinoma Ballet—laid in a sterile abstract operating room representing the hero's unconscious—where the patient, under ether, could wrestle with a malignant cell, only to be rescued by Love in the shape of a gleaming scalpel.

This sort of thing is, admittedly, desperate amusement at best, but already a new musical has arrived which makes my studied eclecticism seem startlingly original: *No Strings*, by Samuel Taylor and Richard Rodgers, is a much more shameless composite than I could ever devise. The work has been advertised as unorthodox, and perhaps I'd better begin by telling you in what its heterodoxy consists. For one thing, the musicians wander dazedly through the action with clarinets, trombones, and flutes, while the actors change the sets—an innovation guaranteed to excite nobody but the theatrical unions who even now are probably planning jurisdictional disputes. And secondly, though Mr. Taylor (less sensitive than I to surfeited themes) has chosen to deal with miscegenation—examining the relations between a high-fashion model and a blocked Pulitzer Prize novelist, both expatriated in France—he dramatizes this subject without ever once acknowledging openly that his hero-ine is a Negress, presumably because it is now an offense against Broadway liberalism to mention even the most obvious racial distinctions.

Spectators will have to be satisfied with these daring depar-tures alone, for the rest of the musical adheres strictly to for-mula. At the end of the first act, the hero and heroine go to bed together (their climax is suggested by a jazz drummer, drenched in blue light, frantically banging away at jungle tom-toms), but they are forced to part at the end of the play—the hero return-ing, for the sake of his art, to his "roots" ("rock-ribbed Maine," as it is called in another of Rodgers' state anthems), the heroine to her presumably enviable career as a Paris clotheshorse. As background for this courageous love story, the collaborators have provided a Hollywood version of the European fashion world (bearded photographers, dumb models, and a wisecrack-ing editor of Paris Vogue, all stolen from a movie called Funny Face), thus permitting the costumer to indulge a misogynistic impulse by dressing the heroine in knickers and the chorus in garments which look suspiciously like long underwear. (Buried in such chic vulgarity, the whole production reminded me of an English debating proposition that "Americans have taste—acres and acres of taste!") The scenic designer, furthermore, using panels, screens, and exposed klieg lights of various horrendous colors, whisks us to places like Honfleur, Deauville, and Monte Carlo—giving the director an opportunity to employ some freeze techniques from John Huston's Moulin Rouge, and the hero a shot at one of those inevitable state-of-mind ballets in which he vacillates between demi-mondaine fleshpots and his officious mistress who keeps urging him to win another Pulitzer Prize. I should add that despite certain Jamesian echoes about the corrupting effect of European culture on innocent Ameri-cans (inappropriate enough to a time which has completely reversed this relationship), the Europe of No Strings is about as

authentic as the Siam, Polynesia, and Israel of previous musicals—an exotic travel poster illustrated with stock types dressed
in native costumes.

As for the music, it has been obvious ever since Lorenz Hart
died that Richard Rodgers is always at the mercy of his lyricist—nothing else will explain the disparity between his former
sophisticated melodies and the sentimental folksy kitsch he
wrote with Hammerstein. Having composed the lyrics for *No
Strings* himself, he is now at his own mercy, and the results are
not very felicitous. Though some of the songs are tuneful
enough (the most melodious one is plugged so hard that one is
reminded of a Woolworth pianist selling the latest sheet music), none show any rhythmic ingenuity and all are self-derivative, while his clichéd lyrics demonstrate that the possibilities
of the love song have long since been exhausted. Reflecting the
play's tendency to line up squarely on each side of every question, the title song celebrates both marriage and love without
any attachments; reflecting what is undoubtedly the animating
motive of the entire work, the others are mainly about money
(in the most frenetic production number, in fact, a Tulsa millionairess stimulates the audience by doing a striptease with
hundred-dollar bills instead of fans). The one virtue of this
musical is Diahann Carroll—exquisite, blithe, and graceful—
who plays the model with a good deal more dignity than the
part deserves. But even she has been forced into imitation.
Expert at a quiet, gentle, restrained style, she has been directed
to growl, gurgle, roll her eyeballs, and pat her thigh sensually
like Lena Horne—presumably to suggest that note of primitive
sexuality which whites generally associate with Negroes while
proclaiming that no differences really exist.

But it is useless to catalogue any further the borrowings, vulgarities, and evasions of this cynical work; suffice it to say, it
makes my own composite hit play seem like a workable possibility for next season. And herein lies the dilemma of the practicing critic. For just as America, according to Philip Roth, has
become too grotesque to be recorded convincingly by a writer of
fiction, so the Broadway stage is beginning to escape the limits
of descriptive prose.

(1962)

VOX POPULI,
VOX BOX

A FUNNY THING HAPPENED ON THE WAY
TO THE FORUM *by Burt Shevelove and Larry
Gelbart, Music and Lyrics by Stephen Sondheim*

■ Fiddled by Walter Kerr while Broadway burns, here is one
of the favorite tunes of the theatrical intelligentsia (music and
lyrics by Vox *Populi*): "Theatre is for the people, and for the
largest number . . . We are told . . . that the only way we
can reach great numbers of people is to stoop or pander to
them. That is not in the least true. Think of . . . Shakespeare,
Sophocles, or Molière." Mr. Kerr has been thinking of these
dramatists for a long time now, invoking their shades whenever
he wishes to deplore the "snobbishness," "abrasiveness," and
"difficulty" of theatrical art since Ibsen. Recently, he has come
to believe that even the commercial drama is "an unpopular
form in America," presumably because it reaches fewer people
than the movies or TV. Seven years ago, Eric Bentley called this
aspect of Mr. Kerr's thinking "democrateering," and it is
heartening to see that the reviewer for the *Herald Tribune* has
never lost his faith in the instinctual good taste of "the folks
out front." Nevertheless, I do not think that his vision of a
quality theatre for "massive audiences" will ever materialize,
especially if it is based on precedents from the past—for such
analogies are full of pitfalls and inaccuracies.

As a matter of fact, even the most popular classical dramatists
never reached "massive audiences": the longest-lived success of
the Greek, Elizabethan, and French Neo-Classical theatres
would hardly have filled a Broadway house for three weeks. Nor
is it true that they never pandered to their audiences—I except

138 / BROADWAY

the Greeks who were writing for a religious congregation, but Shakespeare, for example, certainly made frequent concessions to the groundlings, and blushed over them in his sonnets. The quality of the pandering, of course, depends upon the pander, but it also depends upon the customer; and we must be careful to distinguish between the popular elements of a class society, bound by a common tradition, common interests, and vigorous folk instincts, and the popular elements of a mass society, dehumanized by the mass media, demoralized by industrialism, and degraded by the lack of any common purpose beyond materialistic and status success. If we imagine Shakespeare returning today, as Dostoevski imagined the return of Christ, he would have three possible alternatives: either to withdraw into a "snobbish" and "abrasive" art of revolt against the brutalization of mass man; to conform and write middle-brow Broadway plays for the wealthy theatregoer; or to reach Mr. Kerr's "massive audience" by turning out suburban situation comedy for the *Danny Thomas Show*. But it would undoubtedly extend even Shakespeare's substantial powers to satisfy all modern tastes and himself at the same time—assuming, of course, that the sponsors, producers, backers, networks, agencies, and all the other enemies of honest art (including the reviewers) would even let him try.

Actually, only one modern artist—Charlie Chaplin—ever managed to appeal to all levels of culture, and he succeeded only when he was working in a more popular genre. For if tragedy was too bleak for progressive America, then ebullient comedy was its natural form of expression; and if a serious work like *Monsieur Verdoux* inevitably flopped with its audiences, then the more lighthearted *City Lights* could still be a popular success. Similarly, in the twenties and thirties (when the country was still vigorous) the work of such comic roustabouts as W. C. Fields, Buster Keaton, and the Marx Brothers was also a substantial source of national amusement (though not of national art). Yet, even our unconditioned response to farce and slapstick has been vitiated by the recent domestication of our instincts and the growing pretentiousness of our tastes—until the popular forms have all but disappeared from the popular media, exiled to the work of those "difficult" and "unpopular" playwrights whom Mr. Kerr deplores.

Still, it has not quite disappeared, because a raucous farce just breezed into town, bringing with it the atmosphere of balmier days. A *Funny Thing Happened on the Way to the Forum*, to be sure, has had to be smuggled in disguised as a "musical" in order to be produced at all; but the disguise is so transparent that none but the charity audiences will be deceived. Sticking with surprising fidelity to a number of Plautine farces—situations and characters have been borrowed from *Casina*, *Curculio*, *Miles Gloriosus*, and *Pseudolus*, among others—the work is also flavored with a generous seasoning of Minsky burlesque technique, thus combining Roman convention and American invention in a way that should delight both traditionalists and moderns who still respond to the lowest comedy.

There is a problem with the songs. The essence of farce is uninterrupted movement; yet, whenever the action begins to gather momentum, the lights are lowered and somebody stops short to warble one of Stephen Sondheim's tunes. In addition, the sophisticated lyrics, while superior to the melodies, come from that world of chic which inspires arch Broadway musicals, and are thus in jarring contrast to the wonderful vulgarity of the physical action. Still, the evening is blissfully free of "choreography," and the actors are permitted to be as gross and earthbound as they please, while serving up the farcical ingredients (mistaken identity, female impersonation, double entendre, and the most dizzy chase in years) of this abundant comic potpourri.

If the play seems an evocation of happier years, so do the performances. American actors have never lost their comic talents, but these are so rarely exercised that they almost have to be resurrected; and much of the acting seems the result of expert antiquarian research by the director, George Abbott. Jack Gilford as Hysterium ("slave of slaves") has borrowed the nervous vacancy of Hugh Herbert, twitching with terror as, dressed in female costume, he runs from a lustful old man; Ruth Kobart, as the shrew Domina, has turned to Margaret Dumont for her fine impersonation of a coquettish ogre; Ronald Holgate as Miles ("I am a parade") Gloriosus reminds one of a muscle-bound Nelson Eddy; and David Burns, puffing, blustering, and cooing as the impotent-amorous Senex—a traditional Plautine butt—has reached back to the top banana style of the old girlie musicals.

As for Zero Mostel, playing the prologue and the wily slave who instigates the action, he is indebted to nothing but his own superb imagination. Whether feigning boredom amidst a covey of luscious courtesans (reclining languidly, he plays ticktacktoe on the undulating stomach of the gorgeous Pecunia), declaiming Socrates' hemlock speech while being threatened by an indignant suitor, or transforming his flexible bulk into an inexhaustible variety of animate and inanimate objects, Mostel is responsible for more mischievous and explosive invention than anyone since the splitters of the atom. If comedy is still barely alive in America, we must thank such people as the incomparable Zero who never lost their sense of the ridiculous during the fatuities of the age. And we must thank the authors of this farce who have found the courage to offer audiences little more than joy and laughter in a vanishing form of popular entertainment.

I hope the work presages a trend, but I am inclined to doubt it. Even now there are rumbles (and from Walter Kerr) about its breaches of "taste," and when audiences discover that they are paying $9.90 a ticket for nothing more portentous than another Boys from Syracuse, word of mouth may kill the run. But even if such popular entertainments eventually return, we must not confuse them with dramatic art. As long as the majority remains enfeebled in soul, nerve, and intellect—demoralized in spirit, seeking release in fantasies and opiates—the work of the serious playwright will remain a minority expression, recruiting its spectators from among that "aristocracy of character, of will, of intellect" which Ibsen hoped would resist the cultural degradations of the democratic dogma. The voice of the people is still the voice from the TV box, and he who would have it otherwise must first start a revolution in the consciousness of modern man.

(1962)

BROADWAY REVIVALS

STRANGE INTERLUDE *by Eugene O'Neill;*
TOO TRUE TO BE GOOD *by George Bernard Shaw;*
ARTURO UI *by Bertolt Brecht*

■ A trio of revivals, the first with a note of caution.

Strange Interlude: One of the advantages of the weekly over the daily reviewer is the opportunity he has to temper his immediate responses with more judicious reflections; but on the present occasion, the advantage is wholly lost. Having been cruelly hammered into the ground for five groggy hours—during which time I was too craven to astonish the audience's infuriating piety with a few purgative guffaws—I am still shaking with suppressed rage, four days after the event. I must therefore beg the reader's indulgence for what is certain to be a most immoderate display of spleen.

Strange Interlude is not only the worst play O'Neill ever wrote; it may be the worst play ever written by a major dramatist. One of those ill-born monstrosities O'Neill squeezed out before he began to think like a dramatic artist instead of like a sophomore in psychology, the play examines the bleak mental terrain of some of the most vacant characters ever assembled on a single stage, employing a rhetoric which combines the tremulous climaxes of soap opera ("For the sake of your future happiness and my son's I've got to speak! Your engagement forces me to! It's because the marriage is impossible!"), the gushy confessions found in back copies of *True Romances* ("That last night before he sailed—in his arms until my body ached—kisses until my lips were numb"), and, most painful of all, the anti-language of psychoanalese ("She needs normal love objects for the emotional life Gordon's death blocked up in her"). Actually, O'Neill's characters are stereotypes from pulp fiction (consider their very names: Nina Leeds, Gordon Evans, Edmund Darrell, etc.), who were inspired less by James Joyce, I suspect, than by Molly Bloom's favorite author, Paul de Kock. What O'Neill tried to do was dignify, through psychological complication, a trivial bourgeois she-tragedy about a willful, neurotic woman and the weak men she leads around by the nose (a kind of Nina Faces Life, as one wit put it); but his characters exist less for themselves than for their author's collegiate generalizations about "Life." They are not human beings, but pseudo ideas; and like the windy novelist, Marsden, who tells us fifty times about his mother fixation, they endlessly iterate their single animating concept. Still they are more fortunate than the audience, which is also subjected to their unspoken thoughts (equally dreary), through O'Neill's clumsy, self-conscious use of non-dramatic asides and soliloquies. Nine acts of blah-blah-blah, with a melodramatic climax (son hitting father) to persuade you you've seen a play.

The most charitable way to treat the current production is to say that no actor can fertilize sterile material; but it is difficult to be charitable when the Actors Studio Theatre actually elected to stir these dead remains for its initial production. It was an obvious choice, considering the Studio's quasi-Freudian ambiance. Still, the performance is a shambles: star-infected and under-rehearsed in precisely the manner of that commercial theatre the group is pretending to reform. The actors, though they have been working together for years, give no signs of ensemble consciousness, and all are frozen in the stylized attitudes which first brought them to public attention. As Nina, Geraldine Page has fallen back on her old mannerisms: the neurasthenic fluttering, the quick emotional breakdown, the clicking sounds, the quavering voice rising and falling on selected syllables. Once again, Pat Hingle, as Nina's husband, is playing the loud, brash, All-American simpleton; once again, Ben Gazzara, as Nina's stud, is playing the sinister matinee heavy (though in the process of breaking the role to his movie personality, he does achieve the only few moments of crisp-ness). Franchot Tone is befuddled as Nina's father; William Prince sententiously dull as Marsden; and Geoffrey Horne and Jane Fonda emotionally shallow as a pair of young lovers. David Hays has designed some tacky, transparent settings, possibly as a comment on the play; and José Quintero's direction alternates between the reverential, the ponderous, the ludicrous, and the loud, reaching its decibel climax in the eighth act ("that incomparable comedy scene at the boat races," as Robert Benchley described it, "when people begin dropping dead") in an orgy of screams, shouts, and groans. It was the original Broadway audience that was really responsible for this play, since it pampered and indulged O'Neill's pretensions before his genius had a chance to mature; and since that audience continues to dominate our theatre, the play continues to inspire the perfect middle-brow tableau: hundreds of goofy admirers huddled around an Emperor completely naked of poetry, intellect, or art.

Too True to Be Good: A more accomplished galaxy of star personalities, most of them miscast, are currently whooping it up at the expense of one of Shaw's lesser plays. As read, *Too True to Be Good* has genuine moments of interest, but it rambles aimlessly, has no intrinsic form, and suffers from the author's indecision over whether to write a light Gilbertian comedy or to express the intense, almost nihilistic bitterness which was gnawing at his soul during the dark days of 1932. Not one to disturb the complacency of an audience, Albert Marre, the director, has solved Shaw's dilemma by updating the play to the present, and by cutting out all its more depressing ideas, including Shaw's reflections on disease, the cruelty and madness of World War I, the futility of the Geneva negotiations, the spiritual dislocation caused by Einstein's discoveries, the discouragement of the young, and his own emotional bankruptcy.

Having thus amputated the philosophical limbs of the play, its most interesting features, Marre is able to pass off Shaw's "Political Extravaganza" as what the program calls "A Modern Comedy." It is now a pleasant, apolitical bromide—a cartoon, complete with musical comedy set, merry bridge music, and animated sequences (à la *Oh Dad*, etc.) by Abner Dean—about a group of beach bums loafing on some North African seacoast, unaccountably bored, probably by too much sun and surf. Since this vacationer's comedy could have been written by anybody, one is willing to overlook such problems as Eileen Heckart's unsuccessful struggle with a cockney accent, Cedric Hardwicke's epic battle with his dentures, Robert Preston's identifiably Midwestern charm and energy, and David Wayne's image of T. E. Lawrence as a mischievous leprechaun (though the latter interpretation is one for which Shaw is largely to blame). Glynis Johns, as a screeching invalid, however, and Cyril Ritchard, as a supercilious British Colonel, are so good in a clean Shavian vein that I should like to have seen them in the play the author originally wrote.

Arturo Ui: This is certainly among the weakest of Brecht's plays, an ideological satire on the Nazi era which is totally inadequate to its subject. By identifying the Hitler gang with Chicago "protection" hoodlums, and the Prussian Junkers with American businessmen, Brecht interprets the rise of Nazism as a uniquely economic phenomenon. But this emphasis ignores Hitler's cruelty and madness, and entirely neglects his anti-Semitism. Brecht's incorporation of scenes from Shakespeare's *Richard III* and Goethe's *Faust* is ingenious; some of the clowning is fun in the style of Chaplin's *Great Dictator*, which probably inspired it; and an episode in which a Shakespearean ham teaches Arturo all his histrionic mannerisms emphasizes the connection between cheap theatre and demagogic techniques (later, Lenny Bruce is to imagine a Hitler created entirely to order by M.C.A.). The bulk of the play, however, is literalistic, heavy, blunt; if Brecht, in his early work, could predict the brutality of the Nazis before it even entered history, he later could not face the real thing for what it actually was.

Since David Merrick has a similar difficulty with reality, nobody seemed surprised when he approached *Arturo Ui* as if he were producing another *Gypsy*. For this purpose, he selected George Tabori as adapter, Jule Styne as composer, and Tony

Richardson as director, thus investing the work with a tin ear, a brass voice, and a chrome spirit. With clichés splitting over our brows, electric lights exploding in our faces, horns and percussion pounding in our ears, and scenes whizzing past our eyeballs at the speed of noise, the evening took on the aspect of a Shriners' convention, or a concitation of the backward devils, firecrackers shooting out of their behinds. Christopher Plummer, as Arturo, managed his role with a slithering force and a hangdog charm, but his performance was misconceived, modeled as it seemed to be on Tom Pedi about to lecture a housewife on the virtues of *Dash*.

(1963)

ALBEE AND THE
MEDUSA HEAD

WHO'S AFRAID OF VIRGINIA WOOLF?
by Edward Albee

■ Edward Albee's new work embodies both the failings and the virtues of his previous plays. But its positive achievements are substantial, and I am finally beginning to regard this playwright's future with real expectation. Albee's technical dexterity has always been breathtaking—for sheer theatrical skill, no American, not even Williams, can match him—but like Williams, he has been inclined to falsify his native gifts, distorting experience through self-defensive reflecting mirrors. In *Who's Afraid of Virginia Woolf?*, Albee is still not looking the Gorgon smack in the eye. Still, he has conjured up its outline. And if he tends to focus more on writhing snakes than on the other features of this terrifying monster, then even these quick glances are more penetrating than I have come to expect; and they are always projected in steaming, raging, phantasmagoric theatrical images.

Virginia Woolf is an ambitious play, and it evokes the shades of the most ambitious dramatists. The central conflict—a Strindbergian battle royal between George, a contemplative history professor with an unsuccessful career, and Martha, his bitter shrewish wife—proceeds through a series of confessions, revelations, and interior journeys which recall the circuitous windings of O'Neill's late plays. Glued together by mutual hatred and mutual recriminations, the couple can connect only through enmity, each exposing the other's failures, inadequacies, vices, and secret illusions in language of savagely ironic scorn. Though the climax of the work is built on such an exposure, however, Albee seems less interested in the real history of his characters than in the way they conceal and protect their reality: the conflict is also a kind of game, with strict rules, and what they reveal about each other may not be true. This comedy of concealment reminds one of Pirandello, and even more of Jean Genet. For George and Martha—each by turns the aggressor—shift their identities like reptiles shedding skins. And as the evening grows more alcoholic, and the atmosphere more distended and surrealistic, their "total war" becomes a form of ritual play-acting, performed upon the shifting sands of truth.

The "setting" for this play-within-a-play is a late night party; the "audience" is composed of a hollow young biology instructor, Nick, and his demure, simpering wife, Honey. A conventionally shallow couple, they are at first innocent bystanders, embarrassed by the squabbling of their hosts, then full participants, as George sadistically exposes their guilty secrets: Nick's academic opportunism, Honey's surreptitious abortions. The waspish "fun and games" begin to take the form of ruthlessly aggressive charades. After "Humiliate the Host" and "Get the Guests" comes "Hump the Hostess" as Martha and Nick, in revenge against George, make a feeble attempt to cuckold him in the kitchen. The last episode, "Bringing up Baby," constitutes George's revenge on Martha—not because she tried to betray him (her infidelities are apparently innumerable), but because she broke one of the rules of the game: she mentioned their "son" to strangers. Forcing Martha to recount the child-hood history of this absent youth, George reads the requiem for the dead, climaxing this litany with the announcement that their son has been killed in an auto accident. But the child has never existed. He is merely the essential illusion of the childless Martha, a consoling fiction in her inconsolable reality. The play ends with Honey now determined to have a child, and Martha, submissive and frightened, being comforted by George.

Everyone seems to have boggled at this fictional child; and it is certain that the play collapses at its moment of climax. But the difficulty is not that the author introduces a spurious ele-ment into an otherwise truthful play. It is, rather, that he sud-denly confronts us with a moment of truth after an evening of stage illusions. Albee's theatrical inventiveness rests mainly on incongruous juxtapositions: when George aims a shotgun at his braying wife, for example, it shoots not bullets but a Japanese parasol. These shock tactics are a sure-fire comic technique, but they have the effect of alienating the spectator from the action the very moment he begins to accept it. Thus, when George launches a blistering attack on the evils of modern science, Albee undercuts it with a ludicrous non sequitur: "I will not give up Berlin." And when Martha speaks of her need to escape reality, he has her do so in a broad Irish brogue. George re-sponds to Martha's infidelity by nonchalantly offering her flow-ers; he tells a harrowing story of matricide and patricide which is proved, first, to be autobiographical, and second, to be false; and when asked about the telegram announcing his son's death, he claims to have eaten it. Truth and illusion may be confused, as one character tells us, but after three and a half hours of prestidigitation, we become reluctant to accept one of these magical tricks as the real thing. In short, Albee is a highly accomplished stage magician, but he fails to convince us there is nothing up his sleeve. His thematic content is incompatible with his theatrical content—hi-jinks and high seriousness fail to fuse.

On the other hand, the author has a fine time showing off his sleight of hand, incidentally, I suspect, conjuring his action into the outlines of a classical myth (the evidence is jumbled, and I may be crazy, but I think I can detect elements of the story of Aphrodite, Ares, and Hephaestus, mixed with pieces from the story of Aphrodite and Adonis). And he has been provided with a really superb production, deftly managed by Alan Schneider. I have some quibbles about the set, which is too realistic to suggest the phantasmagoric quality of the action; and two of the characters, Nick and Honey, are too sketchily written to be played with much depth (though Melinda Dillon makes a fine caricature out of the giggly wife). But Uta Hagen and Arthur Hill are astonishingly good as the two slashing, trumpeting domestic animals—Miss Hagen crude, ballsy, relentlessly vicious, with a horse laugh like Martha Raye's; Mr. Hill, by turns meek and malicious, driving toward the jugular with a fury born of despair.

In spite of all the excellences of play and production, however, I am left with my equivocal response. In his latest play, Edward Albee proves once again that he has wit, cunning, theatricality, toughness, formal control, poetry—in short, all the qualities of a major dramatist but one: that selfless commitment to a truthful vision of life which constitutes the universal basis of all serious art. Possibly out of fear of such commitments, Albee is still coquetting with his own talent, still resisting any real identification with his material, so that he tends to confuse his themes, shift his attitudes, and subvert his characters. Yet, a genuine insight, merely sketched in his earlier work, is now beginning to find fuller expression: that in a time of deadened instinct, people will use any methods, including deadly hatred, in order to find their way to others. This, or something like it, may become the solid foundation of Albee's future writing; but whatever it is, I await what is to come with eagerness. For if Albee can confront the Medusa head without the aid of parlor tricks or mirrors, he may yet turn us all to stone.

(1962)

CANDIDE AMONG THE CULTURE-VULTURES

THE BEAUTY PART by S. J. Perelman

■ *The Beauty Part* is an animated cartoon, with satirical shadings, about the American culture industry. It lacks form, focus, or consistent intention—but it is immensely amusing, and there are enough teeth left in its mouth, after the inevitable out-of-town extractions, to provide some bite as well. Patterning his action on Voltaire's *Candide*, S. J. Perelman traces the picaresque adventures of a young Park Avenue idealist named Lance Weatherwax, heir to the Weatherwax All-Weather Handy Garbage Disposal fortune. His mind poisoned by art-appreciation courses, his heart aflame for a loose-living bohemian decorator named April Monkhood, Lance has determined to repudiate his inheritance, and give up his life to Art, convinced that the world of culture is the best of all possible worlds.

To disabuse his hero of this fantastic notion, Perelman shows Lance that culture is the biggest sell of all, mainly by introducing him to a venal gallery of opportunistic artmongers and ostentatious culture-vultures. These include an Action painter who sells out to Hollywood for a percentage of the gross; a vulgar housewife anxious to buy an asbestos painting ("Who cares about the subject matter, so long as it doesn't clash with the drapes?") to beautify her free-floating fireplace; a couple of sensationalist Civil War novelists, one of whom is writing about "the Confederacy as seen through the eyes of a Creole call-girl"; a TV gamester and book publisher of Charnel House, interested primarily in lecture tours and movie sales; and a sculptress who creates portrait busts out of Castile soap on a Procter and Gamble fellowship.

These and others are enough to persuade Lance that the cultural explosion is detonated by the hand of commerce; and after serving his apprenticeship in painting, writing, movie-making, and advertising, he is finally reunited with his now sadly sullied Cunegonde. April has been reduced to entertaining at male conventions; and when she is arrested for "conspiring to come out of a cake and dance with a gorilla," Lance can save her honor only by bribing a corrupt judge. Convinced at last that "the things that matter are the things we can touch," Lance decides to let the foundations arbitrate truth and beauty; he will marry April and cultivate his garden of scratch. The first crop is tenderly displayed by Lance's father, who enters stroking a baby's bassinet, then throws its contents into the orchestra—a sheaf of dollar bills.

The cheerful materialism of this conclusion, though designed to please, will probably find as little favor with the Broadway audience as Mr. Perelman's jaundiced look at its cultural pretensions; and I suspect that the author's personal bassinet would have grown fuller had he chosen a less naked approach to his subject. The middle-class spectator, whatever his private affections, does not usually like to see money stroked in public; and whatever his actual behavior, he still prefers a few gestures in the direction of integrity. Perelman's cynicism, however, is a wholesome antidote to the usual theatrical hypocrisy; and The Beauty Part, like Felicien Marceau's The Egg (which it resembles in many ways), manages to give us a refreshing glimpse into the hidden motives behind our canting ideals.

Other sources of refreshment include a number of farcical interludes which recall the halcyon days of the Marx Brothers; an expert cast performing, under Noel Willman's aptly two-dimensional direction, in a variety of double roles (Charlotte Rae, Alice Ghostley, and Larry Hagman are especially fine); and, of course, the splendidly diversified talents of Bert Lahr. Lahr has a little difficulty wrapping his lips around Perelman's highly verbal wit, but no matter—the play permits him a broad range of comic characterizations. These include Lance's satyro-manic father, sputtering with outraged gentility as he accounts to his wife for a high-pitched off-stage scream ("Really, Octavia, I just had to give our French maid a severe dressing down"); Hyacinth Beddoes Laffoon, a lecherous woman publisher of horror magazines exulting in her power over male editors; Harry Hubris, the Hollywood producer of a musical on the life of John Singer Sargent; Nelson Smedley, of Smedley Snacketerias, who keeps his palsied hand on a direct line to the John Birch society; and Judge Herman J. Rinderbrust, who tries cases on TV, his verdicts influenced by the sponsors, the ratings, and the mammaries of his female defendants.

Most of these characters and situations are burlesque stand-ards—some even appeared recently in that more compromised work, *Little Me*, executed with less success by Sid Caesar. What Perelman adds to the familiar brew is his linguistic flair (compounded of elaborate circumlocutions and Yiddishisms), generous topical references, and sardonic comment. It is the sharpness of the satirical tone which seems new in Perelman, whose writings have always struck me as rather mild-mannered; and there are indications that, seasoned by the affectation and meretriciousness of our age, his cup of bitterness is beginning to spill over. Still, the author is recruiting his audience from the very community he would excoriate; and for this reason, perhaps, his moral position is indecisive, vacillating between ridicule and celebration of the audience's assumed values (the ending, for example, with its half-ironic, half-serious testimonies to money, is particularly ambiguous). Perelman has the capacity to become a very good stage satirist, but like so many writers in his dilemma, he must first be willing to accept an embattled role. One does not war on the cultural pretenders and their publicists by joining ranks with the ex-Philistines who now buy their goods.

(1963)

BRECHT VERSUS BROADWAY

MOTHER COURAGE AND HER CHILDREN
by Bertolt Brecht, adapted by Eric Bentley

■ Brecht's masterly chronicle of the Thirty Years War, *Mother Courage and Her Children*, is often interpreted as a straightforward pacifist document, but it is not simply that. It is also a relentless Marxist indictment of the economic motives behind international aggression. If property is theft in *The Threepenny Opera*, it is rape, pillage, and murder in *Mother Courage*—war, in short, is an extension not of diplomacy but of free enterprise. As for the financier, he is no longer a gangster, like Macheath. He is now a cynical warlord—like the Swedish King Gustavus, who pretends to be animated by religious zeal but who is actually seeking personal gain and territorial aggrandizement. In this atmosphere, where Protestants and Catholics slaughter each other for fun and profit, all human ideals degenerate into hypocritical cant, while heroism shatters into splinters of cruelty, madness, or greed. Brecht works these grim sardonic ironies, however, without bringing a single military adventurer center stage. Like the invisible bourgeoisie of *Threepenny*, the kings and commanders of *Mother Courage* remain in the background of the play, as well as in the rear of the battles. The external conflict is narrated, like newspaper headlines, in legends preceding each scene; but the dramatic action focuses on the lives of the war's subordinates and noncombatants, plying local commerce. "The war is just the same as trading," and "General Tilley's victory at Leipzig" has significance only insofar as it "costs Mother Courage four shirts."

Mother Courage, to be sure, is a pathetic victim of this war—she sacrifices three children to it. She is not, however, simply a passive sufferer, she is also an active agent in her own destruction. Precariously suspended between her maternal and commercial instincts, Courage may curse the war as a mother, but as a businesswoman, she is identified with it. A "hyena of the battlefield," she speculates on the lives of men. And since her canteen wagon is her only means of survival, she treats it as a fourth child, tied to her by a commercial umbilical—the three children of her flesh, significantly, are all taken off while she is haggling. Thus, Mother Courage is another of Brecht's split characters, a compound of good and evil—but one which adds up to more than the sum of its parts. For Courage achieves a third dimension beyond her ideological function. Like Falstaff (her Shakespearean prototype), she is an escaped character who baffles the author's original intentions. Salty, shrewd, hard-bitten, and skeptical, Courage is a full-blooded personification of the anti-heroic view of life. In a moving lyric, "The Song of the Great Capitulation," she traces her progress from a youthful Romantic idealist to a cautious compromiser, marching in time with the band, and, throughout the play, she remains faithful to the doctrine of number one. What she preaches is that the Ten Commandments are a mug's game, and that virtues like bravery, honesty, and unselfishness will invariably bring you low—as indeed such virtues flatten foolhardy Eilif, simple-minded Swiss Cheese, and, finally, kindly Kattrin. Restraining her motherly feelings, Courage survives; yielding to hers, Kattrin dies. But in the world of the play, death and survival are equally dismal alternatives. At the end, childless and desolate, Courage straps herself to her battered wagon and continues to follow the soldiers, having learned nothing except that man's capacity for suffering is limitless. But this knowledge is the tragic perception; and Brecht, for all his ideologizing, has recreated a tragic universe in which the cruelty of men, the venality of society, and the indifference of the gods seem immutable conditions of life.

The ideological structure, however, provides the intellectual spine of the drama; and I have stressed its importance because the current production is intellectually spineless. It is difficult to say why, since it is totally free from the usual Broadway hokum or cynicism. Eric Bentley's idiomatic translation preserves the bite of the German, Paul Dessau's score is sharp and wheedling, and Jerome Robbins' direction proceeds, in all externals, with almost reverential fidelity to the text. Still, the only episode which works is the emotionally charged Drum Scene (virtually stage-proof anyway). The rest of the evening is too often static and labored, and the ironies very rarely register. Certainly, the affluent Broadway audience is partly to blame. Lacking either the wit or the inclination to respond to Marxist mockery, it has a Yahoo's appetite only for blunt obscenities (a soldier's "Kiss my ass," for example, brought the opening night house down)—and no actor is going to press for unappreciated subtleties. Then, again, Mr. Robbins, for all his good intentions, is not enough of a director for a play of this scope, mounted in a four-week rehearsal period. Taking place on a clean bare stage, dressed only with Courage's wagon and occasional set pieces, the action itself seems peculiarly clean and bare. One misses stage business, directorial detail, the bustle of life; the actors do not seem sufficiently at home with their props and costumes; and underneath the surface scruffiness, a hint of American wholesomeness still sneaks through. One of Robbins' effective devices is to project, on a burlap cyclorama, photographs of twentieth-century soldiers and civilians in dusty retreat—but this merely emphasizes the play's anti-war implications, which are already rather obvious.

Even this scheme could have been partially compatible with Brecht's design; but the central role of Mother Courage is disastrously miscast. Ann Bancroft should probably be commended for undertaking a character beyond her years, training, and talents—but like the bravery of Courage's son, Eilif, this often strikes one as mere foolhardiness. Miss Bancroft's impersonation of age is particularly unconvincing, partly because of flat make-up and a form-fitting waist, partly because of her own inexperience. In order to overcome these handicaps, she has been forced into monotonous vocal intonations, which, along with her aphoristic inflections, account for much of the evening's tedium. Beyond this, the part of Mother Courage demands intelligence and a capacity for being unpleasant; Miss Bancroft is an exclusively emotional actress who cannot resist playing for sympathy. Her best moments, apart from her rendering of the songs, come in climaxes of grief, and the final scene, where Courage painfully pulls at her wagon, her mouth agape like a wounded animal, is truly harrowing. For the balance of the play, however, Miss Bancroft has the sound and gestures of a tired Jewish housewife, with no more cutting edge than Molly Goldberg. Zohra Lampert, on the other hand, is expressive, lovely, and poignant as the mute Kattrin (though perhaps too spastic in her movements). And though Barbara Harris lapses into Second City vocal mannerisms as the whore Yvette, Mike Kellin and Gene Wilder contribute moments of crisp humor as the Cook and the Chaplain, and Eugene Roche and John Harkins are vigorous in lesser roles. I have harped on the failures of the production; but there are still sufficient virtues in it to make this an important theatrical occasion. A Brecht masterpiece has been produced with all the care, respect, and expertise that our professional theatre can muster. If this is still not quite enough, we must locate the inadequacy in the nature of the American theatre itself.

(1963)

THE PLAYWRIGHT
AS IMPERSONATOR

Carson McCullers' THE BALLAD OF THE SAD CAFÉ, adapted to the stage by Edward Albee

■ Edward Albee's artistic identity has always been highly uncertain, but he has hitherto managed to exercise his substantial gifts for artistic impersonation. Lacking a developed style or a compelling subject, he elected to model himself on the more spectacular modern dramatists—and his impressions of Genet (*The Zoo Story*), Williams (*Bessie Smith*), and Ionesco (*The American Dream*) were, for the most part, very expert. By the time of *Who's Afraid of Virginia Woolf?*, Albee's gifts for mimicry were so advanced, and his models (Strindberg and O'Neill) so elevated, that he produced an ersatz masterpiece—masterly in its execution, ersatz at its core. And I was even persuaded, for a time, that Albee would soon speak in a firm personal voice. I was mistaken. His latest play shows him still to be imitating—and imitating now an inferior writer. In *The Ballad of the Sad Café*, even Mr. Albee's capacity for impersonation seems to have failed him; and the result is a trivial and a tedious play.

A question springs to mind: Why, when he has all the great artistic roles to choose from, does Albee now decide to play the part of Carson McCullers? Miss McCullers' Gothic stories were modish twenty years ago, but, since they were so obviously written for female readers, they eventually found their proper level among the pages of *Vogue* and *Harper's Bazaar*. For beneath her bizarre costuming, Miss McCullers wears the girdle of the genteel lady novelist—Charlotte Brontë gone sour on too many chitlins and grits. Mr. Albee's new play also belongs in the women's magazines, but whereas Miss McCullers' novella is at least partially redeemed by a suggestive style and a penumbral atmosphere, the playwright's adaptation is unredeemed and unredeemable. *The Ballad of the Sad Café* is a mannerist play without the slightest hint of manner; a work in the Southern decadent tradition by a writer who, apparently, has never set foot in the South.

Consider Mr. Albee's crude way with Southern diction. His dialogue—by contrast with which O'Neill's New England speech seems like a miracle of eloquence—is almost indistinguishable from Basic English. "Cousin Lymon go," mumbles the heroine, "I be all alone." As for me, I be totally unable to grasp the principle behind the author's use of the verb *to be*, which is invariably either omitted from the sentence ("Timber good to have") or left uninflected ("I be partial to collards if they be cooked with sausage")—this is the kind of underwater language one expects to see bubbling from the lips of skin-divers. Mr. Albee's other idea about regional speech is that country folk repeat everything six or seven times, a verbal defect which may not be limited to the rural districts, since Albee's urban narrator is similarly afflicted. This narrator—whose single function is to provide the information which the author has been too lazy to dramatize—is an educated chorus with all his parts of speech in place; but he drones on so interminably with such a gaseous spill of rhetoric that the play gives the impression of being both under- and overwritten, of being too long and too short.

This impression is confirmed by the plot. Concerned with a conventional love triangle—husband, lover, wife—it tries to rescue itself from utter banality by offering us a trio of grotesques. The husband is an ex-convict, who loves and marries a bull dyke, who hates him but loves a dwarf, who in turn adores the husband. "The most outlandish people," gargles the narrator, "can be the stimulus for love." I suppose this is true enough, but their outlandishness does not make them any the less shallow than heterosexual stage lovers; and since Albee neglects to motivate this tripartite romance, or to dramatize the emotions of love and hatred, they are not even very credible. The situation is merely asserted, and, thus, provides barely enough material for a one-act play. The author proceeds to pad this skeleton with a bunch of stereotyped neighbors clacking their tongues, with a series of bewildering flashbacks within flashbacks, with the endless babbling of the narrator, and with a climactic wrestling match in which the husband and the wife—greased for combat—struggle for possession of the dwarf. The husband is victorious and leaves town while the wife withdraws into the dusty sanctuary of her house—a moment, I assume, designed to be pathetic but which, because of my unfamiliarity with dwarf-loving lesbians, was rather lost on me.

This uninspired material has been justly served with a monotonous and commonplace production. Alan Schneider, always an up-and-down director, is in a declension at present, contributing little more to the evening than flat-footed pacing, hollow sound and fury, and cardboard characterizations (to cast

Jenny Egan and Enid Markey as two Mert-and-Marge neighbors is to heap stereotypes on platitudes). As for the rest of the
acting, it is generally superficial. Michael Dunn, a dwarf, fills
the physical dimensions of his role, and acts well besides; since
he is a rather delicate creature, one attends to him with interest.
But Colleen Dewhurst, as the mannish wife, is too cumbrous
and lumpish; Lou Antonio, playing the husband as a cross between L'il Abner and The American Dream, speaks too many
lines with food in his mouth; Roscoe Lee Browne, as the windy
narrator, is defeated by an abstract role with no handle; and
William Prince, in a weak superfluous part, gives another of his
weak superfluous performances. Ben Edwards' grimy interior-
exterior setting seems designed for a more Ingian play than I
think Albee intended; but then I shouldn't presume to read the
author's intentions when he has failed to realize them himself.
Whatever talent Albee displayed in previous work is grievously
absent here, for this sad and sorry ballad possesses neither
music, humor, bite, nor form. If the author wants to talk—God
save the mark!—about unnatural love, then I suggest he find a
less quavering voice than that of Carson McCullers; but if unnatural love is all he wants to talk about, then I suppose any
voice will do. At that level of sound, all voices fade into one
shrill chorus of self-pitying squeaks.

(1963)

THE UNDERGROUND PLAY

NOBODY LOVES AN ALBATROSS
by Ronald Alexander

■ How many Broadway comedies have opened on a hero trading wisecracks with his precocious young daughter and the colored housekeeper? Two thousand by conservative estimate, all
of them preserved for summer stock companies in the cata-

logues of Samuel French. When the curtain rises on a scene like this, you will invariably find me out in the night air before the end of the first act. For I may be helpless to affect the audience's preference for pabulum over whole milk, but at least I don't have to listen to those burps which always follow the swallowing of the formula. *Nobody Loves an Albatross* begins by patting for bubbles in just this manner. And since the author, Ronald Alexander, is credited with a play called *Time Out for Ginger* and a number of television shows, I was just groping for my coat when I began to hear genuine laughter rising from the house—not that expulsion of gas you hear at *Never Too Late* or *Mary, Mary*, but real, honest-to-goodness human sounds.

It is Mr. Alexander's experience in the mass media, I assume, that has taught him to be a strategist; and he is a sneaky one. He has written a play with all the earmarks of a formula comedy, and then proceeded to undermine each and every convention of the genre. Consider his characters and plot devices. Nat Bentley, his hero, is a TV producer—an engaging rascal, naturally, who operates entirely on charm. His boss, a studio empress possibly modeled on Lucille Ball, has given him an ultimatum: create a successful new TV series or be fired off all her shows. The situation is hackneyed, and so is the love interest. For Nat has an attractive secretary who fulfills the two essential requirements of her stereotype: she loves her employer, and she wants him to be true to his ideals. When Nat's stable of writers fails to produce a suitably "warm, human, and touching" script, Nat is given four days to write one himself—inevitably, he succeeds. He is now in a position to marry his secretary, and to irrigate the wasteland with the kind of courageous, meaningful projects she admires (Nat already has one in mind called *Injustice:* "It's about the things that happen to minority groups and the underprivileged in the world"). And thus, we expect him to end up like those hordes of Broadway heroes, covered with glory, love, integrity, and cash.

Our conditioned expectations, however, are disappointed when the author suddenly reveals that Nat has plagiarized his script from an old Shirley Temple movie which has been playing on the *Late Show*. Since his boss has been watching this movie too, he loses his job, his girl, his reputation—everything, in fact, but his instinct for self-preservation, because he cons his way into an even better-paying position with another studio. This is perverse plotting, to say the least, but it is typical of the entire play. For within the shell of formula comedy, Mr. Alexander has constructed a deadly accurate, hilariously funny sociology of the entire entertainment industry and the voracious creatures who feed off it: the venal agents, the compulsive comedy writers, the pretentious teledramatists, the unscrupulous tycoons, the spineless packagers—the whole TV bestiary, in short, as seen by an entirely jaundiced but good-natured zoologist.

Mr. Alexander is aided in this malicious exploration of the animal world by his own ability to raise wisecracks to the level of wit, by a talented cast, and by an extremely inventive director, Gene Saks, who reminds us again that, at its best, the American theatre imagination is essentially comic. So does Robert Preston as the hero, full of roguish energy, shaking his body, shooting his cuffs, snapping his fingers, as he scoots along the stage characterizing himself ("I'm a man of great decision, I go either way"), his female collaborator ("I think she's an entire fag"), his city ("In Hollywood, no matter how warm it gets during the day, at night there's nothing to do"), and the credit-stealing on which American society is based ("Ben Casey does all the work; Dr. Zorba's head of the hospital"). Brilliant, too, are Jack Bittner as a "serious" TV dramatist who disguises his lack of talent by talking "dramaturgy" and the "raison d'être" of a script, Phil Leeds as a dour little man who has invented the laugh machine ("We shape the humor of the American television audience"), and Marian Winters as a loudmouthed, overbearing script writer ("her kids have two fathers and no mother"). As for Will Steven Armstrong's setting, it is a perfect representation of a "decorated" Hollywood apartment, complete with beige walls, fabric panels, Action paintings, and black patent-leather chairs.

The subterranean route taken by Mr. Alexander in order to tell his story is the same underground railway traveled in the past by a number of Hollywood writers and directors. Forbidden by the nature of the mass media to introduce reality or truth into their work, they smuggled a personal commentary on American life into such conventional forms as Westerns, horror fantasies, and gangster movies. *Nobody Loves an Albatross* is the stage equivalent of an underground film, for it has been smuggled past the customs disguised as a conventional and trivial Broadway "hit." Mr. Alexander's expedient may seem a little desperate, but we live in desperate creative times—well. perhaps a little less desperate now that Broadway is supporting a formula comedy which is telling some of the truth.

(1964)

EVERYBODY'S PROTEST PLAY

BLUES FOR MR. CHARLIE *by James Baldwin: Actors Studio Theatre*

> *Let us say, then, that truth, as used here, is meant to imply a devotion to the human being, his freedom and fulfillment; freedom which cannot be legislated, fulfillment which cannot be charted. This is the prime concern, the frame of reference; it is not to be confused with a devotion to Humanity which is too easily equated with a devotion to a Cause; and Causes, as we know, are notoriously bloodthirsty.*
>
> Everybody's Protest Novel

■ James Baldwin wrote these words fifteen years ago in an essay which still stands as the *locus classicus* on the subject of protest fiction; I imagine they sometimes return to haunt him in his dreams. *Blues for Mr. Charlie*, certainly, is the embodiment of everything he once professed to deplore, being "notoriously bloodthirsty" propaganda of the crudest sort, with little existence either as truth, literature, or life. Uncontrolled, hysterical, self-indulgent, employing a clumsy flashback technique and proceeding by means of a surprisingly flabby rhetoric, it is a play of thumbs—fashioned, I would guess, to gouge the eyes of the audience.

It is well known that Baldwin has radically changed his conception of himself over the past few years, suppressing the private side of his character to become an Official Spokesman for a Cause. I have not been among those who admired him in this new role, but I never assumed the decision was easy—or even wholly avoidable, for it may be, as Irving Howe suggests, that the Negro writer cannot find "freedom and fulfillment" until he achieves his Cause. On the other hand, Baldwin's rage, formerly authentic and precise, has begun to seem increasingly mechanical, trumped-up and free-floating, while his self-righteousness has been expressed at the cost of complexity and scruples. In this play, for example, he is—despite a usually delicate awareness of the deadening effect of racial abstractions—dedicated to perpetuating stereotypes, and doing so in a manner which can only create confusion or dissension. The characters have no life apart from narrow racial categories, and the categories themselves are based on prejudice.

No doubt, Baldwin's material is partly to blame. Any work inspired by the Emmett Till case is almost automatically destined to be a melodrama. *Blues for Mr. Charlie*, however, simplifies the historical events even further—the stage is given over literally to a conflict between black and white, or Blacktown versus Whitetown. It is the author's apparent conviction now that all white men are Mr. Charlie, the oppressor, for they are characterized either as sadists and supremacists, burning with hatred for Negro men and lust for Negro women, or as vacillating liberals who befriend the Negroes only to betray them when the chips are down. As for the Negro characters, they enjoy more noble racial stereotypes: the Uncle Tom who redeems himself by fingering the murderer after a lifetime of subservience to him; the integrationist minister who finally determines to keep a gun under his Bible and fight the white man with his own weapons; the strong-minded, white-haired grandmammy of the past generation who believes in religious non-violence; the angry hero who has returned from the North, furious at all the white women who have seduced him, to goad a Southern peckerwood into shooting him; the childhood sweetheart who is rather confusingly persuaded of the necessity for love ("I'm going to learn from Richard how to love! I won't let him die for nothing!") by the hero's angry life and violent death. Since many of these characters are also fixtures of the Broadway stage (Baldwin already manipulates theatrical clichés with the weariness of an experienced commercial dramatist), few of the actors are able to transcend the oppressive conventionality of their roles—though Al Freeman, Jr. is a handsome, vigorous actor, and Diana Sands has an affecting moment of grief—while Burgess Meredith, who directed the Actors Studio production, has been forced to give it the form of a mass meeting in a union hall, especially in the courtroom scene, where black confronts white in angry turmoil, and witnesses detach themselves to deliver impassioned soliloquies downstage.

The most disappointing thing about the play, however, is not its aesthetic flatness but rather its moral and intellectual deficiency. Particularly depressing is Baldwin's curious insistence on the superiority of Negro sexuality, especially since this is a myth which the author himself once took pains to explode. You would never learn from Blues for Mr. Charlie that segregation has social, political, or economic roots; like Tennessee Williams, whose Sweet Bird of Youth his play occasionally resembles, Baldwin has determined that the major cause of anti-Negro feeling is sexual envy. This suggests something of the incredible chauvinism which permeates the work—a strain as virulent here as anything to be found in White Citizens' Councils, and even less honest, since Baldwin attempts to vindicate his own feelings by victimizing his characters. (One finds the same desire to make hatred look virtuous in LeRoi Jones's Dutchman where the chauvinism and violence of the Negro protagonist are forced from him by a white woman who needles, provokes, and finally kills him—but the rage belongs to the author.) Here, for example, is Baldwin ventriloquizing through his hero, when he is crawling on the ground with three bullets in his belly: "White man! I don't want nothing from you. You ain't got nothing to give me! You can't eat because none of your sad-assed chicks can cook. You can't talk because won't nobody talk to you. You can't dance because you've got nobody to dance with. . . . Why are you always trying to cut off my cock? You worried about it? . . . Okay. Okay. Okay. Keep your old lady home, you hear? Don't let her near no nigger. She might get to like it. You might get to like it, too." In contrast with "dried-up piss-assed white women" and "piss-assed faggoty white boys," however, Baldwin's Negroes are all extraordinarily virile, coura-geous, passionate, and alive, even to the point of displaying, during a dance-hall sequence, a natural sense of rhythm.

At this point, the healthiest thing for spectators of both races would be to rise up and repudiate these romantic fabrications, and loudly too; but since the theatre audience is far from healthy, the play merely sinks the white spectator deeper into an impotent, self-defeating guilt. (An index of this is the cow-ardly way in which the play was received by the daily re-viewers—to praise inferior art, simply because it is produced by a Negro, is to let guilt turn into an inverted form of prejudice.) Worse than this, the play attempts to lacerate an ugly rage in the heart of the colored spectator: Blues for Mr. Charlie, for all its conventional gestures toward love, emerges finally as an in-flammatory broadside of race hatred which will profit nobody but the author. If we are locked in the stereotypes that Baldwin conceives, and Negro and white can confront each other only in mutual distrust and anger, then we will have to assume that the Negro "problem" is still too crude for the stage; but such a work as Athol Fugard's The Blood Knot, with its more con-trolled form and deeper understanding, proves there is nothing inevitable about these oppositions at all.

The fault, I am afraid, lies not in the "problem" but in the author. The very terms we use to criticize Baldwin were learned in his school, since it is he, along with Ralph Ellison, who did most to make the Negro visible as a complicated human being.

But considering all that Baldwin once knew and wrote, it is difficult not to conclude that *Blues for Mr. Charlie* is more a work of provocation than conviction—the author has tasted power and is rolling that taste around on his tongue. The ultimate difficulty, then, is not a racial difficulty at all; it is the difficulty of the modern intellectual, torn between the way of influence and the way of truth. This conflict has driven more than one gifted individual of our time to a sorry abuse of his talents, as well as to that almost pathological frustration that usually accompanies it; and I suspect that much of the exasperation in this play stems from Baldwin's inability to reconcile the private and public aspects of his character. Until he does, however, he has ceased to illuminate our consciousness. Early in his career, James Baldwin declared it his ambition to be "an honest man and a good writer." In *Blues for Mr. Charlie* he is neither. There, the complex man of sensibility has been totally absorbed by the simplistic man of power—and that constitutes what Baldwin himself once called "his corruption and our loss."

(1964)

MEMOIRS OF MR. BANG

THE THREE SISTERS by *Anton Chekhov,*
translated by Randall Jarrell: Actors Studio
Theatre

■ The 1963–64 theatre season has concluded not with the razzing it deserves but rather with a cluster of "artistic triumphs"—most of them so unimpressive to me that either everyone has joined a cabal or else I am the Terrible Tempered Mr. Bang. The latest of these pseudo triumphs is the Actors Studio Theatre production of *The Three Sisters,* and I find

myself unable even to manage a minor paean. Without Tyrone
Guthrie's admirable production of the same play last year at
Minneapolis, we might be inclined to accept this lackluster performance as the best Americans can do with Chekhov, but
compared with Guthrie's crisp and confident direction, Lee
Strasberg's is singularly flaccid and limp. Chekhov used to complain that Stanislavsky turned his characters into crybabies—I
can imagine what he would have said about Strasberg, who not
only has them weeping copiously, but also screaming at one
another, and even, at one point, retching in full view (Olga,
complaining that Natasha's bad manners make her sick, proves
it by heaving into the sink!). Actually, Strasberg has left the
play largely undirected and permitted his actors their heads, but
wherever he has bothered to interpret, he has introduced
Chekhovian clichés. This production will confirm the Philis-
tines in their conviction that Chekhov is a deadly bore, for it is
as sluggish and torpid as an early Garbo movie—though the
play is only sixty pages of printed text, it takes the Actors Studio
Theatre three hours and ten minutes to speak it.

The star-studded company is disorganized as an ensemble,
but it is even difficult to single out individual performances for
praise. I would have thought Luther Adler to be ideal as
Tchebutykin, but he is surprisingly apathetic in the role, and
much too prone to Yiddish gesticulation—and Gerald Hiken,
though more vigorous and thoughtful as Andrei, also tends to
translate his character into its Yiddish equivalent (a common
failing in American Chekhov). Other critics have noticed the
confusion of accents in this production—more disturbing to me
is its confusion of styles. Kevin McCarthy, as Vershinin, comes
on like a peppy all-American fullback; Albert Paulsen, as Kulygin, seems to be acting in a Viennese operetta; and Robert
Loggia's Solyony looks and sounds like a TV Mexican *bandito*.
As for the women, Shirley Knight's Irina is delicate, though a
trifle hysterical, but Geraldine Page's Olga is much too warbly,
and Barbara Baxley plays the subtly malevolent Natasha like the
Black Witch of the North. Kim Stanley's Masha has been
highly praised, and her gifts are undeniable, especially in frustration, anguish, and grief, but I have seen this neurasthenic

performance many times now, and it no longer gives me much surprise or pleasure. I am, furthermore, annoyed by Miss Stanley's slackness in the role, a failing which finds expression both vocally—in the extravagant pauses she allows herself in the midst of speeches—and visually—in her physical silhouette. To put it bluntly, Miss Stanley is not in condition—a ballet dancer, or even a lady wrestler would be much more careful about her appearance before performing in public. When we hear how strenuously Sir Laurence Olivier trained to prepare his voice for Othello, it does not seem too much to expect Miss Stanley to prepare her figure for Masha—but perhaps this demonstrates the difference between actors who are disciplined craftsmen and those who are mere self-indulgent stylists.

The company, in general, demonstrates this. In contrast with the debacle at Lincoln Center, the Actors Studio Theatre has had a better season and its choice of plays has been more daring, but this is to compare tinsel with confetti. It is true that Kazan would never have mounted a work like James Costigan's *Baby Want a Kiss*, but then one can hardly fault his judgment there, and, anyway, the Studio hedged its bet at the box office by casting the play with two famous movie stars (both of them, actually, quite good in their roles). I also have my doubts whether a play as badly written as *Blues for Mr. Charlie* would ever have found its way to the stage were it not for the best-selling Baldwin name—and even the Chekhov play, though an excellent repertory vehicle, is hardly a novelty for a training organization whose acting method is based on that of Stanislavsky.

To my mind, the most interesting Actors Studio production of the year was the Arnold Weinstein–William Bolcom "comic opera for actors" *Dynamite Tonight*—a refreshingly naïve and spirited parody of Nelson Eddy and Jeanette MacDonald movies, acted and directed in the wacky style of *Duck Soup*—but this ran into a hostile press and was closed down after one performance. It was the privilege of newspaper reviewers to dislike this work, though Howard Taubman should at least have recognized the excellence of the score (few believe in Taubman's brilliance as a theatre reviewer, but he is rumored to have a little more knowledge of music). But it was shocking that the Studio lacked the gumption to stand behind its own artistic option, especially when Studio productions are largely financed by foundations. *Dynamite Tonight* was the Studio's single gesture toward genuine experiment this year, and I am certain that if the group had stood behind this work, it would ultimately have found its audience. But the Actors Studio Theatre proved, in the end, to be as timid, as panicky, and as success-oriented as the most venal producers, and could not refrain from adapting its policy to the hit-and-miss structure of Broadway. Thus, like its sister institution at Lincoln Center, the Actors Studio Theatre has concluded its first full season, trying to combine artistic prestige with commodity success—trying, that is, to graft the limb of the repertory system onto the trunk of the commercial theatre. Is it any wonder that this limb shakes so dangerously in the wind?

(1964)

FIDDLING WHILE
TALENT BURNS

FIDDLER ON THE ROOF; *Book by Joseph Stein;*
Music by Jerry Bock; Lyrics by
Sheldon Harnick

■ There is an underground song, of which nothing unhappily exists except the title, called "When You're in Love, the Whole World's Jewish"—this could be the leitmotif of *Fiddler on the Roof*. An adaptation of Sholom Aleichem's *Tevye* stories doctored for the musical stage, it bears about the same relation to its source as unleavened cocktail wafers do to Passover matzoth, but it is undoubtedly sufficient to serve the passionate ethnic narcissism of Jewish benefit audiences. Obviously, this demand is amply filled every season—by Chayefsky plays, garment center epics, and Molly Goldberg vehicles—all of which represent the petering out of the great Yiddish theatre tradition. Let us not, however, confuse the appeal of these works with a serious revival of interest in Yiddish culture, for they are popular by virtue of being inauthentic. Trading on the exotic, romanticizing Jewish history for the sake of an easy nostalgia, such Broadway plays are always invested with a trace of condescension. The laughter that invariably greets a pair of hunched shoulders and an upward inflection springs less from racial or religious pride than from a very comfortable assimilation—from a world, that is, in which Manischewitz wine is no longer just for "special occasions" and even Chinamen eat Levy's rye.

Even Chinamen will probably be able to enjoy *Fiddler on the Roof*, since it is slick, colorful, and energetic. The only person it is likely to offend, in fact, is the serious Yiddishist, for it exerts its wide appeal by falsifying the world of Sholom Aleichem, not to mention the character of the East European Jew. Take the plot line, for example. Like the stories, the musical revolves around the marriage of a number of Tevye's daughters to husbands he disapproves of; but now these couplings are all conventional romances, and the most shameful of them—the union of one of the girls with a rich Jewish vulgarian lacking culture or scholarship—has, for rather obvious reasons, been omitted entirely. As for the revolutionary who marries Hodel, and is exiled to Siberia for his political views, his radicalism now has no more content than a belief in mixed dancing, while the Gentile who marries Chava has become a soft-voiced liberal intellectual who gives her lessons in religious tolerance ("Do you feel about us the way they feel about you?"). Sholom Aleichem had a deep suspicion of Russians in general, whom he usually depicted as savage animals in fur caps; but this has now been replaced by the warm glow of human fellowship. The Russians of the musical are mostly kind, courteous, and friendly, and the local constable even warns the Jews of an impending pogrom, apologizing for it as he carries it out.

This pogrom, by the way, is all part of the choreography; it occurs during a wedding, and results mainly in some broken furniture. Hardly enough to cry *gevalt* about, but then nobody in this cartoon Russia is inclined to spit upon a Jewish gaberdine. Boris Aronson underlines the Cloud-Cuckoo-Land quality of the proceedings by designing a set which would be just as appropriate as background for the Three Little Pigs; and you can be certain, whenever some Jews collect together for an ancient ritual, that candles will light up all over the stage, and a chorus will warble one of Jerry Bock's and Sheldon Harnick's Tin Pan Alley tunes. On the other hand, if you are willing to forgive the various distortions of *shtetl* life, you may derive some pleasure from the evening, for it has been organized around an ideal of sensuous enjoyment. Patricia Zipprodt's costumes have just the right touch of style and accuracy, and they make the assorted tailors, matchmakers, butchers, and whey-faced Talmudic scholars look, if not act, authentic. Then, Jerome Robbins has adapted his usual urban razzamatazz to a certain spirited folksiness, especially during some fine Russian *kazatzkes* and Jewish *horas* which leave the stage trembling with energy. He could not resist a touch of pretense at the end when Tevye, having been evicted from the village along with the other Jews, is made to pull his wagon sadly around the stage like Mother Courage; but this merely underlines one's conviction that Broadway musicals, and not serious plays, are really his glass of tea.

Zero Mostel, on the other hand—being the most versatile actor in the land—has the capacity to sip from a variety of beverages, and so I cannot help but regret that he is draining his talents into a benefit-audience musical. Still, my regret is tempered by a sense of delight at seeing him under any circumstances, and his performance, at least in the first act, achieves that sublime breath of reality that the rest of the show lacks. For one thing, Zero is extremely deft at isolating himself from all the brashness and noise—note how cleverly he takes refuge in simple gestures and subtle movements whenever the other actors grow frenetic. And his Tevye the dairyman is a magnificently thick creation. Salty, proverbial, cunning—endlessly misquoting Scripture, and endlessly grumbling (through a massive growth of beard) about his crippled horse, his shrewish wife, and his undependable God—he is the very embodiment of human complaint and human adaptability. When Zero greets the Russian policeman by cocking his finger ambiguously toward his cap and saying, with false heartiness, "Welcome your honor, what's the good news of the world?" we know whatever is to be known about the degradation of the Jews in a hostile environment. What is more, we know the character that Sholom Aleichem originally created, the Jewish survivor par excellence, learning to live with his fate. Nor does Zero slight the demands of the musical itself. He discharges his duties brilliantly as a song-and-dance man, charming us with his almost incredible physical grace, and his thrilling voice. Even Zero, however, cannot wholly disguise the thinness of the material (watch him grapple with a line like "He's as poor as a synagogue mouse" and you will see a soul in agony), and, in the second act, he cannot even rise above it, for he falls back on sly winks and Jewish shrugs for the easy laugh.

Finally, I left the theatre more dejected than exhilarated by this powerful talent, because it is in some danger of being wasted. In a just world and a healthy culture, Zero Mostel would undoubtedly be playing all the great theatrical roles: Falstaff, Dogberry, and Toby Belch, Tartuffe and M. Jourdain, Azdak and Herr Puntila, even Tevye the dairyman in a more faithful adaptation of the stories. Are we now to watch him in an endless succession of long-run musical comedies? It is uncharitable to begrudge this actor his success, since it was obtained after a long period of neglect having nothing to do with his gifts; but I wish he were using his success in a more fruitful way. This is no doubt a very difficult task, since talented Americans are inevitably confronted with a conflict between success and creativity. It is not yet certain whether Zero has resolved this conflict for himself, and his future still remains open. What is certain is that if he does not soon take active control of his talent, it will languish and die.

(1964)

SAUL BELLOW
ON THE DRAGSTRIP

THE LAST ANALYSIS *by Saul Bellow*

■ There is an awful lot of noise issuing from the stage of the
Belasco these days, but the loudest explosion of all can be heard
only with the inner ear: it comes from the head-on collision of a
gifted writer, Saul Bellow, with the crassness and incompetence
of the whole commercial theatre system. Since this has been an
accident with no survivors, and since the vehicle being driven
was smashed beyond repair, it will probably never be known
that *The Last Analysis* was, potentially, a remarkable play, or
that its protagonist, Philip Bummidge, was among the most
flamboyant comic characters ever written for the American
stage. Any interested in rooting around amidst this wreckage,
however, will find the major cause of the accident to be the
complex and ambitious nature of the work itself. There is only
one actor in our theatre capable of realizing the intricacies of its
central character, and that is Zero Mostel—but he has elected
to entertain the Hadassah ladies in *Fiddler on the Roof*.
Sam Levene, who inherited the role by default, apparently
doesn't understand one word of it, and to hide his bafflement,
he plays this one too as if it were written for the Hadassah
ladies, to the crash of splintering intentions. As for directors,
William Ball is the only one I can think of whose touch would
have been equal to the play's delicate balance, but Joseph
Anthony handles himself in the driver's seat with all the grace
of a teen-age drag racer at the wheel of his father's Rolls Royce.
The result is vehicular homicide, for which the major victim,

the author, alone has been arraigned. But never before, in my experience, have a play and its production been so at odds.

I have some quarrels with the work, though nothing that a competent director could not have ironed out with the playwright. It suffers, like much of Mr. Bellow's writing, from a lack of focus; its structure is sprawling; its form is not always integrated with its theme; and its theme is somewhat impacted in the author's ambivalence toward his subject. But it contains, at the same time, some of the most magnificent rhetoric to be heard on the American stage since Clifford Odets, and it is rippling with energy and intelligence. Mr. Bellow is not—as the condescending tone of the dailies seemed to imply—merely another novelist writing dialogue. He has natural dramatic gifts. And in *The Last Analysis*, he is working out a fascinating theatre experiment, trying to combine depth insights with popular American forms.

The form of the play is cartoon farce of that broad knockdown variety common to the thirties—and Bellow's stage is alive with vaudeville jokes and uninhibited action. Despite all the slammed doors, embarrassed confrontations, hidden eavesdroppers, and Jiggs-and-Maggie battles, however, the farce is rather dark, for, inside it, Mr. Bellow is fashioning a melancholy play-within-a-play, somewhat on the order of Pirandello's *Six Characters*. The pivot of the action is Bummidge, an aging, neurotic Jewish comedian, afflicted with the dread plague of "Humanitis," a kind of metaphysical *Angst* over the plight of human existence. This has so infected his career that he is now seeking, through a process of rigorous self-analysis, to undertake "an expedition to recover the lost Self," fishing around in his past for the secret of his life. Being an entertainer, he is preparing to act out his memories over closed-circuit television (piped directly to a convention of psychoanalysts at the Waldorf). And using his family, friends, and parasites as histrionic pack carriers, he begins a safari into the jungle of time, reliving his memories and subjecting them to his own hilariously mordant Freudian commentation.

Moving always back in history, he re-enacts his burlesque and vaudeville days; his marriage to a pregnant girl friend; his early hostility toward his father; his childhood difficulties with his mother ("You didn't want the breast, and your Mamma said, 'All right, I'll give it to the conductor'"); his early toilet training. At last, with the rest of the cast playing Greek chorus to Bummy's Oedipus, he re-enacts his own conception ("Ma, no, no, no! Too late, my number's up"); his development in the womb ("It's great in here. I like it"); and finally the trauma of birth itself ("I hear screams. I'd holler too if I could breathe"). At the climax, resurrected like Lazarus, he rises from a tomb to the playing of "America the Beautiful" and the unfurling of an American flag.

The upshot of all this fine madness is that Bummidge is showered with television offers—but turns them down in order to form a Platonic Academy of Comedy for failing comics like himself; and though his parasites desert him, he is reunited with his family. The ending is shallow and sentimental, inspired more by the conventions of farce than by the pressure of the author's insights, and it demonstrates how the various elements of the play have been improperly fused. For example, Bummy is apparently meant to be a representative of the artist in our time—his need to understand himself, to transcend his sense of futility, to achieve freedom, and to lead an austere life in the midst of American plenty—but we are never told precisely what is typical about a television comic, or why his experience should invite such generalizations. Mr. Bellow states that his theme is "the link between the individual and the universal," but although he tantalizes us with suggestions, he never really shows us how this link is forged.

Still, if Bellow has failed to formulate his play sufficiently, he has certainly created a wild, anarchic theatre piece that would have yielded ample rewards if only his collaborators had not made attentiveness impossible. The cast—with three exceptions (Tresa Hughes as Bummy's wife, Ann Wedgeworth as his mistress, Will Lee as his tailor)—is dismal; and poor Sam Levene, who is almost never off stage, has been abysmally miscast. At a loss with the part, he has fallen back on the only character he has confidence in, the Jewish garment manufacturer, mugging, grimacing, and ogling until he has flattened the values of the play. As for the direction, Joseph Anthony's major contribution is a resounding tumult—typical of which is the recurrent gurgle of a flushing toilet—but he has made no effort whatever to grasp the work, or to clarify its line of development.

Then there are the theatre reviewers who, exposing that awful gap that exists between the theatrical and the literary worlds, dismissed Mr. Bellow as if he were simply another hack writer of the Broadway school. From the tone of some of their reviews, this response was partly motivated by a desire for revenge against those who have kept them in an abject state of inferiority; but its effect, I fear, is to have frustrated a potentially fine dramatist from ever writing plays again. The next time these men begin asking "Where are the playwrights?" let them look at the corpses they have buried under their own reviews.

(1964)

FROM ABROAD

■

■

■

LIBIDO AT LARGE

THE HOSTAGE by Brendan Behan

■ It has been suggested that in *The Hostage* Brendan Behan
is trying to "open up the stage." This is an understatement. He
would like to hack the stage to bits, crunch the proscenium
across his knee, trample the scenery underfoot, and throw
debris wildly in all directions. Like his various prototypes—Jack
Falstaff, Harpo Marx, W. C. Fields, and Dylan Thomas—
Behan is pure Libido on a rampage, mostly in its destructive
phase; and if he has not yet achieved the Dionysian purity of
those eminent anarchists, he is still a welcome presence in our
sanctimonious times. In America, comedy went underground
(i.e., turned "sick") when the various humane societies built a
protective wall around mankind, for an art form based on uninhibited abandon and open aggression cannot long survive the
Anti-Defamation League, the N.A.A.C.P., the Legion of Decency, and *McCall's* Togetherness, not to mention those guardians of cultural virtue who now review theatre, movies, and TV
for the newspapers. But Behan seems to have crossed the At-

177

lantic without any significant accommodation to American tastes, outside of an abrupt conversion from Irish whiskey to homogenized milk.

For the dramatic bludgeon he has installed at the Cort is now flailing indiscriminately at everything in sight, including the British Empire, the I.R.A., the Catholic Church, the Protestant clergy, the army, the police, the F.B.I., and the D.A.R. What these disparate organizations have in common is their orthodoxy: Behan is waging total war on all social institutions excepting brothels and distilleries. But though destructive Libido can be the source of a lot of fun, it is hardly an organizing principle, so the author's assault on order leaves his play almost totally lacking in dramatic logic. Its substance is taped together with burlesque routines, Irish reels, barroom ballads, and outrageous gags (some old, some new, some borrowed, but all "blue"), while its scarecrow plot is just a convenient appendage on which to hang a string of blasphemous howlers. "This is a serious play!" screams a dour, baleful, humorless I.R.A. officer after a typical irreverency. But he convinces nobody. *The Hostage* is neither serious nor even a play. It is a roaring vaudeville turn, too disordered to support any more than a wink of solemnity.

Nevertheless, the plot—which is exhausted the moment you sum it up—does seem serious in its basic outline. Set in a Dublin brothel in modern times, the action revolves around the kidnaping, and ultimate death, of a young English soldier, taken by the I.R.A. because the British are going to execute a Belfast revolutionary. This promises an Irish political drama, and one can easily imagine how O'Casey might have interpreted the same situation. The brothel would become a symbolic Temple of Love, Life, and the Dance; the prostitutes would be "pagan girls" with ample bosoms and free, sensual natures; the comic characters would emerge as personifications of bigotry, indifference, and selfishness; the death of the boy would be an occasion for commentary on the victimization of the innocent by war; and the play would probably conclude with a vision of a better life to come.

But while Behan has turned to O'Casey for his plot outline,

he does not share O'Casey's weakness for adolescent sexuality or utopian social communities. In his illogical, irresponsible view of society, in fact, he comes much closer to Ionesco; in his technique and treatment of low life, closer to the early Brecht. His whores are tough, funny, breezy hookers; the brothel is a sleazy dive run exclusively for profit ("Money is the best religion . . . and the best politics"); and the boy's death is followed immediately by his inexplicable resurrection for a final song ("O death where is thy sting-a-ling-a-ling"). As for the comics—a grotesque gallery which includes a madam and her "ponce" winging standup jokes at each other in the manner of a minstrel show; a religious eccentric goosed in the middle of her hymn by an ex-Postal clerk with a sanctified air and roaming fingers; and two pansies named Rio Rita and Princess Grace ("That's only my name in religion")—they are on stage primarily for what they can contribute to the general mayhem. For Behan's theme is "Nobody loves you like yourself," and his brothel is simply one of the last refuges of privacy where a man can pursue his pleasures and have his laughs.

On the other hand, the poignancy and desperation of the humor aptly illustrate the growing shakiness of this position as the private world becomes more and more circumscribed. Generously spread throughout the play are topical references which change with the latest newspaper headlines (a Russian sailor off the *Baltica* is now one of the customers in the house), anxious glances in the direction of the H-bomb ("It's such a big bomb it's after making me scared of little bombs"), and melodious admonitions to Khrushchev, Eisenhower, and Macmillan ("Don't muck about, don't muck about, don't muck about with the moon"). The forces gathering outside the brothel have now become so overwhelming that they cannot be ignored; and the violence behind Behan's farcical attitudes reveals his impotent frustration at being involuntarily implicated in the frightening activities of the great powers.

Joan Littlewood's production works hard to preserve all the wilder values of this vaudeville whirligig. The company, which has been mostly imported from her Theatre Workshop in England, is an excellent one—in the cases of Avis Bunnage, Alfred

Lynch, and Patience Collier sometimes even inspired. But while Miss Littlewood has developed the appropriate Epic style, and has scrupulously tried to avoid gentility, I still don't think I've really seen the play. Perhaps English actors cannot suppress their instinctive good manners, for while the production rolls along with admirable speed and efficiency, it lacks robustness, coarseness, and spontaneity. But then only a troupe of burlesque comics endowed with the brutal wit of Simon Daedalus and the shameless vulgarity of Aristophanes could hope to catch the proper tone of this sidewinding improvisation. It is an open question whether *The Hostage* belongs on the legitimate stage at all, but considering that Minsky's is out of business, it is important to have it there. Its careless laughter is like a sound out of the past, and Behan's paean to unconditioned man is a wholesome antidote to what Orwell called "the smelly little orthodoxies that are now contending for our souls."

(1960)

A NATURALISM
OF THE GROTESQUE

The Caretaker by Harold Pinter

■ When Harold Pinter tells us that his plays contain no meaning outside of the material itself, I think we should believe him, giving thanks for his unusual, though somewhat self-incriminating, honesty. *The Caretaker*—being little more than the sum of its component parts and dramatic values—certainly seems totally free from either significance or coherence. In this, no doubt, it has something in common with real life. But while the work displays a surface painstakingly decorated with naturalistic details, these are so peculiarly selected that the effect is quite distorted: the play is a slice of life, sliced so arbitrarily that it has lost all resemblance to life. Because of the mystery surrounding Pinter's principles of selection, therefore, suspense is the play's greatest virtue. Pinter manipulates this with considerable skill, tantalizing us with the promise of some eventual explanation—but he stubbornly refuses to deliver. He refuses, in fact, to communicate with us at all. His language, while authentic colloquial speech, is stripped bare of reflective or conceptual thought, so that the play could be just as effectively performed in Finno-Ugric. You might say that *The Caretaker* approaches the condition of music—if you could conceive of music without much development, lyric quality, or thematic content. For the play is so scrupulously non-analytical—so carefully documented with concrete (though pointless) happenings, specific (though atypical) character details, and particularized (though unrecognizable) responses—that it goes full circle from its surface naturalism and ends up a total abstraction.

The basic anecdote is this: A slavish, peevish, vicious old down-and-out named Davies is offered lodging in a junk-filled room, part of a network of apartments waiting to be redecorated. His benefactor, the would-be decorator, is a listless, dull-witted chap named Aston, who has collected Davies in much the same impersonal way he has collected the other useless articles in the place. Aston gives Davies a bed, money, shoes, clothes, and a caretaking job, which the derelict, consumed with defenses and prejudices, accepts or rejects with alternating gratitude and grumbles. Though they live in the same room and share a quality of spiritual paralysis (Aston wants but is unable to build a tool shed; Davies is desirous but incapable of going to Sidcup for his papers), they cannot connect. Nor do they connect with Aston's brother, Mick, a mordant young entrepreneur who hardly says a word to Aston and who relates to Davies mainly by baiting him with cruel practical jokes. Following Aston's confession that shock treatments had addled his brain (a confession alien to the style of the play), Davies tries to form an alliance with Mick to evict Aston from the room. Mick first encourages Davies' scheme; then, smashing his brother's statue of Buddha for emphasis, ridicules it. After a petty altercation between the two roommates over Davies' noisy sleeping habits—which climaxes when Davies, flourishing a knife, lets slip some unfortunate remarks about Aston's "stinking shed"—Aston asks him to leave. Whimpering like a rebellious slave whipped into submission, Davies begs to be allowed to remain.

That, apart from a wealth of equally mystifying details and a few comic episodes, is the meat of the play; and I'm perspiring from the effort to extract this much coherence. One is forced to respect Pinter's command of the stage, since he has composed scenes of substantial theatrical force dominated by a compelling air of mystery, but his motive for writing the play escapes me. I would be delighted to be able to tell you that Pinter nurtures some of the seeds he plants in the work—that The Caretaker is about the spiritual vacancy of modern life, the inability of slave types to achieve dignity, or (favorite theme of "sensitive" contemporary playwrights) the failure of human beings to communicate with one another. But I cannot honestly conclude that it is about anything at all, other than itself. The situation, apparently ordinary, is so special, and the characters, apparently human, are so unrepresentative, that we are totally alienated from the events on the stage; and finally begin to regard these creatures as a bacteriologist might examine germ life on another planet.

For this reason, the present tendency to couple Pinter and Beckett is more misleading than it is illuminating. Pinter has obviously borrowed some of Beckett's techniques and conventions—the tramp figure, the immobility of the central characters, the repetitions in the dialogue, the occasional vaudeville stunts, the mixture of comedy and seriousness—but he has used them for totally different purposes. In Waiting for Godot, the action is metaphorical and universal; in The Caretaker, it is denotative and specific. Beckett's play reveals the feelings of a metaphysical poet about the quality of human existence. Pinter's, excluding both feeling and thought, bears almost no relation to any known form of human life, and is so impersonal it seems to have written itself. What Pinter has created, in short, is a naturalism of the grotesque wrapped around a core of abstraction—something less like Beckett than like Sherwood Anderson, though lacking the compassion of either.

The production takes full advantage of ample theatrical opportunities. Donald McWhinnie approaches the play, quite correctly, as if it were a perfectly conventional kitchen drama, adding a note of casual imperturbability with his direction which enhances the oddness. Brian Currah's setting—an artfully arranged hodgepodge of vacuum cleaners, lawn mowers, broken-down beds, paint buckets, and other articles of junk— provides the proper air of imprisonment. And the acting is further proof that the new English proletarian style is now more flexible than our own. Pinter, who writes succulent parts for actors, has created a really juicy character in Davies, excellently played by Donald Pleasence with a kind of shambling, sniveling, corrosive nastiness. But for me the best performance of the evening is contributed by Alan Bates as Mick, whose alternating cruelty, irony, wit, and injured innocence are etched with such assurance that one is almost convinced that there is something of consequence beneath the baffling exterior of the part.

But the surface refuses to budge. In *The Caretaker*, Pinter has gone beyond the most extreme theories of the most radical Existentialists: he has created a work in which existence not only precedes essence but thoroughly destroys it. Without some hint of the essential, all judgments must be relative, and a critic of the drama becomes as useless as those critics of Action painting who are given to analyzing their own subliminal responses to a work instead of the work itself. My subliminal response to Pinter's play was a growing irritation and boredom, somewhat mitigated by admiration for his redoubtable theatrical gifts. If these gifts can someday be combined with visionary power, beauty, heart, and mind, then we shall someday have a new dramatic artist and not just an abstract technician of striking scenes for actors.

(1961)

CHRONICLE OF
A RELUCTANT HERO

A Man for All Seasons by Robert Bolt

■ After some years of neglect, the chronicle history play has been enjoying a rebirth among the more literary English and French dramatists. Up till now, the results have been rather indifferent, but in Robert Bolt's A Man for All Seasons we finally have an effective example of the genre. A faithful account of the martyrdom of Sir Thomas More, this work is too diffuse to be completely successful; yet, compared with more vulgar dramatic biographies like Anouilh's Becket and Osborne's Luther, it shows remarkable intelligence, historicity, theatrical ingenuity, and good taste. I confess that the work took me by surprise, for nothing in Bolt's last entry, an inept piece of contemporary realism called Flowering Cherry, prepared me for the kind of form and substance he handles with such authority here. Yet, I can think of at least two reasons why he and his contemporaries are now turning to history for their subject matter. As Bolt unwittingly demonstrated in Flowering Cherry, modern man has become so trivial and uninteresting that he has lost his power to involve us, while modern mass society has inhibited even the superior spirits from expressing themselves through significant action. When human destinies are arbitrated primarily by bureaucrats, "Creon's secretaries," to quote Duerrenmatt's wistfully beautiful insight, "close Antigone's books." In an age without heroes, artists can lament our vacancy and spiritual undernourishment, like Samuel Beckett, or invent subjective heroic fantasies, like Jean Genet, or rake in the embers of the past for adequate human material, like the new dramatic chroniclers. Or, when they have no past, no history, no tradition, they can congratulate us on our triumphant mediocrity, like the Broadway dramatists—but this approach is beneath discussion.

A second reason for the growing popularity of the history play has to do with the influence of Brecht, who brought new eyes to the past and new techniques for putting it on the stage. It is Brecht's spirit, tempered by the spirit of Elizabethan drama and of More himself (whose writings, transcripts, and proverbialisms appear as dialogue in the play), that hovers over Bolt's new work, just as it is the spirit of Teo Otto, Brecht's scenic designer, that inhabits Motley's setting—a handsome unit of simple polished Tudor stairs, located by various signs, emblems, and props dropped from the flies. For the purpose of setting the stage, bridging transitions, and commenting on the action, Bolt has supplied a Brechtian Chorus, who also plays all the lower class characters—a greedy, ironic, calculating opportunist called (with none of the usual Broadway toadying to this type) the Common Man. And just as Bolt's Chorus assumes some of the functions of the Story Teller in *The Caucasian Chalk Circle*, so Bolt's interpretation of More—the great humanist, lawyer, statesman, and saint, who lost his life for opposing Henry VIII's divorce and the English Reformation which followed it—recalls Brecht's concept of Galileo, another historical figure hounded by authorities.

More (whose conversation, according to Erasmus, was "all of jesting and of fun") has usually been treated on the stage as a madcap: the Elizabethan play, *Sir Thomas More*, even has him cracking jokes on the scaffold. Without scanting More's wit, Bolt interprets him more as a melancholy intellectual aristocrat, desperately trying to preserve some corner of private conscience, while preserving his life at the same time. Unlike some of the rasher spirits who surround him, More is prudent and discreet ("Our natural business lies in escaping"), and inclined to protect himself behind legalistic subterfuges. When asked to swear to the Acts of Succession, establishing Henry's divorce and his control over the English Church, he simply maintains silence. Determined not to be a martyr if he can help it, he could probably defend his strategy with the same aphorism as Brecht's Galileo: "Unhappy is the land that needs a hero." More, however, is reluctantly nudged into heroism when all escape routes have been closed. Imprisoned and brought to trial by Henry's minister, a "dockside bully" named Thomas Cromwell, More is goaded to break his silence; but only when he has been convicted on the basis of a witness' perjury does he rise to declare the new Acts "directly repugnant to the law of God." As he delivers himself to the headsman, the Common Man tells the audience, with a salacious wink: "It isn't difficult to stay alive, friends—*just don't make trouble!*" More's death, the wages of integrity, is for the ages; but the moral is for our own time, when the common man ("the master statesman of us all") preserves his skin through compromise and accommodation.

Noel Willman's production is excellent—tight, fluid, graceful, by turns both rowdy and dignified—and the entire cast is impeccable, from George Rose's sardonic Common Man, hastily burrowing in a basket for his various costume changes, through Albert Dekker's Norfolk, played with the robustness of a growling Tudor mastiff, Keith Baxter's Henry, cast against type as a lithe, muscular, egocentric golden boy, and Leo McKern's Cromwell, a pudgy Machiavellian humorist of astonishing dexterity (at one audacious point he leaps backward upon a table). But the play is really a tour de force for Paul Scofield, who superbly endows the leading role with that most elusive of all acting qualities: sheer intelligence. Looking like Holbein's portrait, dowdy, laconic, wry, sweet, mellow, dreamy and humorous (his irony is reminiscent of Olivier's), he tells us almost as much about the quality of More's mind as the play itself, and a good deal more about the quality of More's emotions—especially in one scene where he breaks down quietly over a custard that his wife has brought him in prison. It is a soft expressive moment in a performance of exquisitely subtle modulation (Scofield raises his voice only once in the entire evening); and, if the play tends to fade a little after its initial impact, Scofield's More remains indelibly fixed in your memory.

(1961)

GERMAN GUILT
AND SWISS INDICTMENTS

ANDORRA by Max Frisch; THE FIREBUGS
by Max Frisch

■ For any drama with an accusatory tone, the Germans have become the most receptive audience in the world; whenever the finger points, they obligingly answer with a chorus of *mea culpa*. How would you respond if you felt you had gotten away with mass murder? To feel absolved of a crime, a guilty Calvinist demands some commensurate punishment. But the enormity of Nazi crimes makes absolute justice unthinkable, and even relative justice has been mocked by American political expediency, as Germany becomes an ally in the East-West struggle, and the Nazis are returned to public office. As for the Eichmann trial, this only demonstrated the hideous absurdity of trying to pin on one man what Hannah Arendt calls the "moral debacle" of an entire nation. And lacking a suitable scapegoat, the German people are left without the luxury of expiation. Like the German hero of Sartre's *Les Séquestrés d'Altona*, they must contemplate not Allied vengeance but rather their own unprecedented prosperity—after such knowledge, what forgiveness? Anguished by the mad, insufferable quality of this knowledge, Sartre's hero commits suicide; his countrymen go to the theatre, and weep over the fate of Anne Frank. Such tears are purgative, but let us not confuse these lachrymose calisthenics with genuine remorse. As Brecht's widow, Helene Weigel, told Kenneth Tynan, after witnessing the *Anne Frank* spectacle: "I know my dear Germans. They would do this again. Tomorrow." Meanwhile, the Germans exhibit their guilt with as much national pride as their Volkswagens, and much of the European theatre is given over to guilt-provoking myths.

The most persistent toiler in the guilt industry is Max Frisch, a Swiss playwright recently represented here by two of his works. One of these, Andorra, is currently prosecuting audiences in fifty-three German cities (not to mention sixteen other countries), but the indictment was quickly thrown out of court in New York when spectators refused to accept the summons. This recalcitrance was partly caused by Frisch's Broadway process-servers: Michael Langham's direction managed to make even an occasionally exciting scene look static and labored, and George Tabori's clumsy translation, Boris Aronson's surprisingly artless setting, and the superficial acting of the cast were not much help. While I can imagine a more theatrical event being culled from the play, however, I cannot imagine a more convincing one. As a piece of construction, Andorra seems to have been put together with thumbtacks and bailing wire; it is largely lacking in subtlety and totally lacking in grace; and its dramatic ideas often resound with self-righteous yodeling and liberalistic bellows.

The subject of the work is anti-Semitism, its causes and effects, couched in the form of an allegory. In a mythical land named Andorra (Western Europe), which borders on a hostile country of militant anti-Semites called the Blacks (Nazi Germany), a young man is brought up to believe himself a Jew. Although the Andorrans are proud of their democratic heritage, they subject the boy to prejudice, hatred, and contempt, demanding that he behave according to rigid Jewish stereotypes—cowardice, rapacity, shrewdness, etc. When it is finally revealed that the boy is Gentile—the illegitimate son of his "adopted" father and a Black woman—nobody believes the truth. And partly because he has begun to accept the stereotypes thrust upon him, the boy refuses to believe it too. The Blacks invade Andorra. When the Jew Inspector arrives to make the country judenrein, he instinctually identifies the boy as Jewish. The boy is executed; and the Andorrans must live with their guilt.

Instead of doing violence to the play, a bare outline is the kindest way to describe it, since Frisch is obviously less interested in creating a textured, ambiguous art than in making bald statements. Only some of these statements, however, strike me as true. It is possible to argue that all of Europe is implicated in the death of six million Jews, and it is beyond argument (i.e., obvious) that racial stereotypes are bad. But the play also suggests that the Jew has been invented by the European Gentile—that the Jew, in short, does not exist. I am as unwilling to concede this as to believe that the Negro does not exist (the predominant cliché of the American stage). It seems to me far healthier to accept the differences among people than to pretend that we are really all the same, especially when we remember that it was in the country of most successful Jewish assimilation—Germany—that the Nazi madness began. Well, at least I should like to have heard some arguments for the other side.

This inability to keep two ideas in his mind at the same time is also apparent in Frisch's *The Firebugs*, which recently expired from similar internal and external causes. The director, Gene Frankel, mauled the work into the shape of a Mack Sennett farce, and was responsible for some extremely self-conscious acting; but one felt again that no great masterwork was being violated. The hero of this play is Biedermann (upright citizen)—a bourgeois Everyman who permits a trio of arsonists to send up his house in flames, while a chorus of firemen keep an ineffective watch. Biedermann's passivity before his own destruction—an event he helps to bring about by trying to establish a proletarian comradeship with the firebugs—is a consequence of his personal guilt: he has grown rich by stealing a hair tonic formula from a former employee. As an explanation for the rise of totalitarianism in capitalistic countries, this idea might have had some cogency if it were not so simply stated, but once again a suggestive dramatic metaphor degenerates into a literalistic, and rather smug, allegory. Frisch has been compared to Brecht, whom he acknowledges as his master; but, lacking Brecht's poetry, ambiguity, and inwardness, he seems more akin to the German Expressionists of the twenties and thirties. His is an ideological mind without an ideology, creating activist myths which prescribe no action. A dynamic interrupted or unfulfilled can only produce guilt, Frisch's primary subject and the one emotion his plays provoke. And because of this emphasis on guilt, Frisch provides wet whips for a Germany repulsively eager to flagellate itself.

(1963)

THE HEALTHINESS
OF SICK COMEDY

BEYOND THE FRINGE by and with Alan Bennett, Peter Cook, Jonathan Miller, and Dudley Moore

■ In an article entitled "Sicknik Time," Benjamin DeMott anatomizes the satire of the so-called "sick" comedians, which he finds irresponsible, unclarified, and socially ineffectual. To illustrate this, Professor DeMott lumps together such diverse sources of humor as Nichols and May, Lenny Bruce, Jules Feiffer, Pinky Lee, Joe E. Lewis, and Mad magazine, all rendered into the same unappetizing bowl of sour farina. This reductive method tells us little about the specific style and attack of the individual comics, but it is DeMott's intention to consign them all to a generalized sociological category; and the most impressive part of his essay catalogues the themes and conventions which sick comedy usually assails: racial subjects, bourgeois domesticity, commercialized religion, politics, public relations, and cultural improvement. Alas, DeMott the social scientist is only a torso supporting the disapproving head of DeMott the moralist; and it is not long before he is scoring all his subjects for their "lack of a moral center," their scorn for healthy family life, their nastiness, their preoccupation with nuclear disaster, their "universal hostility . . . to all positive assertion," etc.—finally dismissing them for their failure to affirm that man can change his time.

This demonstrates, I think, what happens when an essentially anarchistic art falls into the critical hands of liberal-humanists: it is spanked for not serving the social hopes and ethical ideals of the community. More sophisticated than, say, President Kennedy, who tends to regard artists and entertainers as soldiers in the cold war, DeMott, nevertheless, seems to share the official desire to impress private expressions into public service, which may end by emasculating culture altogether. Though I suspect that DeMott's strictures could be applied to almost any Juvenalian satirist (is Lenny Bruce, for example, any more scurrilous than John Marston?), they are valid—as valid as Plato's discovery that the artist was subversive of the Republic—but they are also irrelevant. Most satire is, by its very nature, destructive and impractical. The satirist is an immoderate man who is often repelled by the very idea of civilized society. And if he has any positive social function at all, it is purely purgative: relieving the spectator of his outrage and frustration over the forces which manipulate his fate. If sick comedy is prone to explore hidden areas of experience, then this is because these forces have severely limited the remaining avenues of freedom; and if its response to the time is excessive and extreme, then this is because the danger, terror, and insanity of our age have almost reached the breaking point.

I bring this up in order to introduce a discussion of *Beyond the Fringe*, the first British equivalent of American-type satire to reach our shores. This scorching review has all the qualifications of sick comedy as defined by DeMott. It roasts all his categorical turkeys, it has no firm moral center, it is immoderate, irresponsible, and totally destructive, it affirms no changing world, and—if I may be permitted an unDeMottian judgment of value—it is violently funny. The sketches certainly contain echoes of Jules Feiffer and Nichols and May, even occasional hints of Lenny Bruce, along with that rebellious tone and contempt for authority which one associates with the work of Amis, Osborne, and J. P. Donleavy. *Beyond the Fringe* has not yet been identified with sick comedy, perhaps because the community it attacks is not our own; but even now, I suspect, English critics are expressing sociological disapproval over its anti-social behavior.

The review's title suggests its stance: that posture of disaffiliation from the system which DeMott seems to deplore. Beyond the fringe are four extremely talented and alienated young men; within the fringe are all the pieties, platitudes, and prejudices of the last English generation; and the sketches consist of venomous darts hurled over the boundary line. The major political target is Prime Minister Macmillan: one episode finds him, ancient and confused, describing the youthful vigor of Kennedy, while pawing, arthritically, at a globe of the world; another represents a duel between a Russian and a Briton, the weapons a chorus of raspberries for their respective leaders. Commercialized religion also gets the Bronx cheer as a TV theologian, who bubbles like a social worker, speaks of channeling juvenile violence toward God (a later sketch shows a vicar explicating a passage from the story of Jacob in terms of class distinctions). The English worship of royalty is assailed; play censors and censors of pornography are identified with the perversions they would suppress; an African statesman is made to look as venal, corrupt, and self-serving as his European counterparts. Four homosexuals admire one another's hair and clothing before launching into a singing commercial for a man's cigarette; two linguistic philosophers trade "how questions" and "why questions" with examples from "real life"; a Beaverbrook journalist and an adman discuss ways to express dissent (the journalist titters at the boss behind his hand).

Two members of the company are especially gifted: the pianist, Dudley Moore, a kind of cultured Jimmy Savo, who does wicked takes on Art songs, Benjamin Britten, and the endless codas of Romantic German composers, and the raconteur, Jonathan Miller, a perpetually unbalanced whooping crane whose fertile imagination can turn the most commonplace news story into a weird comic fantasy. As a group, however, the company excels in its longest numbers. The first act finale, "Aftermyth of War," satirizes the blood-and-beaches attitudes of the English under Churchill, complete with stiff upper lips, unending cups of tea, and futile sacrifices, finally collapsing into utter desperation as the war generation hands the world over to the youngsters. And the funniest sketch of all satirizes Shakespearean productions (especially Olivier's *Henry V* and the current Old Vic), and even Shakespeare himself—reducing the clown scenes, duels, and choral speeches to bluster and bombast, and the blank verse to absolute nonsense.

If all these subjects lie within the fringe, there is one subject that extends beyond: the H-bomb—and it is under the shadow of this monstrous birth that the entire review is played out. The evening is studded with nuclear references, and two sketches deal with the bomb directly: in the first, a panel group, addressing itself to the question "Kill or Be Killed—or Both," prescribes brown paper bags as a defense against radiation, thus suggesting the absolute idiocy of civil defense; in the second, and final sketch, "The End Is Nigh," a group of fundamentalists are revealed, sitting on a mountaintop, awaiting apocalypse. It is this expectation of nuclear annihilation which accounts for the fury and savagery of much of this review, as it partly accounts for the extravagance of our own sick comedians. For if the young seem negative and irresponsible, then this may be because their positive and responsible elders have left them such a poisoned inheritance. And it is a measure of health, not sickness, that their inevitable anger and resentment can still be disciplined within a witty, sharp, and purgative art.

(1962)

THE ANTI-ESTABLISHMENTARIANS

THE ESTABLISHMENT *by the Cast and*
Peter Cook

■ Despite the serio-comic efforts of Richard Rovere to uncover one, there is no American Establishment, only a changing guard of Influentials rising periodically from a multitude on the make. A true Establishment—based as it is on order, tradition, and hierarchy—exists independently of favor or fashion, but our power structure is a moving target which is always changing its outline. I mention this in partial explanation of why English satire is political and ours is not—since we have no ruling classes, there is never sufficient distance established between the electorate and its representatives. Instead of being isolated figures—objects of awe, veneration, or resentment—our politicians are almost indistinguishable from ourselves, and the gap is narrowing all the time. American political satire seems to cope effectively only with generals, Southern senators, and F.B.I. agents—that is to say, with men who are either mad, moronic, or malevolent. Only extreme types are able to jar the satirist out of his political apathy into genuine indignation.

Fortunately for partisans of satire on great persons, the English have a ruling class which has survived all leveling democratic processes, though I am not sure it will survive its representation on the stage of the Strollers Theatre-Club: *The Establishment* sends off a volley of grapeshot which leaves no political turn unstoned. The invisible mastermind of this review is its writer-producer, Peter Cook, a young man who impersonates Prime Minister Macmillan in *Beyond the Fringe.* And though *The Establishment* is more uneven than its distinguished model (it is also more radical), it obviously involves the same civilized discontents. Macmillan, once again, bears the heaviest burden of mockery. The most palpable hit is a filmed sequence in which the PM unwittingly satirizes himself, muddling through an extremely smug, confused, and halting speech; but his "razor-sharp mind" is exposed to much the same advantage in a murderous skit, modeled on *Advise and Consent,* where, palsied and gerontic, he attempts to deal with a homosexual (therefore potentially Communist) member of his government. Macmillan's regime is also blamed for the recent British humiliations in foreign policy: one sketch finds his cabinet minister, Peter Thorneycroft, reporting on his recent trip to Bermuda, justifying the C.I.A. ("the Cuban Invasion Agency"), the Anglo-American "partnership" ("Mr. McNamara put forth his view as clearly and forcefully as he could— and I agreed with it"), and the advantage of having short-range Blue Steel missiles without the long-range Polaris submarine ("If there's ever any trouble in Scotland—!").

When the cast wearies of Macmillan, it turns to a number of related subjects, demonstrating, for example, the social advantages of a good Establishment accent ("crude compared to your system," notes the narrator, "which is based on money"). Proper diction helps you get away with murder, rape, and imposture, and was even useful to Christ, who is portrayed as an upper-class Englishman, crucified between two grumbling cockneys ("You're the one who's getting all the vinegar sponges"). A long and rather labored sketch shows the Labor party trying to improve its fading image through advertising gimmicks and public relations slogans ("If you don't vote Labor, your genitals will fall off"); and an extremely funny one reveals Kenyatta, ostensibly being questioned about a football match, describing his ambition to be "perhaps the first Negro man to be Queen of England," while happily envisioning Buckingham Palace swimming in an ocean of blood.

The non-political sketches, though not necessarily the least effective, are the most derivative. One sequence, which owes its inspiration to Nichols and May, reveals the gauche, clumsy, and apologetic nature of upper-class courtship, as a boy and girl make intellectual small talk in preparation for a mutually embarrassing good-night kiss. Some material employs the shock tactics of Lenny Bruce—particularly a filmed clip which shows all the gory details of stomach surgery, and turns out to be a cigarette commercial. And the songs owe a lot to Brecht and Weill: one affirming that all those who believe in justice, charity, love, and mankind will go to the wall; another synchronizing conventional love lyrics with filmed shots of world violence and brutality, concluding with an explosion of the hydrogen bomb. The cast is young, good-humored in its savagery, and very talented in an unpolished sort of way; the writing is always literate and intelligent; and the atmosphere invokes that amiably jaded cynicism which has become the characteristic tone of the world's dissenting and disaffiliated young.

(1963)

THE BACKWARDS BIRDS

LUTHER by John Osborne;
CHIPS WITH EVERYTHING by Arnold Wesker

■ The new English dramatists are very odd birds. They awwk and screech and holler as if they were cocks of the walk, and they lack no confidence in their capacity to soar—but they always seem to be flying backwards. Compared with preening peacocks like Coward, Rattigan, and Fry, these plainer specimens look like lusty fowl indeed, and it is satisfying to see Osborne, Wesker, Delaney, and Arden chasing such feathered fops from the coop. But beside the eagles which are trying their wings in France, the English sparrows seem quite gray. While their plumage is modest, it is also a little threadbare; while their calls are sharp, they are occasionally harsh and strident. Even by our own limited standards, the current English pecking order seems like a throwback to an archaic stage of poultry development.

The fact is that the theatrical revolution generated by the "angries" has come about thirty years too late—that is, for any country but their own. To embrace naturalism long after the more advanced dramatists have repudiated it; to discover the nobility of the working classes long after almost everyone else has ceased to believe in it—these vestiges of American social realism are native to every new English dramatist except Pinter, who imitates Beckett. It is a relief to be spared from polished Sussex drawing rooms on the English stage; but Birmingham canals, Manchester slagheaps, and Brighton boardwalks are now becoming equally conventional. Perhaps the recent success of *Tom Jones* will put an end to those innumerable plays and movies which focus so relentlessly on the grimy sludge of industrial cities, before concluding with testimonials to the indomitable spirit of lower-class England. For all their emphasis on external "truth," such documentaries are essentially false and sentimental, and, for all their fine acting, without art or imagination. The new English drama, like the American drama of the thirties, possesses a brilliant intensity and a passionate sense of engagement; but its naïve progressivism and proletarianism embarrass us with memories of our past. In their attempt to identify with the working classes, Osborne and Wesker are constantly invoking the shades of Odets, just as Tony Richardson is beginning to remind us of Kazan.

Osborne shares with Odets the same nervous energy and the same keen ear for common speech—but also the same intellectual deficiencies, the same lack of control. All of these qualities are apparent in *Luther*, a work which is just as unfocused as Osborne's previous efforts, and—despite its religious-historical setting—just as parochial. Osborne has finally abandoned lowerclass England; still, the only consistent line in the play is its class line. After a soporific first act—during which Luther is initiated into the Augustinian order to the accompaniment of plain song, prayers, and directorial Elia Kazanjammers from Tony Richardson—Osborne proceeds to characterize the Protestant Reformation as the revolt of a peasant monk against an upper-class Church, followed by his subsequent betrayal of the class from which he sprang. As portrayed by Albert Finney, in a shuffling, colloquial, writhing, and electric performance, Luther emerges as an angry Midlands miner, determined to take the mickey out of his aristocratic bosses: the Papal Legate, played by John Moffat with subtle superciliousness; the mountebank Tetzel, an effete salesman of indulgences; even the Pope himself, an indolent courtier in hunting clothes, enjoying the privileges of the landed gentry.

Osborne understands that the Reformation had wider reference than this, and includes some extra-social material as well, but none of it is very coherent. There is some suggestion that Luther's ambivalence toward authority was formed by his attitude toward his father. A few epileptic fits provide theatrical climaxes. And references are made—excessively, some have charged—to Luther's difficulties with his bowels. Actually, Osborne's anal obsessions are quite subdued when compared with Luther's (the central Lutheran inspiration—the famous Thurmerlebnis or "experience in the tower"—occurred to Luther on the latrine); and the playwright's scatalogical imagery is almost all lifted from Luther's sermons or his Table Talk. Osborne, however, fails to use this material for any other purpose than to spice up his dialogue or to show his hero in the torments of constipation. But any Freudian can tell him, and Norman O. Brown in Life Against Death has brilliantly demonstrated, that Luther's anality was intimately connected with his attitudes toward the Devil, toward usury, and toward religion itself— theological problems which Osborne hardly mentions, though they are crucial to his subject. Thus, a magnificent possibility dwindles into a sketchy, narrow, and inconsequential tintype, neither fully written nor fully thought through.

Arnold Wesker's Chips With Everything is a much more finished and feeling play, though it suffers from the same social astigmatism. Wesker is animated by a profound political faith which gives him emotional intensity at the expense of artistic finish: his plays are always threatening to fall into socialist propaganda. *Chips With Everything* is no exception, but it has been vastly enhanced by an interesting military setting, and a superb production by the English Stage Company. Under the expert direction of John Dexter, every role becomes a cameo and every scene a unity; the play takes on an uncanny rhythmic precision as the conventions of time and place are dissolved in the snappy cadences of marching men.

The plot concerns the unsuccessful rebellion of the aristocratic Pip Thompson against the R.A.F. caste system; an enlisted man by choice, he refuses to betray his companions in the ranks by becoming an officer. The officers believe the enlisted men are mindless louts; Pip believes them to be dignified human beings—and to prove it, he encourages them to recite Burns's poetry and to sing folk songs instead of drinking, quarreling, and dancing the Twist. Pip even begins to establish a clumsy fellowship with some of the men; but the more attractive he becomes to the recruits, the more the officers determine to make him join their ranks. When they discover his true motive for "slumming"—his unconscious desire to be a "messiah to the masses"—they break his spirit and make him submit; and he immediately adopts the condescending prejudices of his caste. Much of this is reminiscent of *The Mint* where T. E. Lawrence, another fugitive from his class, tells of his efforts to lose his personality in the ranks of the R.A.F.; and when Wesker is writing of the intellectual's unhappy failure to merge with the masses, he uncorks a subject which is both moving and, one suspects, deeply felt. But too often, Wesker's ideology dominates his personal experience, so that preachment begins to replace perception and the ugly head of agit-prop starts to waggle, while his characters tend to develop into caricatures from Marxist melodrama.

For all this, *Chips With Everything* is a real development for Wesker who is beginning to grope his way, tentatively and bashfully, toward deeper wells of emotion—if only his awareness were also deeper. The strength of his sincerity has always been powerful, and his sense of conviction makes me mourn my lost innocence—but I wish he would lose some of his. Crude, unsophisticated, unskeptical, the new English dramatists un-wittingly demonstrate that politics and art can no more be syn-thesized than dogma and truth: what their ideology gives them in vitality, it takes away in complication. They are birds of a feather—if only they could lose the flock, and learn to fly alone.

(1963)

SHAKESPEARE
WITH A FEW TEARS

HAMLET by William Shakespeare; A COMEDY
OF ERRORS and KING LEAR by William
Shakespeare: Royal Shakespeare Company

■ In honor of Shakespeare's four hundredth, three candles were recently lighted on the birthday cake: Sir John Gielgud's production of *Hamlet*, with Richard Burton in the lead, and the Royal Shakespeare Company's versions of *A Comedy of Errors* and *King Lear*. Of these, the *Hamlet* flickers most feebly, partly because of an unfortunate directorial choice by Gielgud, who has designed the performance to look like a final runthrough. The stage is bare, except for some unfinished steps and platforms; sandbags hang from the flies; a canvas flat has been painted to simulate the brick back wall of a theatre; and the actors wear rehearsal outfits and street clothes. The purpose of all this ostentatious simplicity, I suppose, is to introduce some spontaneity into a familiar work, withdrawing the play from history and returning to the actors what has been ex-propriated by costumers and set designers. But the informality is too calculated, and it is ultimately self-defeating. When Gertrude appears with a mink draped over her shoulder, and Claudius sports a blazer, the action, instead of being left unlocated, is automatically transferred from Renaissance Denmark to twentieth-century Suburbia; and when the curtain rises on a rehearsal, one begins to suspect that this particular *Hamlet* is not yet ready to open.

This suspicion is confirmed as the evening proceeds. As often happens with pickup casts, the actors all seem very strange and well bred and uncomfortable with one another. Some of the performances are simply amateur; others are hamstrung by the obstacles of the production. Still, Hume Cronyn's Polonius is interesting to watch: a cranky, rheumatic, avuncular but forthright and sagacious counselor. Cronyn undoubtedly knows that this interpretation is wrongheaded—he is obviously unwilling to repeat the cliché of the "tedious old fool"—but although he thereby sacrifices Polonius' comic possibilities, it is a pleasure to observe him at work. Cronyn approaches a part like a textual scholar doing a critical gloss; every word is crisply interpreted and cleanly communicated. Since his vision is fresh, his technique certain, and his intelligence wide, he teaches us plenty about a role, even in the act of misplaying it.

Whereas Cronyn illuminates and clarifies, Burton darkens and shades. One performance is all line, the other is all color, like an Action painting. The resources of Burton are almost entirely emotional, with the result that his Hamlet is chancy and erratic—effective from moment to moment, but lacking a consistent design. Some of Burton's difficulties are technical; his voice, for example, is limited in range and squeezed and issues mostly through his nose. He sniffs, brays, and barks too much; and he is more dour and surly than truly melancholy. Burton, furthermore, is not of the natural nobility; his Hamlet is less a scholar-courtier than a virile peasant, poetic but slightly musclebound. Still, for all these limitations, he occasionally achieves some startling effects, primarily through abrupt changes in volume and rhythm, and he does not lack for daring. What he is best at is ironic self-hatred. He builds the soliloquy "Oh what a rogue and peasant slave" toward a hysterical climax in the manner of John Barrymore; but after turning his hand into a hideous claw on the word *vengeance*, he examines the gesture with wry amusement, then lets his hand fall with disgust. This shows thought, but too much of the performance is thoughtless, breathless, and febrile—less a Hamlet than a Hamlet Coloring Book. The colors are brighter than those he painted on the part in 1953 with the Old Vic; but they are still splashed. I should like to see him do it again in a few years with more competent support.

The Royal Shakespeare Company is performing *A Comedy of Errors* within a *commedia dell' arte* framework which has been borrowed almost intact from Giorgio Strehler's famous production, for the Piccolo Teatro di Milano, of Goldoni's *Servant of Two Masters*. The concept, actually, has been too closely imitated to have much punch or freshness, and since *A Comedy of Errors* is more Roman than Italian, it is not even very relevant: the *commedia* techniques have obviously been dragged in to beef up a dull play. There is one wacky scene, however, involving the conjuror Pinch—brilliantly improvised by Michael Williams in a long scarf, fingerless gloves, and tattered tailcoat, a raggle-taggle magician baffled by his own smoke pots—which is in the *commedia* tradition; but the character belongs more to the actor than to the playwright.

As for Peter Brook's *Lear*, it has been justly praised. The production is a work of admirable intelligence, carefully conceived and beautifully executed; even its coldness, a quality which restrains one's enthusiasm, is part of a considered pattern. Drawing his inspiration from Samuel Beckett, Brook has superimposed the world of *Waiting for Godot* and *Endgame* on that of *Lear*: the action takes place on an isolated, infertile, and forbidding terrain which is not even worth dividing. The emphasis, visually, is on empty space—a single geometric sheet of corroded metal is suspended near stretched canvas (three of these abstract shapes will later hang down and rattle during the storm scene)—and also on primitiveness and decay—the costumes are of patched leather, worn with age. Empathy has been forbidden—compassionate speeches, including Edmund's repentance, have been excised. The pacing is sluggish and numbed and full of pauses; the spiritual landscape is frozen and dead. The battle scene is a series of off-stage noises, heard while the blinded Gloucester sits on the stage in misery, decaying before your very eyes, and the duel between Edmund and Edgar is like a prehistoric ballet, performed by two sleepwalking animals, pressing each other silently to earth. There is so little genuine activity in the production that when a scene erupts—as does the banquet scene, with Lear overturning a table, and his knights demolishing the chamber—it seems as if pandemonium has broken loose. At the cost of substantial tedium, in short, Brook has emphasized values of futility, waiting, exhaustion, cruelty. Since these are already present in the play, it is not really necessary to validate the work by evoking Samuel Beckett; but this presentation does demonstrate how much the modern existential dramatists have learned from *King Lear*.

The acting is very much at the service of Brook's concept, for the actors appear less like characters than like dolmens—ancient, broken, irregular stones. Irene Worth gives, I think, the most intense and original performance of the evening, playing Goneril as a tight-lipped malevolence, exhausted by evil, breaking under a burden of horror and despair. Like Tom Fleming's Kent, a character which gradually turns from an upright human into a bent, gnarled oak, her Goneril undergoes a physical transformation—a wilting silhouette, literally malformed by the power of Lear's terrible curse. As for Paul Scofield's Lear, it is an awesome, if not entirely satisfactory, achievement. Scofield has purposely limited his resources for the part, adopting a monotonous vocal inflection which he does not vary much, and he conscientiously refuses to thunder and rage. What he achieves, magnificently, is the feel of old age. Looking at first like a retired Prussian Junker, then like a wretched and confused vagrant, he is the very image of stiff antiquity—arthritic, soughing, dazed, and self-involved. Since the life of this Lear is almost entirely passive, it is almost entirely internal, and Scofield has developed the most extraordinary capacity for looking inward, his lip hanging with pain and regret. This occasionally evokes a wrenching pathos—Scofield's first scene with the Fool (played with ethereal sadness by Alec McCowen) is surely one of the most affecting moments in the modern theatre—but a

Lear without rage is a diminished Lear, and most of the play is oddly unmoving. Thus, one comes away from this performance aroused but unsatisfied, having witnessed not the definitive production of the play but rather a fascinating essay on it by a brilliant modern commentator, one which raises new questions without answering the old.

(1964)

HISTORY AS DRAMA

THE DEPUTY *by Rolf Hochhuth, adapted by Jerome Rothenberg*

■ Rolf Hochhuth's *The Deputy* reads like a German doctoral dissertation in verse: two or three epigraphs precede each of the five acts, the acts themselves are divided into discrete sections and titled as if they were chapters, discursive passages and author's asides are generously mixed in with the dialogue, and sixty pages of prose, called "Historical Sidelights," are appended at the end, accompanied by footnotes. The presence of so much scholarly paraphernalia in a published dramatic work suggests, for one thing, that the author has prepared himself for trouble ahead. And since *The Deputy* deals with an extremely inflammatory subject—the failure of Pope Pius XII to condemn unequivocally Hitler's extermination of the Jews—he has acted wisely: the work is born unto trouble, as the sparks fly upward. There is no need to rehearse here the controversy that *The Deputy* has provoked in Europe and America; the slanders, the innuendo, the protests, the riots. Suffice it to say that the customary conditions following the publication of an unpleasant truth have prevailed, and humanity has managed to disgrace itself again.

Hochhuth's painstaking research, on the other hand, does

raise difficulties of a quite different kind, for although The Deputy is a remarkable work in many ways, it is an animal amphibium—a compound of fiction and fact which can be classified neither as good history nor as good literature. While Hochhuth's historical facts are unassailable, for example, some interesting questions have recently been raised about his interpretation of these facts, particularly his assumption that the silence of the Vatican—though partially determined by Church policy, which held the Bolsheviks to be the greater danger than the Nazis—would have been broken had another Pope (say, Pius XI) been in power. Guenter Lewy has suggested that, on the contrary, Vatican policy was the logical culmination of Catholic anti-Semitism, while Hannah Arendt has emphasized that it was Pacelli's predecessor who first praised Hitler and signed the Concordat with Nazi Germany. The temporizing of Pacelli over the fate of the Jews, even as they were being rounded up under his window, then, was not an isolated instance of passivity in the face of evil, but rather reflected the general moral and spiritual collapse of European Christianity, Protestant and Catholic alike.

Hochhuth's tendency to make the individual accountable for the failures of the institution is a heritage of his German idealism, an influence which can also be seen in the shape and substance of his play. The Deputy is written in the ponderous heroic style of Schiller, full of vaunting speeches, generous sacrifices, and externalized emotions—angry confrontations dominate each scene, the verse pitches and rolls, and indignation keeps the tone at a high boil. As for the characters, they are larger than scale, and, therefore, not always very convincing. When the author permits himself artistic license, he can create an interesting and complex individual—the Doctor, for example, whose fatigued cynicism, experimental cruelty, and intellectual arrogance make him a figure of absolute evil, a creation worthy of Sartre or Camus. But more often, Hochhuth's characters are members of a cardboard nobility: Gerstein, for example, the compassionate German who joined the S.S., risking his own life to help the victims of Hitler, or Father Riccardo Fontana, the anguished Jesuit priest, who pinned the Jewish star to his cassock when the Pope refused to protest, and accompanied the Jews to Auschwitz.

Although Father Fontana is fictional, Kurt Gerstein is based on an actual figure whose heroism Hochhuth wished to celebrate in his play. But this is one of the difficulties: historical fact does not always make for very profound art, unless it is supported by a good deal of invention. This is even more obvious in Hochhuth's characterization of Pacelli who appears, a cold, forbidding diplomat, in a climactic obligatory scene, endorsing checks from the Society of Jesus, discussing the various financial holdings of the Church, condemning the Allied bombing of San Lorenzo, and composing a highly ineffectual Article against suffering and misfortune which never once mentions the Jews by name. By adhering so faithfully to contemporary accounts of the Pope, Hochhuth has protected himself, as he must, against charges of tampering with history, but he has left us with a superficial and shadowy character, whose motives remain unplumbed. Unlike Hannah Arendt, who was able to create an extraordinarily complex portrait of Eichmann because the materials were so abundant and her insight so acute, Hochhuth is limited by a scarcity of information about his subject, and by his own apparent lack of interest in the inner workings of character. Cataloguing his personages almost exclusively according to their attitudes toward the Pope's silence, Hochhuth preserves the moral integrity of his work, but at the cost of its aesthetic weight and complexity.

The New York production, however, preserves no integrity at all, and I have confined my discussion to the printed play because the Broadway production is beneath discussion. The adapter, first of all, has confused the need to cut this six-hour work with the license to butcher it, for he has hacked away at the most interesting feature—its intellectual heart—exposing the weakest part of the anatomy—its melodramatic bones. Aside from excising four whole scenes, two of them essential to the theme, decimating characters (the Doctor and Gerstein are mere shadows now), and cutting out just about every literary, historical, political, and religious reference in the text, the adapter has also methodically proceeded to soften the horror of the work and weaken the accusation of the author, sometimes by rewriting whole portions of dialogue. What the adapter has left undone in the way of carnage, the director and actors have completed. Were it not so sloppy and unfinished, Herman Shumlin's direction might remind one of certain Hollywood Nazi movies of the forties, because it features exactly the same clichés: the jagged line of prisoners, rags carefully arranged, moving stagily behind barbed wire, threatened by guards; the immaculate Nazis, cracking whips against their boots and curling their lips contemptuously at their victims; the idealistic martyr-heroes, striking lofty postures, pumping up emotion, and spilling righteous rhetoric. Except for Emlyn Williams, whose characterization of Pacelli is suitably frozen and fastidious, none of the actors gives more than a stock performance, and so many different styles are being used that everyone seems to be performing in a separate play. Broadway may have had the initial courage to produce The Deputy, but it has not finally been able to transcend its ingrained cowardice and artistic inadequacy.

Still, the play is available in published form—a document of power and persuasiveness, whatever its aesthetic and interpretive shortcomings. If Hochhuth has not entirely proven himself yet as either a historian or a dramatist, he has certainly proven himself as a man of discriminating moral intelligence and outstanding courage, and this alone makes him a rare and valuable figure in the modern world. Appearing at this time, The Deputy may, as one American religious group complained, endanger the cause of "harmonious inter-faith relations," but if such a cause is contingent on the suppression of truth, then we are better off without it. As Hannah Arendt has observed, after suffering her own ordeal at the hands of groups with special interests, the truth always seems to come at the wrong psychological moment, but in the words of the Catholic historian whom she quotes at the conclusion of her article, "Only the truth will make us free. The truth which is always awful." I am not so certain that the truth will make us free, but a courageous confrontation of the terrible is still the most exhilarating thing I know, and the greatest source of metaphysical joy.

(1964)

COMPANIES

■

■

■

REPERTORY FEVER

■ Over the past few years, the educated classes of America have developed a new sense of responsibility toward the arts, which, in the theatre, has been reflected in a growth of enthusiasm for the various repertory companies burgeoning in and around New York. Such companies, of course, are hardly novelties in the city, but the amount of excitement generated by them today is practically unprecedented. In the past—while other areas were offering varying degrees of hospitality to permanent groups with high ideals, like the Barter Theatre, the Actor's Workshop, the Arena Theatre, and the Pasadena Playhouse—New York theatregoers were content merely to support the isolated and ephemeral commercial entertainments on Broadway. And, with the exception of the Theatre Guild, which has now turned commercial itself, and the Group Theatre, which eked out a precarious existence throughout the thirties, New York companies having more extended visions were usually permitted to expire after a season or two of poverty

209

and neglect. For the past five years, however, quite a few companies have managed to survive the indifference of the majority audience. Operating in such outlandish places as Greenwich Village, Second Avenue, and Central Park, they have frequently brought real distinction both to dramatic classics and to experimental plays, thereby substantially enlarging the possibilities of repertory as an artistic force.

Partly as a result of their success, repertory enthusiasm has begun to spread like a fever rash. Tyrone Guthrie is forming an ambitious new company in the Midwest; other groups are preparing to open all over the country; and even the traditionally Philistine State Department is coughing up $150,000 as propaganda money to send some American stars overseas under the management of the Theatre Guild's Lawrence Langner. But the most highly publicized realization of the idea is still a few years off. In 1963, when the Repertory Theatre Association begins operations as a part of the Lincoln Center for the Performing Arts, American repertory will become a national institution. Provided with foundation support, private subsidies, a brandnew theatre, abundant Broadway talent, a ready-made audience, boundless good will, and the blessings of John D. Rockefeller III, the Lincoln Center company is proof that the once unpopular repertory ideal has now become the basis for favor, fashion, and influence.

The theoretical cause of this repertory fever is easy enough to determine. It has at last become sufficiently obvious, at least to those who care about the theatre as an art form, that America will never develop a satisfactory dramatic tradition until it can develop a unified company with plenty of rehearsal time and a vigorous, intelligent, and continuous artistic policy. Conscious of the examples of France and Britain, which supplement their Boulevard and West End showshops with state and locally supported art theatres, increasing numbers of disgruntled spectators have grown out of patience, if not out of pocket, with Broadway products, and have begun to seek a headier vintage of dramatic wine than the hit-flop vendors of Times Square can afford to provide. The Lincoln Center project comes in response to this demand, its purpose to extract the professional advantages of the New York stage without suffering the economic disadvantages. But while external conditions seem ripe for the formation of such a company, something more than good intentions, high hopes, and financial generosity are needed to make it an effective reality. For, unlike France and Britain, which draw on an already fixed dramatic heritage, America has been without a responsible theatre for so long that the transition from the commercial to the repertory system will undoubtedly uncover unique problems which may prove difficult to solve. First suggesting what some of these problems are, let us then examine how the Lincoln Center organization is preparing to approach them; and then we may be in a better position to speculate about its future possibilities.

The first great threat to the native repertory system lies in the inner nature of the American theatre artist. The repertory system demands the absolute submission of the individual to a high ideal; yet, the majority of our theatre eminences are primarily interested in the advancement of their own careers. Self-aggrandizement, a primal characteristic of American life, can hardly be called the exclusive property of the American theatre, though it is exacerbated there by the public's insatiable thirst for "personalities." But while personal ambition may be an asset to a business organization, it can be fatal to a theatre unit based on co-operation, selflessness, and humility. For, if a repertory company is ever to function properly, its members must subordinate their own aspirations to the demands of the company, working in perfect harmony for the sake of a balanced and unified artwork.

Our commercial theatre encourages quite a different form of behavior. On Broadway, a famous "name" can affect the obtaining of a theatre, the form of a play, and even whether a work gets on at all. Taking advantage of this central position, established stars tend to choose their vehicles for the length and attractiveness of their roles; they enforce revisions designed to fatten their scenes and point their entrances; they influence the casting of supporting roles so they will not be eclipsed by someone else's youth, beauty, or talent; they ingratiate themselves with the audience instead of adapting themselves to the play; they are notoriously unco-operative about rehearsals; and they are obsessively preoccupied with salary and billing. And this kind of careerism is hardly confined to our stars, for many directors, designers, and supporting players as well have developed ingenious methods for attracting attention to their own particular specialties. In this atmosphere—where the majority ignore Stanislavsky's admonition to love the art in one's self rather than one's self in art—the commercial theatre has come to resemble a glittering showcase window, inhabited by glamorous dressmakers' dummies. And though such a theatre may appeal to those who like to gape and gawk at the latest fashions, it is hardly the proper setting for dramatic art.

The second threat to repertory success lies in the fact that even some of our best and most dedicated professional actors lack histrionic range. In a company presumably dedicated to performing the plays of many countries and periods, versatility and virtuosity of technique are basic requirements. Yet, the current Broadway practice is to cast actors for their personal characteristics rather than for the ability to adapt themselves to the needs of each role. In England, Olivier, Gielgud, and Guinness are accustomed to playing characters of every age, class, and quality. In America, where actors are forced to repeat themselves from role to role, Olivier would probably be persistently cast as a romantic leading man, Gielgud as a prep school headmaster, and Guinness as a grocery clerk in the A. & P. For American actors survive by intensifying a single personality trait which has managed to capture the fancy of the audience; and, in consequence, many American playwrights create characters along already established type lines, and many theatrical agents turn away gifted performers unless they conform to these types. It is no wonder that our actors tend to imitate one another.

Of course, a good training program, along the lines suggested by Michel Saint-Denis in his stimulating book, *Theatre: The Rediscovery of Style*, might teach the American actor more diversified techniques. But our existing programs are woefully inadequate. For example, it is probable that the Lincoln Center company will be drawn mainly from the Actors Studio, not only because of Kazan's association with that group but because the Studio has helped produce some extremely gifted performers. But while the Studio has made undeniable contributions to American theatre—promoting dramatic truth, eliminating staginess, and developing a native acting style—it is the worst possible training grounds for a repertory actor. I am not just thinking of the limitations of that famous Studio stereotype, the lower American primate, scratching his proletarian lice and mumbling erotic incoherencies into his ripped tee shirt, for the Studio can boast of achievements greater than these. I am referring to the inadequacy of the Studio Method. Based primarily on self-analysis, the Method has increased emotional authenticity at the cost of all poetry, imagination, and style, and finally reduced acting to mere imitation. For the Studio actor, developing those psychological aspects of character which conform most closely to his own experience, has become unable to make that essential imaginative leap into another's life, with the result that he tends to play himself over and over again. Thus, the Studio Method is most appropriate to the commercial theatre where type-casters seize on a single salable commodity for merciless exploitation.

Under these circumstances, the vast majority of American actors are competent only in narrow naturalistic roles, even though the masterpieces of the drama were all written in other modes. One shudders to think of people like Ben Gazzara, Pat Hingle, Kim Stanley, or Shelley Winters being confronted with Greek tragedy, Shakespeare, Italian commedia, or French Romantic drama, when even such recent contemporaries as Ibsen, O'Casey, Shaw, and Anouilh seem to be sources of bafflement. To be sure, there is a substantial number of American actors, trained in European schools or hinterland repertory companies, who are better equipped to play classical roles. But many of them, discouraged by present conditions, have left New York, and the handful which achieved some recognition here has not been able to develop. The limitation of the professional actor is one of the most serious hurdles in the path of repertory success. If it is not quickly removed, the American repertory company— failing to cope adequately with the great dramatic literature—

will be forced to settle for the mediocre works it is competent to perform.

The third threat to repertory is the most subtle one of all, for it lies in the nature of the American theatre audience. A repertory company can develop a great vision only if it is supported by an intelligent, imaginative, and enthusiastic audience, but the typical American theatregoer of today is the most passive, immobile, and moribund spectator in the world. He may go to the movies for escape or pleasure, but when he rouses himself to go to the theatre he expects to be neither stimulated, enlightened, or entertained, for he sits out three hours in a cataleptic trance, coming to consciousness only to applaud the star's entrance, his exit, and his curtain call. The stupefying vacuity of the Broadway audience is the direct result of economics. With ticket prices soaring into the stratosphere, the audience has become dominated by the prosperous business classes, most of whom attend the theatre not because they want to but out of some external pressure. Going to a play is now a form of conspicuous consumption, the play itself less important than the circumstances surrounding it.

In consequence, the New York theatre audience is composed mainly of two types of spectators. The first makes up the matinee, benefit, and convention audiences, and goes to a play for the sake of charity, business, or sightseeing (for him, Broadway serves up such gooey fudge sundaes as *The Sound of Music*, *The World of Suzie Wong*, *Auntie Mame*, *Take Me Along*, and *A Majority of One*). The second type is the cocktail party celebrant who, fearful of drawing an embarrassing conversational blank, trails Kulchur down every neon alley in Times Square (for him, Broadway invokes the more pretentious glories of *J.B.*, *Dear Liar*, and *The Miracle Worker*; the cumbrous opulence of overweighted productions like the recent *Heartbreak House* and *Caligula*; and the summer "festivities" of the American Shakespeare Festival). Going to the theatre for cultural improvement, charity purposes, or expense account entertainment hardly signifies a very vital relationship between the spectator and the stage; and it does not motivate theatregoers to exercise much intelligence or judgment in evaluating plays, which is probably why the works are so bad and the opinions of the reviewers so sacrosanct. Any repertory company which plans to tap the existing audience, instead of creating an entirely new one out of those multitudes who now stay home out of penury, apathy, or disgust, is doomed before it opens its curtain. It will be merely an extended arm of Broadway, pointing in the direction of Broadway mediocrity and pretense.

These, then, are the major problems which the Lincoln Center company must solve if it is ever to be anything more than a fashionable plaything for the opulent and the bored.

And though we can only speculate about its intentions from the numerous policy statements circulated in the press by Kazan and Whitehead, these statements make the future direction of the company fairly clear. "We intend to make a theatre that is interesting, exciting, vital to us in contemporary terms," said Kazan in a recent interview. "If we do a classic, it has to have a meaning for us today and it's got to be exciting. . . ." In more precise terms, Kazan and Whitehead affirm that their repertory program will "avoid the smell of the library" by ruling out things like "pseudo-realistic productions of The Wild Duck, always that same damned Wild Duck." Instead, the company will perform an annual program of two new plays by "leading American writers," two revivals of "classical European plays," and one revival of "an American classic" ("Everyone," adds Kazan, "should see Death of a Salesman every five years"). Moreover, the repertory might include sweeping dramatizations of such novels as Werfel's Forty Days of Musa Dagh, Dreiser's Sister Carrie ("We recreate the social background of that era . . . an environment out of which came the America of today"), and Zola's Germinal ("What a play that would make. The coal mines of Belgium. A real Van Gogh feeling about it. A love story there, and a story of labor struggles"). The company itself would consist of thirty "leading" American actors, paid anywhere between Off Broadway minimum and the maximum of a Broadway star, and would spend eight months before out-of-town audiences experimenting with a number of plays in the hope of selecting the first two or three. Finally, the directors are sure that Lincoln Center, though subsidized, will prove no unfair competition to Broadway, because its box office scale will be "almost as high as Broadway's." And with this plan, Kazan hopes to attract "a lot of my intellectual friends [who] have stopped going to the theatre."

At the risk of sounding prematurely harsh, let me now explain why Mr. Kazan's intellectual friends will probably prefer to stay home.

1) *Classics vital in contemporary terms.* In theory, a high-sounding ideal; in practice, always an excuse for a director to spread his personality over a play. The only way to make a drama meaningful "for us today" is to find your way past both convention and contrivance to the heart of the author's intention, but for such a task, Mr. Kazan does not seem very well qualified. He has yet to direct anything but commercial American plays, and two years ago he announced that he would never produce Shakespeare because "I am more interested in the life that is around me." This curious statement, along with other evidence, suggests that for all his brilliant craftsmanship and psychological intuition, Mr. Kazan's concept of the drama is purely environmental. I suspect if he does direct a classic, it will end up either with an American setting or an American social-psychological interpretation: something on the order of *The Wisteria Trees*. I am not sure the Lincoln Center directors are aware that while you can doctor second-rate works to suit your own prejudices, you don't meddle with masterpieces.

2) *Avoid the smell of the library.* If the library smells, it is from lack of human habitation, for it is rarely aired by our theatrical eminences. Yet, this odoriferous area contains most of the works worth doing by a subsidized repertory company. It would be interesting to tally how many times "pseudo-realistic productions of *The Wild Duck*" have been performed in this country compared with pseudo-realistic productions of *All My Sons*, pseudo-poetic productions of *J. B.*, and pseudo-pseudo productions of *Sweet Bird of Youth*. Lincoln Center may succeed in filtering out the "smell of the library" by introducing the stink of the cashbox.

3) *The repertory.* The two new plays by "leading American writers" would be more appropriate to Broadway than to a

subsidized art theatre. Plays by new or experimental writers would be more to the point. The cycle of "American classics," after two or three plays by O'Neill, and (this is a generous estimate) one each by Wilder, Williams, and Miller, will be totally exhausted. The "two classical European plays" might have some merit, but what works could be chosen when all the great European dramas "smell of the library"? Kazan's plan for dramatizing novels might prove a contribution to the theatre, but hardly to the drama; up till now, such adaptations have been the province of the writers of musicals.

4) *The company.* "Leading American actors"? With pay scales up to the astronomic portions of a star? Look out! So far, Christopher Plummer and Geraldine Page, both versatile actors, have been announced for the company; the rest will probably come from the less resourceful ranks of the Actors Studio. My guess is that, in consequence, within a year or so the repertory will consist exclusively of American plays.

5) *Experimenting out of town.* Evidence that Lincoln Center will be more inclined to follow public taste than to lead it. Out-of-town tryouts are a peculiar Broadway custom, invariably resulting in the revision of a play to suit the demands of the audience. Is it utopian to expect a subsidized company to revise its audience to suit the demands of the play?

6) *Box office scale almost as high as Broadway's.* This makes it a safe prediction that Lincoln Center will attract precisely the same audience as Broadway; it is already preparing the same kind of fare. In its projected ticket prices, as in almost every one of its announced plans, Lincoln Center—three years before its opening date—is effectively undermining the basic purpose of subsidized repertory.

The prospect, therefore, despite all the love, sweat, and money being poured into the project, is not very heartening. The motives of Mr. Kazan and Mr. Whitehead are undoubtedly above reproach, and it is certain that they are among the most gifted men working in the commercial theatre. But for them the standards of art have hitherto been confounded with the standards of Broadway, and you do not easily change the habits of a lifetime. One may wonder—when it is commercialism that is debasing our theatre—why the Lincoln Center project was handed over to two men who up till now have shown no great interest in any other system. But it is an American custom to analyze a problem correctly, and then come up with the wrong solution.

Meanwhile, other companies—without fanfare, funds, or fabulous theatre buildings—are working their way through to the right solutions. For while Americans will blunder under the most favorable conditions, they can also come through with striking and imaginative achievements against the most overwhelming odds. Lincoln Center may suggest that our current repertory fever is only the hectic of an old disease, but for such companies as The Living Theatre and Shakespeare in the Park, it is more like the blush of a bright and clean beginning.

(1960)

WHAT'S WRONG
WITH THE PHOENIX?

PEER GYNT by Henrik Ibsen

■ The intentions of the Phoenix company, which aspires to create a repertory of "time-honored and modern classics," are lofty and honorable, but their productions this year have overwhelmed me with fatigue, impatience, and gloom. My anguished imagination is now subject to a fearful hallucination in which I see the finest works of the greatest dramatists strewn about the Phoenix stage like so many violated corpses, while a chorus of newspaper reviewers gleefully sings dirges in the wings. Perhaps it is unfair to blame anyone but the reviewers themselves for the absurdities they write about Aristophanes and Ibsen; certainly, journalists—occupied with exalting the present—have always been inclined to knock the past. Yet, it cannot be denied that the Phoenix has provided a generous supply of corks for this pop-gun fusillade.

For it seems to me that the Phoenix, while outwardly more deferential toward the past than the reviewers, is inwardly just as indifferent to it. Instead of letting these plays stand on their own legs, the company's policy is to hale them into the twentieth century by the nearest available appendages. In *Lysistrata* this resulted in extremely painful attempts at topicality (as when an assorted collection of pneumatic females chanted "Sex Almighty, Aphrodite, rah, rah, rah!" or an ungainly chorus carried placards across the stage announcing that "Athens is a Summer Festival"). In *Peer Gynt*, the effort is less clumsy but no less obfuscating—a varnish of "theatrical values" is spread thickly over the surface of the play. The Phoenix production never betrays the slightest hint that *Peer Gynt* has an intellectual content, a consistent theme, or, for that matter, any interest at all beyond a histrionic sweep. Stuart Vaughan, the director, has staged the mad scene, for example, as a frenetic phantasmagoria which is quite chilling in its effect, but one has not the vaguest idea what such a scene is doing in the play. With the directorial emphasis on stage effects, crowd scenes, and occasional "Method" touches in the relations between characters, what was conceived as a masterful play of ideas emerges as just another stage piece, and a pretty boring one at that.

But *Peer Gynt's* claim to "classical" stature does not rest on the fact that it provides fat parts for actors, compelling scenes, or the opportunity for designers, directors, and technicians to display their wares; nor is the play particularly distinguished by any profound psychological insights. Considered strictly as *theatre* (a word which is coming to mean the very opposite of *drama*), the play undoubtedly has severe defects, especially in form. But like all great works, *Peer Gynt* survives because it transcends the facile notion of "theatre," because it is larger than its characters or its effects, and because what it has to say about the nature of existence remains both wide and deep.

In fact, *Peer Gynt*, written nearly a hundred years ago, tells us more about our own condition than almost anything written in America in recent times, for Peer's concern with Self is one of the central problems of our national life. A fanciful story-teller with a prancing imagination, Peer might have developed into a great man, but he is too absorbed in appearances to become anything more than a great illusionist. As rapist, as honorary troll, as slave trader, as entrepreneur, as prophet, he is the incarnation of compromise, the spirit of accommodation, the apotheosis of the middle way. He whirls giddily around the glove, justifying his absolute lack of conviction and principle with the protest that he is being true to himself. The inevitable conclusion to this maniacal egotism is insanity (where the ego turns in upon itself completely), and it is in the madhouse that Peer is crowned Emperor. Neither saint nor sinner, Peer finally learns he has been a worthless nonentity who existed only in the love of a faithful wife, and at the end of the play he is waiting to be melted down, like all useless things, by the Button Moulder. "He who forfeits his calling, forfeits his right to live," wrote Kierkegaard, who believed, like Ibsen, that careerist self-absorption and mindless self-seeking are the most monstrous waste of life. Or, as the Button Moulder puts it: "To be yourself, you must slay yourself."

"To be yourself is to kill the worst and therefore to bring out the best in yourself" is the way the passage reads in the Phoenix production, which will give you some idea how easily a profundity can become a copybook maxim. But although Norman Ginsbury's doggerel, inaccurate rendering makes William Archer's Victorian bromides seem sublime and precise, the adapter is not exclusively to blame for the general amorphousness of the evening. Stuart Vaughan's cutting is almost guaranteed to make the work incomprehensible, and the central roles are all pretty well miscast. If the Phoenix were a true repertory company, Fritz Weaver would have been ideally placed in the part of the Button Moulder; since it is not, he plays the leading role. A heroic actor with a fine gift for irony, Weaver begins to make sense when Peer gets older; but his heavy style is inappropriate to the younger, quicksilver Peer who is turned into an earthbound swain with monotonous speech inflections and a clumsy pair of hooves.

In brief, we must be grateful to the Phoenix for wanting to mount this play, at the same time wondering what the animating impulse was to do so. In the past, the Phoenix had no policy other than to survive; today, its brochure speaks of creating a "new tradition in the theatre." But since the Phoenix has developed no new methods of staging, no new methods of playing, no new interpretative approach, I am puzzled about what this new tradition will be. There seems to be an authentic desire, as yet unrealized, to create a "working, professional group that can grow as a unit," but we have yet to see any sign that the "time-honored and modern classics" will function as anything more than showcases for the company. Alas, the trouble with the Phoenix is the trouble with the American theatre at large; isolated within its theatre walls, it shows no willingness to abandon itself to any purpose higher than its own existence. In this regard, Ibsen's play remains a cogent lesson; for if the American theatre is ever to be a place for art, it must learn to slay itself.

(1960)

BACK AT THE PHOENIX . . .

HENRY IV, *Parts I and II*,
by William Shakespeare

■ Henry IV has always seemed to me the work of two collaborators with conflicting notions about the value of individual freedom in the corporate state. Shakespeare in his history plays is a nationalistic chronicler concerned with the welfare of England; and officially—as E. M. W. Tillyard has correctly observed—the two parts of *Henry IV* constitute an extended morality play about the Redemption of a Prodigal Prince who eventually evolves into the ideal English King. Prince Hal, in his father's eyes, seems wholly given over to riotous living and evil companions, but the audience knows from the beginning that Hal is preparing for a dramatic reformation. In this morality structure, Falstaff functions as a Vice figure—Sloth and Vanity in the first part, Disorder and Misrule in the second— who must be suppressed so that the new king may act with efficiency and heroism. The rejection of the old knight on coronation day is a prologue to England's glorious victory on the fields of France.

But contending with the public historian was a private artist who preferred to write a great Aristophanic farce about the exuberant anarchy and instinctualism of unconditioned man: Falstaff's character—like his capacious guts which are continually spilling over his belt—cannot be contained within the formal design. In this farce, Hal looks less like a perfect prince than a perfect prig, and Falstaff's resistance to civic virtue becomes a triumphant defense of natural man against all the domestic, national, and spiritual claims that are made on him. George Orwell, discussing the comic postcards of Donald McGill, has unwittingly provided the best description of Falstaff's appeal: "He is your unofficial self, the voice of the belly protesting against the soul . . . the lazy, cowardly, debt-bilking adulterer who is inside all of us . . . who sees very clearly the advantages of staying alive with a whole skin." Clearly, Falstaff is not a very inspiring presence when there are wars to be won, wives to be supported, children to be fed, laws to be enforced, and order to be maintained; and, since man must live in a social unit, his ultimate fate is inevitable, and, in a certain sense, just. Yet, he is the source of our greatest humor, and the dramatic embodiment of our eternal rebellion against institutional demands.

The Phoenix is now performing the two plays in repertory, and my difficulty in reviewing the productions, I suspect, is similar to Shakespeare's in writing the plays: an irreconcilable conflict between my private and public selves. Officially—which is to say, in the interests of good box office, dramatic literature, and the perpetuation of the theatre—I suppose I should join in the unanimous chorus of praise for the company's present work, shouting Best Damn Show I've Seen in Years, A Knockout, Long Life, Get Ye Down There, and all the other quotable gobbets which are currently being gouged out of the journalists' meaty prose. But unofficially, I feel compelled to admit that, taken as a whole, the two productions bored me stiff, and that if I'd had my way I would have been some place where things were more lively, possibly at Gadshill taking a purse with the old knight.

Now, since the Phoenix *Henrys* are undoubtedly the best work the company has done all year, what could be wrong? Surely, the plays are handsomely costumed and, if one doesn't notice that the set looks like a gallows, tastefully designed. As for the direction, there are not any striking interpretive blunders, aside from the fact that Stuart Vaughan has paced some scenes with irritating slowness, invented too much coy mischief for Falstaff's page, and sentimentalized the tougher relationships—Hotspur and his wife are continually making love, and Hal is forced to cover and kiss Falstaff when he is asleep behind the arras and fight for control during the rejection scene. Similarly, while a few roles are miscast or misplayed, a few others come close to being definitive. Hotspur is less a gruff, seasoned soldier than an extravagant lyricist still wet from his adolescence, and Hal mouths his lines like a bumpkin giving lip-reading lessons to the deaf; but John Heffernan's gray and twinkly Shallow, though sometimes a trifle too sweet, is full of brilliant comic invention; Franklin Cover's Silence is a gem of palsied and owlish somnambulance; Patricia Falkenhain plays Doll Tearsheet like a disordered, staggering Picadilly whore; Ray Reinhardt as Pistol firks and foins with robust salacity; and Gerry Jedd, Fritz Weaver and Juliet Randall are quite wonderful in other roles.

Yet, except for these scattered performances which give life to some of the comic scenes in Part II, there is no consistent fun or art in the productions, for the plays have been unconscionably tamed and domesticated. One feels this everywhere, but especially where least expected, in the part of Falstaff. Eric Berry looks the role and walks it, but in his fastidious hands the knight is an impostor, imported from a Restoration play. For

Berry's Falstaff is less concerned with amusement than with elocution, always a little too delighted with himself for having pronounced his words with the proper B.B.C. inflection. Laughter becomes *lofter*, not, *nut*, past, *pahhst*, and the r's are trilled until your ears ring; one begins, in short, to listen to diction rather than sense. A group of school children, I am told, who came to the Phoenix expecting to see a *bad* man, were delighted to find that Falstaff was really *nice*. And that, I fear, is the word to sum up the performance. Shakespeare's con man has been converted into an ingratiating old fella with a tendency to foppishness but no more subversive than your Uncle Cyril from Bristol.

And Berry's upper-class mannerisms set the tone for the entire production. Shot through with moth holes of dullness and amateurism, the two evenings are characterized by an academic gentility that reminds one too often of the Old Vic. The Phoenix ends its season having developed a few actors of real talent and power, but still a long march from a unified company with a meaningful direction. Its ideals are still only unfulfilled hopes, for the Phoenix has not yet dared to let go of the old traditions and rampage into the new.

(1960)

O FOR A DRAUGHT ...

HENRY V; MEASURE FOR MEASURE; THE
TAMING OF THE SHREW: *New York Shakespeare
Festival, Central Park*

■ With the help of an underground acquaintance named Charon, I managed this summer to get my hands on a two-gallon jug of lethe water—a brew which, when generously laced with nepenthe, is absolutely invaluable in helping you to forget

your more harrowing experiences. This infernal cocktail worked
so well for me that I was able to blot out not only the horrors of
the last Broadway season, but some of the atrocities of the early
summer as well. I remember going in July to see Jackson
MacLow's *Marrying Maiden* and Sophocles' *Women of Trachis*
at The Living Theatre. But aside from a few details (I recollect
that the first featured dialogue selected at random by a throw of
the dice, drowned out anyway by cacophonous sounds on un-
identifiable instruments, and that the second was translated by
Ezra Pound into colloquialisms which would have seemed
dated during the War of 1812), my memory of them is a merci-
ful blank. I think I went to Stratford, too, for I recall watching
Katherine Hepburn, in what was advertised as a production of
Twelfth Night, impersonate Captain Horatio Hornblower in a
setting laid in Brighton by the Sea. Remembering that previous
Stratford performances had been placed in Spanish Texas and
nineteenth-century Vienna, I conveniently forgot to see Robert
Ryan support Miss Hepburn in *Antony and Cleopatra*. I admit
to a little irresponsibility there, but I expect to catch the movie
version which, no doubt, will be laid in a cigar factory near
Rome, Georgia.

After a few visits to the free New York Shakespeare Festival
in Central Park, however, I am now petitioning Mnemosyne,
goddess of memory, for an antidote—never have I so bitterly
regretted the impermanence of the theatrical occasion. Through
love, intelligence, imagination, and sheer doggedness, Joseph
Papp has built this company into an ensemble comparable to
any in the world, a group so virile that it makes the Old Vic
look like a collection of Bennington girls doing their junior year
field work. The company has, thank heaven, developed no stars,
so the first production was somewhat hampered by a certain
monotony in the leading role; but this *Henry V*, directed by
Papp himself, was so muscular, masculine, and leathery that, in
retrospect, I began to think Olivier's film version (which always
seemed to me definitive) a little soft and sentimental. To name
only one of the insights of this strong interpretation, the
wooing scene became, in Papp's conception, less a piece of
romantic badinage than a practical act of policy, less a love

contest between a skilled suitor and a coy, yielding kitten than a political contract between a clumsy, ambitious, good-natured king and an ironic, occasionally bitchy princess who will not easily forget how many of her kinsmen were killed on the battlefield.

The Festival production of *Measure for Measure* was less impressive—not so much a miscarriage as something which was never conceived. The director, Alan Schneider, hadn't much idea about how to solve the problems of the play, and he didn't know how to use Eldon Elder's handsome and functional setting. As for the acting, the supporting company was quite good, especially in the lowlife scenes, but for the leads Schneider imported an Antonio who expended too much energy impersonating Gielgud, and an Isabella still too green and sanguine to capture the sudden shifts of this difficult creature—together, they capsized the show into a little pond of tedium.

The third production, a spirited performance of *Taming of the Shrew*, was the season's triumph, and a triumph for the American theatre. Though superlatives have a habit of sticking in my throat, I must not temporize here: this was the finest production of a Shakespeare comedy I have ever seen. The director, Gerald Freedman, is new to me; yet, I have no hesitation in saying, from this job alone, that he is one of the most gifted theatre men in America. With admirable daring, he flipped tradition (which is to say, cliché) on its back, substituting a joyous, exuberant farce style which drew on the Marx Brothers, Mack Sennett, and animated cartoons, while choreographing the set changes and crowd scenes in a manner introduced, I think, by Gene Frankel, but now brought to its stylistic perfection. From the first moment that Christopher Sly was catapulted out of an alehouse by an angry Amazonian barmaid, the production roared along with a speed and inventiveness which I have seen surpassed on the stage only by the Piccolo Teatro di Milano. Like that inspired group, the *Shrew* company never lets the audience forget it is in a theatre—very aptly, since Shakespeare's play has Italian roots, the whole performance is in the presentational style of *commedia dell' arte*. It is impossible to describe all the splendid *lazzi*, including pratfalls, beatings, tumblings, and brawls, which made this production such an uninhibited delight, so I will merely say that I remember them with the same intense gratitude that I remember certain devices of Chaplin, Keaton, Fields and all the other greats who knew how the physicalness of man could be the source of our wildest laughter.

For the abundance of comic genius collected in the Park is reminiscent of the heyday of silent films. Frederick Warriner, as a quaking, shaking, bone-breaking ancient who gets down on his knees to catalogue his possessions and locks agonizingly into position; John Call, as a bristling turkeycock of a retainer, ecstatically warming his frozen behind over a fire, ogling, raspberrying, and abadabadabaing when he is aroused; Joseph Bova, as a mischievous, devious, electrified servant, telling his master how much he loves him while feeling the sumptuous fur on his master's costume; John Heffernan, as the Tailor, swallowing his pins after having been clapped on the back, and, as the Pedant, anxiously fingering a bunch of celery, his perpetually agape mouth finally stopped with a cork from his sack bottle; Harry Singleton, as a reluctant page forced to impersonate Sly's "Madam" in a broken voice and ill-fitting gown, squeezing his "husband's" cheeks in fury and braining him with a fan whenever he makes a pass—these are only a few hors d'oeuvres from the general feast in Central Park. As for the main dishes, Barbara Ann Barrie and Robert Vail succeeded in the difficult task of making the Bianca-Lucentio subplot more than a pallid interlude; and Jack Cannon, playing Petruchio as a splenetic, acquisitive, swashbuckling Italianate blackguard, and Jane White, making Kate a mercurial, whip-brandishing, and (after she has been starved half to death) whip-eating hellion, are the only actors I know who can keep these characters so funny, wild, and real without ever accommodating to the more tender marital notions of the modern audience.

Without enormous funds or large foundation grants, Papp has beautifully succeeded where so many more fashionable producers have failed: he has created a uniquely American Shakespeare style which is both fresh and faithful to the text, and built a company of which we can all be proud. For this alone, Mnemosyne, let your draught be pure.

(1960)

DEFECTS AND VIRTUES

MUCH ADO ABOUT NOTHING; A MIDSUMMER
NIGHT'S DREAM; RICHARD II: *New York
Shakespeare Festival, Central Park*

■ Since the New York Shakespeare Festival filled me with
much satisfaction this summer, I am perhaps ungrateful to
insist on the total euphoria I experienced in previous years; but
the 1961 season failed to invoke that feeling of beaming beati-
tude I have learned to expect from this remarkable troupe. In
the defection, before the summer began, of his most gifted
director, and in the apparent desertion of his most dependable
comic actors, Joseph Papp suffered losses which undoubtedly
impaired the quality of his productions; yet, more profound
difficulties than mere problems of personnel could be detected
in the season's offerings. Granted that a few individual performances were not as inspired as usual this summer, the company as a whole still managed to display its customary virtues:
the trouble was that, through a complex of circumstances, the
defects of these virtues had finally become apparent as well.

The special trademark of Papp's group, and the quality which
makes it so peculiarly American, has always been its volatile,
ripsnorting, rough-and-ready style. But while broad comedy,
boisterous physical action, colloquial speech patterns, and
broken line rhythms are perfectly appropriate to Shakespeare's
more masculine and action-filled plays, one begins to hear the
tinkle of shattered china when these techniques are applied to
works of delicacy, lyricism, and grace. Similarly, Papp's laudable
disdain for the star system has helped to turn his company into
one of the smoothest ensembles in America, but he has not yet

developed an actor commanding enough to interpret the larger Shakespeare roles with as much expertise as the smaller ones are always played. In previous seasons, a shrewd balancing of the repertory managed to disguise these limitations, but this summer's program sometimes seemed beyond the company's present range.

Much Ado About Nothing, directed by Papp himself, was located in Goya's Spain where stiff-backed caballeros in cocked hats and grand ladies in mantillas and lace played shuffleboard, pursued butterflies, and flourished fans against a background of amorous intrigue, their conversation punctuated by the castanet-snapping and heel-clicking of Flamenco dances. Though it sometimes inclined perilously toward the gimmickry associated with the American Stratford, this production was distinguished by a color, dash, and verve which made it far more expansive and balletic than Gielgud's static treatment of three seasons ago. Papp directed the work as if he were aware of the obscure pun in the title (Nothing was once an Elizabethan homonym for noting or observing), carefully heightening the various eavesdropping sequences which further and complicate the action; and his playful handling of the Claudio-Hero plot not only rejuvenated these usually tedious episodes but even made certain related scenes seem more crisp and gay (Beatrice's "Kill Claudio," for example, was read, and actually assumed a crazy relevance, as a laugh line). Despite the skillful modulations of Nan Martin's laconic Beatrice, however, the wit badinage was rather heavy and flat. Jack Cannon apparently confused his Benedick with Petruchio, a role he had successfully essayed the previous season, because he roared, rasped, and croaked his lines with such misogynistic spleen that they sounded like instruments of aggression rather than the armor of a vulnerable heart; and his pacing was so eccentric that it muddled the rhythms of the entire production. Without this deft clash of wits, Much Ado is a hollow shell of plot; and all the ingenuity in the world will not redeem the work from dullness.

A Midsummer Night's Dream, the second Festival production, skirted as close to disaster as anything I can remember seeing in the Park. With all the lyric speeches either trimmed or cut completely to accommodate some inordinately long and relentlessly unfunny spurts of horseplay, this bodiless and dreamlike creation assumed a gross, waking physicality which made it seem peculiarly lumpish and sensual (these qualities even penetrated the forest scenes where Puck was found necking with some sprites and Titania could be seen bussing Bottom on the hairy mouth of his ass's head). What is more, the lovers were too frenetic; the court too vulgar; the rustics too strained; and the fairies either too elephantine (Oberon's train) or too fussy (Titania's). Most of these gaucheries were attributable to Joel Friedman's awkward direction, but some were the result of casting, the most baffling in the Festival's history. Albert Quinton, gifted enough as a character actor but no comedian, was a dull Bottom; John Call, the more obvious choice for Bottom, grappled with Puck, playing him like an exhausted clown too lethargic to pull his weight, much less to put a girdle round about the earth in forty minutes; and Philip Kenneally, as Theseus, seemed to have gleaned his notions of regal dignity from a reading of *Ubu Roi*. And so I had the unhappy experience of seeing one of Shakespeare's loveliest and most fragile works so badly mauled and crunched that the stage seemed littered with mangled limbs.

The last production of the season, *Richard II*, was also the most compelling, especially in the initial acts where the play hinges on ceremony and external conflict. Making admirable use of Eldon Elder's simple, flexible setting and Lewis Brown's illustrative costuming, Gladys Vaughan, the director, populated Richard's court with gypsies, jugglers, dwarfs, magicians, and effeminate courtiers, thus evoking an atmosphere of Oriental splendor which contrasted with the manly simplicity of the Machiavel, Bolingbroke, and his followers, and thus emphasizing visually Shakespeare's undramatized suggestion that Richard's parasitical caterpillars are eating up the commonwealth. In the second half of the work, however, which shifts into an internal study of Richard, Mrs. Vaughan's production was somewhat less successful. Ben Hayes created a frivolous, self-indulgent, quixotic ruler who, in glorious golden armor, looked like a magnificent sun king; but he failed to capture the narcissistic aspect of Richard, who is, after all, an actor and a poseur (he is always setting a dramatic scene and then assuming the leading role). Therefore, in the deposition scene, Hayes—instead of suggesting the enjoyment Richard takes in his self-pity and attitudinizing—played for straightforward emotions of sincerity and grief, thus robbing the character of its most interesting psychological quirk. Nevertheless, this was a firmly controlled production, in which Papp's company so effectively demonstrated its celebrated gifts as an ensemble that I left the theatre convinced there were no problems it could not ultimately solve, considering the care, taste, imagination, and originality with which it was so plentifully endowed.

(1961)

NIGHTS
WITH THE OLD VIC

MACBETH by William Shakespeare;
ROMEO AND JULIET by William Shakespeare;
ST. JOAN by Bernard Shaw

■ For years, the Old Vic has been the sturdy repository of a rich English dramatic tradition, but like most institutions dedicated to preserving the past, it is now in danger of becoming a museum. Having begun its Shakespeare seasons in 1914, the Old Vic climaxed its auspicious history in the forties, when Olivier and Richardson were heading the acting company, and Michel Saint-Denis was training talented recruits in the now unhappily defunct Old Vic school. But ever since the brilliant 1945–46 season—with its superb productions of Henry IV and Oedipus Rex—the Old Vic has been gradually stiffening into attitudes of piety, gentility, and conventionality, a process greatly accelerated when Michael Benthall took over the directorship in 1953. During Benthall's tenure, the company began to attract sensitive, moody leading men and ethereal, well-bred young ladies (such roughneck alumni as Harry Andrews and Joyce Redman would find no comradeship in these high-toned circles), thus limiting the effective repertory to Shakespeare's lighter works. For, in the more powerful tragic roles, the actors were forced into obvious impersonations—the men padding their costumes and gruffening their voices, the women kicking their skirts viciously on turns. Lacking penetrating performances, therefore, the Old Vic soon became a director's rather than an actor's theatre, concentrating on novel interpretations of standard works. But despite attempts to "jolly up" Shakespeare's content, the techniques of the resident directors remained stolidly traditionalist. And except for fresh re-evaluations by occasional visitors (such as Tyrone Guthrie's memorable *Troilus and Cressida*), the Old Vic's Shakespeare has been a stale and musty waxworks—elegantly spoken and heroically postured but no more vigorous than an exhibition at Tussaud's.

The current productions of *Macbeth* (directed by Benthall) and *St. Joan* (directed by Douglas Seale) represent the Old Vic at its lowest ebb. In these works, the company looks as shabby as that actor-manager unit Donald Wolfit used to bring over, except that it is not even dominated by a strong personality. Both productions lack luster in performance, direction, and setting; even the make-up and sound effects ("Sound the alarum," cries Macbeth—Clink, clink, comes the reply) are sloppily designed. In *Macbeth*, Benthall has gestured toward the primitive by dressing his Scottish warriors in sheepskins and horned helmets—but the masquerade is over as soon as these elegant savages begin to speak with polite, cadenced diction. John Clements, too lightweight for Macbeth, avoids the embarrassment of the character's torment by substituting a delicate irony, while Barbara Jefford turns his Lady into a long-haired Chelsea bohemian who probably served time in the Wrens (she does parade turns in the sleepwalking scene). In its stiff and formalized groupings, the production generates no terror at all—nor pity either, since Macduff's son, enacted by a youth in his twenties, is played like a retarded nitwit—and the entire work takes on the cold, processional quality of the witches' masque of kings.

In *St. Joan*, Miss Jefford shows off her versatility by playing the Maid like Viola in *Twelfth Night*: pert, pettish, and swashbuckling—a saucy young thing in drag. La Hire (also in drag, since he wears more crepe hair on his face than Lon Chaney during a full moon) shouts at one point that he could follow Joan through hell, but it is doubtful if anyone ever followed this Joan anywhere, except down a dark street in the hope of a pickup. Embodying a nubile quality which is not in the part, Miss Jefford lacks the charismatic quality which is. And because she is too ladylike to do any more with Joan's peasant awkwardness than round her r's (Shaw's impossible dialect does not help here), the first three scenes fall flat on our face. The only scene that really works, in fact, is the colloquy between Cauchon and Warwick (played by Clements with Machiavellian bite and humor), where Shaw offers his amusing, elementary history course in the rise of Protestantism and Nationalism. As for the rest, the production exposes all the weaknesses of the play but few of its strengths, consigning Shaw, ironically, to that same oblivion that Shaw used to reserve for Shakespeare.

In Franco Zeffirelli's celebrated version of *Romeo and Juliet*, however, the waxworks comes alive. The action—opening on hoarse-voiced fishwives and bored loungers sweating and steaming in the lazy Italian sun—erupts almost instantly into frenetic swordplay, where bodies leap and thud as in a dangerous ballet whose theme is the death of men. Despite the fact that this action rarely flags, however, the real rewards of the evening are not in its galvanic violence but rather in its visual and atmospheric effects. In Signor Zeffirelli's setting, the ancient stones of Verona take on a muddy, granite physicality, against which Peter Hall's dark brown and green costumes (Juliet's tomb nightgown is the only touch of white) evoke a quality of Rembrandt chiaroscuro. As figures in heavy brocades move in an eerie charade through misty yellow light, one is struck by a feeling of muted terror—terror, as it were, in halftones.

Still, for all its splendor, I cannot believe that Signor Zeffirelli's interpretation will satisfy any but those who detest the play, for it is thoroughly devoid of lyricism, romance, or grace. Either the director doesn't understand the lines or he has perversely chosen to ignore them, because he has merely used the text as a scenario for a work of his own—naturalizing the action, literalizing the age of the lovers, and thus producing still another *West Side Story*, this time in the style of Italian neorealism. The lovers, acted with hot eagerness by John Stride and Joanna Dunham, have been made to behave like a couple of gangly adolescents playing post office; Romeo climbs Juliet's balcony with his behind stuck out, and after giggling inanely, they smack away at each other like two erotic woodpeckers. As for Mercutio—played by Edward Atienza in a voluminous cape which he flourishes like an effeminate Batman—he has been robbed of his manhood, and even of his imaginative powers, since he muffles his speeches by munching apples and engaging in irrelevant horseplay. Much of the work, in fact, has been cut to accommodate Zeffirelli's passion for illustrative business; and the verse that remains is invariably read as if it were prose. Reduced to its action, the work—like many neo-realistic movies—eventually begins to look operatic. And because of the obtrusiveness of his effects, we come away remembering the director rather than the play.

What we do not remember is the company, for, despite occasional lapses into virility, it is much too weak to make a lasting impression. One wonders why, when the English theatre is beginning to develop in new directions, the Old Vic lags so far behind—why it has not assimilated into its ranks such promising talents as Peter O'Toole or Albert Finney. For it is strong performers that the company lacks—and gifted directors who, without violating the text, would be able to mold this strength into something fresh and true. Without this, I fear, the Old Vic will remain just another overloaded pillar of the Establishment, toppling under the weight of the mighty past.

(1962)

AT WORK AND AT PLAY WITH THE APA

THE SCHOOL FOR SCANDAL *by Richard Brinsley Sheridan;* THE SEAGULL *by Anton Chekhov, newly translated by Alex Szogyi;* THE TAVERN *by George M. Cohan: APA Repertory Company*

■ On a recent visit to New York, the Association of Producing Artists—an itinerant repertory troupe known less pretentiously as the APA—deposited three productions on our doorstep, collected a number of favorable reviews and some enthusiastic partisans, and then departed for the interior, just when audiences were beginning to map out the arduous route to the Folksbiene Playhouse. The APA's decision to regard our city as simply another temporary stop in a tour shows admirable selflessness, but it is also quite shrewd: New York, for all its theatrical activity, is the city least likely to support an unsubsidized permanent repertory. Local audiences, conditioned by a competitive system, are attracted to successful plays, not to aspiring companies; and local companies have thus been forced to commercialize their operations, suspending continuity whenever a single play succeeds (only the free Shakespeare Festival in the Park has never trimmed its program to the winds of fashion). As for the local reviewer, he presides over hits and misses, not continuous development. And even when he is sympathetic to repertory ideals, he is powerless to advance them. Torn between a cultural objective (permitting a permanent company to perfect itself) and a critical objective (evaluating each production strictly on its own merits), he can keep a group in business only by lowering his standards; but here he finds that objective criticism and booster journalism are separate and contradictory functions.

Lacking the power to influence audiences, I am not beset by the temptations of boosterism, but prodded by the spirit of charity (an unfamiliar demon), I did decide to reserve judgment on the APA until I had seen the full program. Familiar with most of the actors through their work with other repertories like Group 20, Brattle, Antioch, and Stratford, I knew them to be among the better classical performers in America; but their work with the APA I found surprisingly erratic. Last year, I had seen the company at Princeton, performing *King Lear*—a production which would have been more convincing if the men and women had exchanged roles (can you imagine a Lear who stamps his foot when he grows angry?). And this year, one of the New York productions was so agonizingly miscast, misdirected, and misplayed that I began to think that "artist" was merely a euphemism for actors unschooled in the rudiments of their craft.

I refer to the APA production of *The Seagull*—a garbled, semi-modernized version which looked as though someone had dropped the play in a time-place machine and whirled it in several directions at once. The costumes (a hasty collection of tennis shorts, blazers, red cummerbunds, and sweater-skirt ensembles) were confusing enough; and it was disconcerting to find Masha smoking cigarillos instead of taking snuff. But with the translator employing the colloquialisms of the 1960s and the director the style of the 1920s—with some of the actors performing in a Gilbert-Garbo silent film and others in a stock-company treatment of *Private Lives*—we seemed to be by turns in Hollywood, Brighton, and Westport, and nowhere very long. Needless to say, the sense of vacuity and isolation inherent in Chekhov's provincial Russia had totally evaporated in the general bubbliness. And gone, too, were the farce and pathos of the play, for instead of alienating us from the absurd posturing, self-pity, and aimlessness of the characters, the director had chosen to make them all extremely ingratiating, vigorous, and self-aware (both Masha and Treplev, for example, were always making fun of their despair). Of the numerous silly-clever ideas substituted for Chekhov's tragi-comic intentions, I shall mention only one: Treplev's domination by his mother was turned into a passionate Oedipal affair which ended with mother and son kissing each other hungrily on the lips.

The other two APA productions, however, made me rather glad I had withheld judgment on the group. In these, the actors displayed that affectionate sensitivity to works of the past which is the major justification of a repertory company. Both, it is true, were performances of comedies; and it may be that the APA—like its director, Ellis Rabb, who is a brilliant clown but a perfectly awful tragedian—is primarily qualified for works which do not demand much emotional depth. At any rate, the APA *School for Scandal*, while not entirely satisfying, had moments of real enjoyment, especially in the second part when plot began to take precedence over character. It must be admitted that some of the acting was not grotesque enough (the actors playing Snake and Lady Sneerwell, for example, neither snaked nor sneered), and George Grizzard, amusing enough as the sanctimonious Joseph Surface, rather neglected the unctuousness in the role. But Rosemary Harris as a teasy Lady Teazle and Clayton Corzatte as a rakish Charles played with spirit and boldness; and the screen scene moved with such vigor, invention, style, and surprise that the entire production was redeemed.

For sheer entertainment, though, the high point of the repertory was the company's superb treatment of George M. Cohan's farce-melodrama, *The Tavern*—an inspired piece of vintage hokum and a fine example of the kind of entertainment that used to abound in the commercial theatre before the great deluge of middle seriousness. Following the usual procedure in such cases, the APA endeavored to remove the play's cobwebs by exaggerating the melodrama; but since Cohan himself obviously regarded *The Tavern* as a theatrical joke, the external comment served to heighten rather than to patronize the intentions of the work. Lloyd Burlingame's setting, in which characters warmed their hands before a painted fire after emerging, strewn with paper leaves, from a wind-machine storm, was the perfect picturization of the exaggerated acting style; and Ellis Rabb's direction sometimes moved with such speed and grace that it almost became choreography (as, for example, when a fainting matron was whirled dizzily from one end of the room to the other, and finally deposited, floatingly, on a couch). As for the actors, they made up a large gallery of hilarious caricatures: Tucker Ashworth as a cretinous lover; Page Johnson as a villainous unshaven hired hand; George Grizzard as a red-nosed rogue who moves the action and comments portentously on life and the theatre; Gerry Jedd as a dazed, heavy-lidded, slow-thinking victim of the storm who identifies every man she meets as the one who ruined her; Rosemary Harris as a lisping, empty-headed aristocrat, fluttering in amorous ecstasy and wrinkling her nose with giggles—the entire company, in fact, contributed to the general amusement with ensemble work of the highest quality.

Such plays as *The Tavern*, of course, are holidays for a repertory company; and it cannot yet be said that the APA's workdays are quite so impressive. Still, the company is young, visionary, and willing to take risks; it is composed of undeniably strong talents; and, best of all, it has the opportunity to perfect itself through experiment and error. It is in such companies, for all their erraticism, that the theatre still realizes its possibilities, just as it is in the love of dedicated actors, for all their failings, that the great classical works continue to survive.

(1962)

ENGLISH GARDENERS
AND AMERICAN GARDENS

HAMLET by William Shakespeare; THE MISER by Molière; THE THREE SISTERS by Anton Chekhov; DEATH OF A SALESMAN by Arthur Miller: The Minnesota Theatre Company

■ The Tyrone Guthrie Theatre in Minneapolis is a cultural seed planted by an English gardener in the rich, untilled soil of the Midwest; and in its very first season, it has already sprouted into a handsome plant. Mr. Guthrie, who also plowed and cropped in Canada, obviously has a green thumb—but the fruits of his American endeavors are oddly varied: sometimes delicious, occasionally without much taste. One begins to suspect that his theatre is a transplant, producing hybrids—it looks for all the world like a British repertory, though it has been largely staffed with American actors. Guthrie has taught his company to speak a clear, spirited English; and, aided by Douglas Campbell, his assistant artistic director, and Tanya Moiseiwitsch, his hugely gifted designer, he has shaped a couple of memorable productions. But I do not think he has solved, or even bothered to confront, the problem of an American classical style. Standard diction for heroes and cockney for clowns; characters based on the English class system; updated Shakespeare with reference to recent English history—these are the techniques we have come to associate with Stratford-on-Avon and the Old Vic. The Minnesota Theatre will soon be equal, I think, to most of the repertories in England (it is already superior to the Old Vic), and so it probably seems ungracious to complain; but I rarely sensed that it was native, and to our manner born.

Within these limits, however, the company functions admirably. Though it may not be the most impressive acting ensemble ever formed in America, it has apparently been inspired by the really excellent conditions under which it works. The theatre building, for example, is a beautiful steel, wood, and glass structure, and the house is designed both for intimacy and for grandeur. The audience looks down on the action, sometimes from a dizzy height, but it surrounds the stage on three sides (no spectator is ever more than sixty feet from the apron), and is always being directly addressed by the actors. As for the stage, an asymmetrical platform of polished oak, it is not only an aesthetic object in itself but also a keen precision instrument as functional as costumes or props.

Guthrie's production of *Hamlet*, set in some recent period, probably Victorian, used this stage to great advantage, but it was not always very coherent. With Hamlet delivering his soliloquies in smoking jackets and Italian suits, with Laertes costumed like an I.R.A. man in trenchcoat and boots, with the Danish soldiers in Graustark uniforms and the ministers in cutaway coats, and with Fortinbras dressed like the German Kaiser and his aides-de-camp in the khakis of the British Expeditionary Forces, I was never very clear about which country was embroiled in which squabbles at what particular time and place. Some years ago, Mr. Guthrie illuminated *Troilus and Cressida* with much the same approach, but in *Hamlet*, he only made us conscious of puzzling anachronisms: ghosts in an age of rationalism, swords in an age of dynamite, peculiar hostilities between Norway and Poland, etc. Although Zoe Caldwell's Ophelia was too heavy and Jessica Tandy's Gertrude too light, some interesting performances were occasionally inspired by the scheme: Lee Richardson's Colonel Blimp of a Claudius, played like a Crimean general about to recount the campaign at Balaklava, Robert Pastene's bureaucratic Polonius, Ed Preble's cheeky gravedigger, John Cromwell's Player King, an actor in the school of Forbes-Robertson. And whenever external action was called for, the play ignited, especially in the play scene—a panic of scrambling courtiers blinded by leiko lights—and the duel scene—the most exciting version of the Hamlet-Laertes fracas I have yet witnessed. But the internal action was neglected, partly because the production lacked psychological detail, partly because George Grizzard (who would have made an excellent Rosencrantz) was a callow Hamlet: sullen instead of noble, peevish instead of witty, self-pitying instead of melancholy.

The next two shows—Douglas Campbell's production of *The Miser* and Guthrie's of *The Three Sisters*—were fine work indeed. Campbell turned the Molière work into a *commedia dell' arte* scenario, with masked harlequins improvising doors and windows, *inamorati* making stylized love, and servants being beaten with slapsticks, all climaxed by a hilarious recognition scene which became a dizzy, madcap dance. Mr. Campbell's comic invention occasionally flagged, but Hume Cronyn's Harpagon was a performance of such versatility that the *lazzi* seemed superfluous anyway. As Mr. Cronyn is only rarely permitted to show, he is one of the most gifted character actors in America. His Harpagon was of such epic stinginess that even his movements seemed prodigal, though he scurried about the stage like a ravenous rodent sniffing out cheese. His climactic scene—in which his strongbox is stolen, and, suspicious of everybody (including himself), he rends his clothes—combined just the right helpings of hysteria, pathos, and farce.

If *The Miser* was essentially virtuoso work, the ensemble work of *The Three Sisters* left one with the sense that the group had been acting together for ages. Mr. Guthrie, who is not always so diligent in the service of a text, devoted himself faithfully to Chekhov's intentions, and the result was a clean, crisp, precise performance without a single blurred edge, offered in a translation (by Guthrie and Leonid Kipnis) which may be the most actable version extant. Guthrie repeatedly struck that note of banishment which is the leitmotiv of the play—banishment from hearth and from heart—but without exaggerating the pathos: the tempo of each of the four acts was as varied as the four movements of a classic sonata. As for the acting, two or three parts were played without distinction, but the rest was of the highest quality, especially Claude Woolman's eager, stuttering Tusenbach, Hume Cronyn's twinkly Tchebutykin, Jessica Tandy's slightly hysterical Olga, and Clayton Corzatte's sweetly foolish Kulygin. *The Three Sisters* was the triumph of the repertory and the climax of the Minneapolis season.

Death of a Salesman, however, was its denouement, and a sorry conclusion to an otherwise distinguished program. I have never been convinced that this is a very important work, and I am certain that it is too familiar to need reviving (so is a better play, *The Glass Menagerie*, which Guthrie has announced for next season—the choice of repertory at Minneapolis is hardly audacious). Old Broadway plays are better left to the commercial visionaries at Lincoln Center; and, as a matter of curious fact, the Miller work proved least popular of all. The Minneapolis actors were simply too refined for their roles, and Hume Cronyn, though occasionally powerful, was too sophisticated to catch the *lumpen* desperation of Willy Loman. Douglas Campbell's production was further hamstrung by an extremely precarious and unwieldy set (the only one not designed by Moiseiwitsch)—an abstract steel structure which forced the play into a style of misty Expressionism. This was also the style of a more competent production that I saw last summer at the Brandeis Forum Theatre, but it is a mistake. *Death of a Salesman* is essentially a realistic problem play, in which even Willy's hallucinations have the quality of factual flashbacks, since most of them are recalled accurately. The spectacle of American actors stumbling over the most familiar kind of American play suggests that there are problems to be overcome at Minneapolis, despite its substantial achievements, and that until it can forge a classical style out of the American experience, it will not be a theatre we can truly call our own.

(1963)

ARTHUR MILLER'S
MEA CULPA

AFTER THE FALL by Arthur Miller:
Repertory Theatre of Lincoln Center

■ Despite the notoriety connected with his name, Arthur
Miller has always seemed one of the more reticent and dignified of American celebrities, while his plays, for all their hidden
private references, have appeared to be relatively impersonal. By
some perverse law of overcompensation, however, After the Fall
is a three-and-one-half-hour breach of taste, a confessional auto-
biography of embarrassing explicitness, during which the author
does not stop talking about himself for an instant, while making
only the most perfunctory gestures toward concealing his identity. Thus, the hero is named Quentin rather than Arthur; he is
a lawyer instead of a Broadway dramatist; and in place of a
famous play, he has written a "majestic" legal brief. Behind this
transparent curtain, however, Mr. Miller is dancing a spiritual
striptease while the band plays mea culpa, a performance which
is not concluded until every sequined veil has been snatched
away from his sexual and political anatomy. Some of the more
juicy turns in this exhibition include his arguments with his par-
ents, and his mother's emasculation of his father; his quarrels
with his first wife over her coldness in bed and his suspected infidelities; his continuing loyalty to his ex-Communist friends,
one of whom throws himself under a subway train; his break
with Mickey (Elia Kazan) over the latter's decision to name
names to a Congressional committee; his affair, marriage, and
tortured life with Maggie (Marilyn Monroe), concluding with

her suicide; and, finally, his decision to build a new marriage with Holga, a German woman he met abroad.

This, in short, is the kind of document that playwrights publish posthumously, if at all, since it implicates so many people living, and so many recently dead. What makes this invasion of privacy even more wanton is that most of these characters are in the public eye—indeed, one of them is actually directing Mr. Miller's play! Antonin Artaud used to complain that the bourgeois theatre turned the spectators into Peeping Toms: what would he have said about *After the Fall?* Although the author has obviously convinced himself that his life is typical of his generation, and that he has "universalized" his experience into a parable of guilt and innocence, the fact remains that he has created a shameless piece of tabloid gossip, an act of exhibitionism which makes us all voyeurs.

Now voyeurism is, admittedly, a stimulating business, but *After the Fall* is not even effective as titillation. Having discharged my duties as a moralist, let me now try to examine why such potentially fascinating material should be so intrinsically dull.

The play, first of all, is a wretched piece of dramatic writing: shapeless, tedious, overwritten, and confused. The secret of the autobiographical drama—as Strindberg learned in *To Damascus*, and O'Neill in *A Long Day's Journey into Night*—is to find some objective theatrical image for your subjective emotional state; but Mr. Miller is too close to his material to assimilate it properly, and he still has not managed to dramatize it. Too eager to uncork his self-revelations, he is too impatient to let them ferment in significant action, so his play lacks form or plot or forward movement. It is, furthermore, composed of endless palaver. While Miller has borrowed techniques from *Death of a Salesman*, moving his hero through time and space from childhood to maturity, he has taken his most obtrusive device from *View from the Bridge*: the static oracular Chorus. Since the hero and the Chorus are one, the play seems like an uninterrupted monologue, which is not completed until Quentin exhausts his vocabulary and runs out of steam, pontificating hoarsely to the very end. As a result, Jo Mielziner's blue space stage becomes completely useless: *After the Fall* could have been just as effectively produced from a lectern at the Y.M.H.A.

Let me mention, now that we are on the subject, that the whole Lincoln Center apparatus is irrelevant to this play. One of the advantages of the repertory system is a longer rehearsal period, since this enables the actor to probe his character more deeply and to work out his relations with the other performers—but Mr. Miller's characters are too shallow to be plumbed, and they are functioning most of the time in a state of total isolation. Zohra Lampert, for example, usually a fine actress, does a minor bit with less confidence than some longer roles she has worked up on one week's notice, while Salome Jens, Mariclare Costello, and Ralph Meeker, in other parts, are merely fobbing off character clichés or bad habits from the past. As for the direction, it is so spare and empty, so lacking in conviction, power, or concentration, that I began to toy with the mischievous notion that Kazan was purposely undermining the play; after all, whatever his artistic faults, he has never before directed a boring performance. On the other hand, when an actor as gifted as Jason Robards starts repeating his emotional cycles over and over again—rearing his head, raising his voice, and punching his climaxes in the thankless role of Quentin—I have to reject the conspiracy theory, and conclude that the material is simply intractable.

Now I must perform a distasteful labor, and deal with the subject matter itself, a job more appropriate to a gossip columnist than a drama critic. But it must be observed that an important reason for the tediousness of the evening is the author's superficial treatment of his most promising character: "Maggie" Monroe. It is astonishing that a playwright, whose major business is perception, could live with this unfortunate woman for over four years, and yet be capable of no greater insights into her character than those made by Maurice Zolotow, a professional theatre columnist. But Mr. Miller is too confused in his feelings toward his former wife to be very complicated about her, as he sometimes concedes ("My bitterness is making me lie"), and out of his ambivalence, he has created a contradictory portrait. As played by Barbara Loden on a shrill, one-dimensional note, Maggie changes character as rapidly as she changes wigs, beginning as a giddy, simple-minded, generous creature who only wants to love—an image created by her press agents, and by Mr. Miller himself in *The Misfits*—and then developing into a raging, screaming, suicidal shrew, firing subordinates and demeaning her husband, while groveling on the floor with a bottle of Jack Daniels and a fistful of pills—*vide* Chayefsky's movie, *The Goddess*. The only new insight I was able to glean from these familiar episodes was that Mr. Miller must have talked his wife's ear off, since even in the act of viciously throttling her, he is explaining why she hates life, why she drinks, why she married him, and why she is trying to commit suicide.

This excessive self-consciousness is itself a form of dishonesty, and dishonesty remains the worst flaw in the play. *After the Fall* claims to drill right down to bedrock, and its only structure is a sequence of revelations dredged out of ruthless self-examination; but I often sensed somehow that the real discoveries were being concealed or had yet to be made. Thus, while Mr. Miller is eager to scourge himself for his inability to love, he is still conducting an involuntary vendetta against the former objects of his love: there is a misogynistic strain in the play which the author does not seem to recognize, nor does he recognize how much self-justification is hidden in his apparent remorse. Then, for all the talk about "truth" and "honesty," few of the insights of the play sound genuine. I will pass over Quentin's motives for marrying Maggie ("She is like a flag to me—a proof that people can win"), as well as Mickey's reasons for informing on his friends ("I want to lead a straightforward open life"), though these are the murkiest moments in the play. But it is difficult to ignore Miller's foggy political discussions. As the title suggests, the author thinks that he has emerged from a prelapsarian state of innocence into a state of anguished experience, but he still conceives of politics in the simple-minded language of the thirties. All of the ex-Communists in the play, for example, are merely "fighting injustice," while the friend who commits suicide is "a decent broken man that never wanted anything more but the good of the world." No wonder these men were duped when they know so little abcut their own political motives. After all these terrible years, is Miller still defining Stalinism as if it were a sentiment without any reference to ideas, ideology, or power?

Well, it is obvious that Arthur Miller's world is disintegrating: *After the Fall* chronicles its moral, political, and artistic collapse. By writing the play, the author has not changed my mind about his talents, which have never seemed to me much more than minor; but, in lacking the wisdom to suppress it, he has seriously compromised his reputation for rectitude, taste, and dignity. As it is, the play will unquestionably exercise a strong appeal as an indecent spectacle—which makes it, I would say, perfectly typical of the commercial theatre at large. The generation which Mr. Miller discredits in *After the Fall* is one that eventually came to control Broadway, passing off its ambition as altruism, its expediency as honesty, its avarice as integrity, its lust for fame as love of art. Now, grown fat and prosperous and exhausted, it has institutionalized the bankrupt Broadway vision in the fashionable culture emporium of Lincoln Center. Recently, S. N. Behrman, who will provide the third radical experiment offered by the Lincoln Center repertory, mused, "I'd rather wait for Lefty than wait for Godot." Well, while Lefty is being awaited by the playwrights, directors, technicians, and actors of this forward-looking group, the rest of us had better find some empty basement theatre in which to wait for Godot.

(1964)

SUBSIDIZED RUBBISH

LINCOLN CENTER

■ For over four weeks now, I have been trying to write about the last two offerings at Lincoln Center, but whenever I begin a review, my typewriter fails me. The keys stick, the ribbon jams, the carriage jumps—obviously my reluctance is being communicated to my machine. This sounds like anger—and I wish to God it were, because a fierce raging assault upon this whole deadly enterprise would, at least, relieve my feelings—but it is actually something closer to torpor. To sit through the successive evenings of the current Lincoln Center season is to progress from boredom to apathy to total numbness. To attempt to write about the individual productions is to SToMth&%#wHt-TeFB . . . Well, you see what I mean.

You may ask why a theatre critic, whose experience of meretricious drama is certainly vast, should suddenly become immobilized by plays and productions no worse than some of those on Broadway. But this is precisely the point. Lincoln Center attempts to dignify Broadway; it transforms commercial commodities into cultural pseudo events. Were *Marco Millions* and *But for Whom Charlie* to be produced under normal Broadway auspices, one would have the option of ignoring them completely; but produced at the Repertory Theatre by a permanent company on an apron stage—catapulted into our consciousness with so much artistic posturing and policy fanfare—these works ask to be treated as if they were really worthy of serious consideration. This I simply cannot do. Contrary to the popular notion that critics enjoy roasting turkeys and squeezing lemons, there is absolutely no reward at all to be had in writing about bad theatre. Were I to elaborate upon the innumerable mistakes and blunders committed by the actors, directors, and writers at Lincoln Center, it would probably demoralize me more than it would the company.

The question arises, however: Who was naïve enough to expect anything better? From the moment that Elia Kazan and Robert Whitehead were appointed producing directors, the prospects of this venture perceptibly dimmed. I do not set up as a prophet, but this was obvious enough to me three years before the first Lincoln Center production, because, in December 1960, I was already wondering "why—when it is commercialism that is debasing our theatre—the Lincoln Center project was handed over to two men who up till now have shown no great interest in any other system." After examining the policy statements of the two directors, in fact, I concluded that "within a year or so the repertory will consist mainly of conventional American plays." At the time, I feared I was being prematurely harsh, but as it turned out, I was not harsh enough. Even from my pessimistic perspective, I could not foresee that my prediction would be fulfilled the very first season, and that Lincoln Center would soon be featuring the trivial maunderings of S. N. Behrman.

This outcome was inevitable, however, because of the superficial assumption underlying the selection of Kazan and Whitehead: that the troubles with American theatre were exclusively external. The original reasoning might have gone something like this: Broadway actors, directors, and playwrights function under impossible artistic conditions; change these conditions, and the quality of their art will change. For years, Walter Kerr and Brooks Atkinson had been hammering away at the proscenium stage, declaring that it was responsible for the mediocrity of our drama, and that only an open stage could inspire American masterpieces. Similarly, the uneven quality of American acting was said to be the consequence of the star system, pickup casts, and inadequate rehearsal periods, while the paucity of great classical works on Broadway was attributed to crazy theatre economics, where each play had to be a runaway hit in order to pay back costs.

Now there was some truth in this analysis, but only a very small portion of the truth. For instead of being hamstrung by

hostile conditions, the Broadway professional was actually functioning in a system which he had helped to create, and which
was perfectly tailored to his needs. Consider, for example, the
question of the proscenium stage. It is, of course, absurd to say
that the physical theatre is largely responsible for empty playwriting, but, aside from this, it should have been clear that the
proscenium is perfectly adequate to our contemporary plays,
because most American drama is essentially realistic, even when
it takes place in "the mind, thought, and memory" of its protagonist. Similarly, the inability of American actors to merge
into an ensemble owes a good deal to Method training, which
encourages the performer to concentrate primarily on internal
problems of the self, while the disappearance of great plays
from the commercial theatre has as much to do with the ignorance, incapacity, and indifference of the professional as with
the venality of the producer. The career of Kazan himself is a
perfect illustration of this. For years, he was in a position to
direct any play he wanted, and for years he limited his objectives to the works of Williams, Miller, Anderson, MacLeish,
and Inge.

At Lincoln Center, where external conditions are supposed to
be ideal, Kazan's objectives have, if anything, narrowed. An
open stage has been designed for him by Jo Mielziner—a pallid
affair, I might add, beside the sturdy aprons in Canada and
Minneapolis—and Kazan mounts plays which would be more
effective behind a proscenium. He has the freedom to choose,
for a "classical revival," from among the greatest works in dramatic literature, and he selects an early outrage by Eugene
O'Neill, presumably because it is a costume drama (thus qualifying as a "classic"), and because it satisfies a certain superficial
nostalgic radicalism by satirizing businessmen. For "experimental" new works, he turns to a monstrosity by Miller and a
banality by Behrman, both of which have less to do with reality
than with the personal lives of those represented at Lincoln
Center (Miller's play is partly about himself and Kazan, and
Behrman's is partly about O'Neill and his children—it is too
bad, for the sake of symmetry, that O'Neill did not write a play
about S. N. Behrman and Arthur Miller). Kazan has the opportunity to pick his permanent company from among the most

versatile performers in America, and he picks a group so limited that a stock actor like David Wayne can walk off with the honors, simply because he has a sense of character, and a loud clear voice. All that early training in diction, and the players still have marbles in their mouths; all that fencing, movement, and dance, and they still stumble about like sleepwalkers; all that rehearsal time, and they are still so mannered and remote. What is worse, none of these people is even displaying that professional competence they once commanded in the commercial theatre. This is especially true of Kazan who leaves us with the final irony that Lincoln Center has gained a bad director, and Broadway has lost a good one.

So as not to deprive Broadway of one of its few genuine assets, I would like to see Kazan returned to his original hunting grounds, and Lincoln Center handed over to a more capable producer. The purpose of a repertory theatre, as almost everyone knows, is to stage the interesting works of the past, and the stimulating works of the present; it is not to transplant commercial plays into more congenial surroundings. At the APA, for example—a genuine repertory troupe in theory if not ideal in practice—the works of Pirandello, Molière, George M. Cohan, and Gorky are running in sequence, so that the more popular play is able to support the one that has not attracted an audience. At Lincoln Center, where none of the plays deserves support, the repertory system functions only to perpetuate bad art, and to keep the shame of the actors cruelly on display. If Lincoln Center is not utterly committed to the subsidy of rubbish, it must be willing to countenance a complete change in personnel. Three years ago, I suggested Joseph Papp as head of the classical side of Lincoln Center; as the experimental troupe, I should like to propose The Living Theatre or the Actor's Workshop. There are many other competent groups, even the APA, which have developed standards and aspirations superior to those at Lincoln Center; any of them would be preferable. For if Americans are really serious about developing a genuine culture and not mere cultural pretense, then we will have to start institutionalizing our artistic virtues instead of our commercial vices.

(1964)

WE ARE
TWO CULTURAL NATIONS

THE CHANGELING by Thomas Middleton and
William Rowley: Repertory Theatre of Lincoln
Center; THE OLD GLORY by Robert Lowell:
American Place Theatre

■ This has been a week of dejection and exhilaration, of
baffled promise and shining possibility, of grinding failure and
monumental achievement—a week that has shown us the worst
and the best of our cultural times. For, within three days after
the Repertory Theatre of Lincoln Center exposed to public
shock and ridicule an outrageously incompetent production of
The Changeling, the American Place Theatre opened its doors
on a fascinating pair of plays by Robert Lowell, brilliantly
written, superbly directed, and acted with incomparable grace,
taste, and style. The conjunction of these two events is a portent of more than passing significance, because it heralds the
eventual supersession of something worn-out and sterile by a
force of genuine vitality and intelligence. Since most of the
local reviewers were predictably dull-witted about both plays,
both were misrepresented in the press. But although the impact
of these two events will therefore take a while to have its effect
on the public consciousness, some issues are being clarified
which have hitherto been inchoate and confused. These issues
are crucial, for they concern the whole future direction of the
serious American stage. The present theatre establishment is
now in a state of crisis, collapsing from within and sieged from
without, and, at the same time that a new foundation is just in

process of being built, the old, eroded masonry is falling in ruins about our heads.

The rubble has certainly collected on the stage at the ANTA Washington Square Theatre, where the Lincoln Center Company is currently doing a wrecker's job on The Changeling. This is Elia Kazan's first experience with a non-contemporary, non-American play, and, as one of those who has been exhorting this director and his company to stage the great classical works, I feel acutely embarrassed at having to discuss the results at all. To put no fine point on it, the production is a debacle. Mr. Kazan obviously hasn't an inkling of what The Changeling is about, nor, apparently, the slightest interest in trying to find out. Instead of plumbing the depths of this profound work, he has chosen to assault it from without, imposing on its delicate Gothic lines his own heavy Broadway scaffolding.

Since the play was completely buried under the debris, few members of the audience seemed to realize it was a masterpiece, especially when most of the reviewers made it an occasion for Philistine sneers. Even Walter Kerr—who periodically pays homage to the Elizabethans when he needs a club with which to beat Ibsen and Chekhov on the head—called the play a "pop melodrama," and subtitled it "The Case of the Vicious Virgin." To clear the work of such edifying epithets, perhaps some textual discussion is in order, however brief and superficial, for The Changeling is generally acknowledged, by scholars of the drama, to be the most subtle psychological tragedy in English outside of Shakespeare. Written in simple, ungorgeous verse, and in that impersonal manner which is the hallmark of Middleton's style, the play—if we ignore the silly subplot contributed by Rowley—is the closest thing to a realistic tragedy in the Stuart canon. Actually, the play foreshadows Strindberg's Miss Julie, for it concerns the spiritual degeneration of a young gentlewoman named Beatrice-Joanna, and her gradual habituation to sin, as a result of an uncontrollable appetitive will.

Following the various changes in Beatrice's affections (change is the key word of the play), the action opens when she has already transferred her feelings from her first love, Alonzo Piraquo, to a second, Alsemero. Since she is already betrothed to Piraquo, she can marry Alsemero only by murdering her fiancé; and for this purpose, she hires a creature she instinctually detests, the ugly dispossessed gentleman, De Flores. But De Flores also has a will, and demands, as payment for the deed, her maidenhead (thus the significance of his name—the Deflowerer). This horrifies Beatrice, whose peculiar ethical blindness lies in valuing her own virginity over everything, including human life ("Why, 'tis impossible thou canst be so wicked/Or shelter such a cunning cruelty/To make his death the murderer of my honor!"). But the more balanced and self-aware De Flores is adamantine, and in a magnificent scene that mixes equal strains of brutality and tenderness, he leads her to her fate, promising "Thou'lt love anon/What thou so fear'st and faint'st to venture on."

Now comes the real audacity of the work. For as the action proceeds, De Flores' prophecy is slowly fulfilled. Beatrice experiences the dawning of genuine love for this loathsome henchman, primarily because he is concerned for what she cherishes most, her outward reputation. When Alsemero discovers her kissing De Flores, she is willing to confess to murder rather than to blemish this reputation; but when all comes out, De Flores kills her and himself, becoming her true partner in death and shame. Thus, The Changeling is a variant on the story of Beauty and the Beast, where Beauty is a moral beast, and Beast achieves a certain heroic beauty. Out of a sequence of Tussaud horrors, Middleton snatches a Petrarchan lyricism, making the deaths of these two monsters into a curiously moving Liebestod.

Needless to say, the production captures none of this, because Mr. Kazan will not let us hear four consecutive lines of verse before he is introducing his own interpolations—crawling mendicants, hysterical madmen, cavorting monks, scurrying hunters, carousing guests—or shoving his actors into a bed that has been placed conspicuously on the stage. Where Mr. Kazan got that particular piece of furniture I cannot say; maybe it was left over from Cat on a Hot Tin Roof; there is certainly no such bed in the text. But this director is obviously willing to sacrifice everything—plot, character, theme, language, the sense of the past—

for the sake of a few prurient giggles from the gallery. Take, as an example, his sorry abuse of the subplot. Now I do not hold that Rowley's witless scenes in the madhouse are essential to a play which would have more formal unity without them. But the subplot serves a dramatic function beyond its grotesque humors: Isabella's relationship to the disguised Antonio is designed to mirror Beatrice's relationship to Alsemero, with a servant, in both cases, putting in for his share. The parallel, however, involves an ironic contrast—while Beatrice falls, Isabella remains chaste—but in Mr. Kazan's version, Isabella bounces merrily into the sack as well, even though this is a direct violation of the whole purpose of the scene. Well, I suppose it is fruitless to discuss thematic purpose when the director is so much more preoccupied with undressing his female characters, and having them copulate before our eyes.

It is also fruitless to discuss the acting: such a performance would have disgraced the theatre club at South Dakota Subnormal Junior High. Barbara Loden has been singled out for special obloquy, and it is true that she is pathetically inadequate to the part of Beatrice. But her vocal and temperamental deficiencies are shared by almost the entire cast, and they have surely been aggravated by the mindlessness and vulgarity of the production (for example, wasn't it possible to advise Miss Loden that you do not express loathing for someone by sticking out your tongue?). Because there are scores of experienced classical actors scattered around the country, the principles behind the hiring and training of this company escape me. But the blame for this particular failure must be spread wide—not only among those responsible for The Changeling, but also among those who have dictated the direction of our stage for the past twenty-five years. The social-psychological theatre of the thirties, which culminated in the Actors Studio and Lincoln Center, has now proved itself utterly incompetent to deal with a serious work of the imagination, or anything other than Broadway and Hollywood commodities. And the American theatre will never find itself again until all these outmoded methods and limited visions have been swept away.

Just such a renewal seems to be occurring now at the American Place Theatre where Robert Lowell's *The Old Glory* is currently enjoying an inspired production by Jonathan Miller. *The Old Glory* consists of two short plays (formerly three), held together by the unifying symbol of a flag—*My Kinsman, Major Molineux*, based largely on the Hawthorne story, and *Benito Cereno*, after the novella by Herman Melville. Mr. Lowell has accomplished the extraordinary feat of adapting these stories with relative fidelity to the originals while making them wholly and uniquely his own work. Invested with the author's sharp historical sense and marvelous gift of language, the source materials assume the thickness and authority of myth; American history takes on the quality of metaphor and ritual; traditional American literature begins to function like Greek mythology, as the source and reflection of contemporary behavior. What Mr. Lowell has done so subtly is to superimpose the present on the past, so that the plays manage to look backward and forward at the same time. The works are not easy, for the author has purposely adopted a style which is chilling, measured, and remote, but they are charged with flinty intelligence and taut emotion, and they work on the spectator with the suggestive power of non-discursive poems.

The first and more difficult of the two plays is an eerie parable of the American Revolution, experienced, as in a nightmare, by a Deerfield youth and his twelve-year-old brother. Arriving in Boston, the "city of the dead," to seek their kinsman, Major Molineux (a "lobsterback" who symbolizes the British forces in continental America), the two innocents watch in astonished horror as the Revolution is born out of indecision, hatred, resentment, and self-interest. The struggle, which culminates in the murder of Molineux, is embodied in the Union Jack and the rattlesnake flag of the incipient republic, and the semi-mythic characters—including a Charon-like ferryman, a vacillating clergyman, a man whose face grows bloody as the bloody event approaches—are identified through their attitudes toward these two significant emblems. Jonathan Miller has directed the work in a harrowing manner, using the hallucinatory style of Hogarth drawings or political cartoons by James Gillray: all but the two youths are dressed in blacks and whites, their countenances pastied and topped with powdered wigs, their movement stylized and spasmodic. Aided by an impeccable cast, illustrative costuming by Willa Kim, and spine-tingling musical effects by Yehudi Wyner, this production is surely one of the most brilliant theatrical events since William Ball's *Six Characters*.

Benito Cereno, however, is a good deal more than theatrically impressive: it is a cultural-poetic masterpiece, built on a strong suspenseful narrative. Melville's story largely concerns the shadow cast over a civilized mind by the primitive darkness: Lowell heightens this theme, examining along the way the ambiguous American attitude toward slavery and servitude. The plot concerns the visit of the Yankee merchant captain, Amasa Delano—a typically complacent, chauvinistic, wry, and generous American—to a mysterious slave ship anchored off South America, and captained by a noble Spaniard named Benito Cereno. The ship is a shambles, and the slaves are roaming freely about the deck. When Delano's curiosity and disapproval are aroused, Cereno—dogged and prompted always by his officious, unctuous, smiling slave, Babu—tells a halting, semi-hysterical story of calms, disease, and the loss of most of his crew.

But the story doesn't satisfy Delano, and, upset over the squalor and strangeness of the ship (so shocking to his Yankee sense of order), he finds himself being gradually demoralized by the swelling undulation of the waves, the spontaneity of the blacks and their ominous droning, the buzzing of the tropical mosquitoes, and the confused indirections of the obviously anguished Spanish captain. A series of enigmatic rituals and ceremonies are enacted before him, including the humiliation of an African king; he watches Cereno, terrified, being shaved by Babu with the Spanish flag used as an apron; and he begins to realize that, for all his belief in American ideals of freedom, in his heart he wants slaves. At last, he learns that Cereno is actually a prisoner on his own ship, which the revolting slaves have captured, murdering most of the crew. And when Babu unmasks himself as the leader of the rebels, forcing Delano's mate to kiss the lips of a ghastly skeleton and demanding that

Delano sail the ship back to Africa, the Yankee shoots him down, crying "This is your future!" The final confrontation of Babu and Delano looks forward to the confrontation of black and white in modern America, while the insidious effect of the slave ship on all the whites recalls those horrifying images of primitive envelopment in Conrad's *Heart of Darkness.*

Miller has paced this play with an eye to its half-languorous, half-ominous atmosphere, finally letting it explode into a shocking climax; and he has pulled performances out of his company which are nothing short of marvelous. Three actors in particular—Roscoe Lee Browne, alternating between Calypso sunniness and sinister threat as Babu; Frank Langella, a stately but trembling wreck as Cereno; Lester Rawlins, suave and self-satisfied as Delano—are giving the performances of their careers, but the entire cast works with the kind of precision and power we have learned to expect only from well-established repertory companies. It has been a long time since a simple set has been used in such a fluid manner, and even longer since a new playwright of such transcendent artistry has met a new director of such superior imaginativeness on common creative ground.

Instead of rejoicing over this signal occasion, the reviewers for the New York *Times* and *Herald Tribune* devoted their columns to lecturing Mr. Lowell and Mr. Miller on the requirements of conventional theatre, Mr. Kerr even suggesting that the evening would have benefited from a little Broadway "pressure." Thus, no doubt, did contemporary critics reproach Chekhov for ignoring the old theatrical formulas, and thus have the guardians of the tried-and-true always responded to the advances of the creative spirit. Well, let us confront the implications of these events squarely—in a cultural sense, we are two nations. Our theatre has maintained a monolithic mediocrity for so long that men of intelligence have all but disappeared from both sides of the proscenium. But now that Robert Lowell, Jonathan Miller, and the American Place have found one another, they must be permitted to find a suitable audience, and develop their vision in appreciative surroundings. How this can be achieved when the newspaper reviewers are still arbitrating success and failure in the theatre, I cannot say, but I am willing to make a practical suggestion in the form of a pact. If Mr. Kerr and Mr. Taubman will promise never again to review a serious work of dramatic art, I for one will offer never to cover another musical, commercial comedy, or melodrama. This may sound like a desperate notion, but the fiasco at Lincoln Center and the triumph at the American Place have taught us that we must now be willing to accept the consequences of a split culture. The dramatic imagination will never be permitted to expand in this country until it can function independently of the present theatre establishment; and that establishment is now discrediting itself so completely that one begins to have faith, at last, that such an expansion may soon take place.

(1964)

MUDDY TRACK
AT LINCOLN CENTER

INCIDENT AT VICHY by Arthur Miller:
Repertory Theatre of Lincoln Center

■ Arthur Miller has a new entry in the Guilt Sweepstakes. It is called Incident at Vichy, and it runs a muddy track in an hour and a half, huffing all the way. Unlike After the Fall, his previous contender at Recrimination Downs, this one is a standard steed, but it contains the same noisy virtue and moral flatulence, and it has about as much vigor and beauty as an old dray horse about to be melted down for glue.

Incident at Vichy takes place outside an improvised police station in occupied France. Sitting on a bench are a number of recently apprehended prisoners, arguing over the possible reasons for their arrest, and their eventual fate. All but two of the prisoners—a gypsy, and an Austrian nobleman arrested by mistake—are Jews, therefore destined for the death camps. And the structure of the work is based on the gradual decimation of the bench sitters as, one by one, they are led into the police station and examined for circumcision by a Jew Inspector and a German Major.

Although all the characters have names, professions, and little dramas, it soon becomes clear that they are not so much private men as public speakers, each with a symbolic role: a Humanist, a Marxist, a Coward, an Artist, a Businessman, an Aristocrat, etc. By the time the group has dwindled to a Jewish psychiatrist (the Humanist) and an Austrian prince (the Aristocrat), arguing over the nature of racial prejudice, it has become obvious that Mr. Miller has given us not so much a play as another solemn sermon on Human Responsibility.

The trouble with Mr. Miller's sermons, apart from the fact that they are tedious, glum, and badly written, is that they are so uncomplicated. Only one character has an option on the Truth, which the others will eventually take up with a cry of *Eureka!* Here the playwright, using the psychiatrist as his megaphone, brings the Austrian aristocrat to the realization that the persecution of the Jews by the Nazis merely reflects a more universal system of persecution. "Each man has his Jew," he cries, "it is the Other." This is the single line in the play to approach eloquence, and it is followed by the single discovery to approach a dramatic revelation—that the Austrian has a Nazi cousin! Having established everybody's complicity—presumably excepting his own—the psychiatrist then shouts, "It's not your guilt I want. It's your responsibility!" Instead of finding this demand presumptuous in the extreme, or replying that he is not to be held accountable for the politics of his relatives, the Austrian is only permitted his cry of *Eureka!* Hitherto a disengaged aesthete, he now proceeds to sacrifice his life so that the psychiatrist may escape.

Howard Taubman has announced that this play "returns the theatre to greatness." It returns the theatre, more accurately, to the thirties, a period the author seems never to have left. Miller's Jew Inspector is borrowed from Max Frisch's *Andorra,* and his German Major—a decent person who has turned cruel because "there are no people any more"—is a simplified version of a character in Rolf Hochhuth's The Deputy. But the real inspiration for this play comes from such liberal melodramas as Robert Sherwood's The Petrified Forest, where the Uncommitted Hero must be convinced of his Duty to Humanity, and give his life for a Cause. As for the ideas of the work—the only elements capable of raising it above the level of a Warner Brothers anti-Nazi epic starring Conrad Veidt—these have been hopelessly watered down.

It is apparently Mr. Miller's fate to stumble upon Pressing Questions long after more subtle minds have exhausted their possibilities, and then to pass them off as Profound Revelations—but all he adds are the Capital Letters. The theme of Incident at Vichy, for example, is nothing but half-understood Hannah Arendt. In Eichmann in Jerusalem, Miss Arendt showed how all of Europe was implicated in the fate of the Jews, but she hardly exculpated the Germans. In Incident at Vichy, however, Mr. Miller compares the treatment of the Jews by the Nazis with the hounding of the middle classes by the Russians, the exploitation of Africans and Indians by the British, and the suppression of Negroes by the Americans—and somehow manages to get the Germans off the hook. If everybody is guilty, then nobody is guilty, and the extermination of six million can be attributed merely to the universality of human evil, another agency recently discovered by the author.

Harold Clurman's production almost transcends the limitations imposed upon it by the writing, but since the action is mainly restricted to a bench, it cannot help being static for long periods and melodramatic for short ones, and the acting sometimes seems as dated as the play. Joseph Wiseman, who may be the spookiest actor in the American theatre, would be ideally cast as Dracula, but only this company would think of giving him the role of a rationalistic and humane psychiatrist. It is a credit to Mr. Wiseman that he manages to restrain his sinister vibrato for so much of the play, but he loses control in the final scene, warbling his lines in a rich bel canto manner, flapping his arms, and descending upon the Austrian as if he were about to suck his neck. David Wayne as the nobleman and David J. Stewart as a flamboyant actor are effective, and Hal Holbrook as the German Major is, to my pleased surprise, considerably more than that, contributing a performance of authentic anguish and complexity. But most of the cast speak in those slack New York tonalities that we have come to think of as the Lincoln Center style.

This style, to be sure, has been largely created by Arthur Miller, whose two plays constitute, for the moment, the only presentations at the Repertory Theatre. I see no reason why Mr. Miller should not have his own company—or Tennessee Williams, Murray Schisgal, and Jean Kerr too, for that matter—but I think we ought to stop pretending that what is going on at Lincoln Center has anything to do with the repertory idea. Certainly, the artistic director of the company seems to have no clear notion of what this idea is: "We've been working one year and produced two hits, Arthur Miller's *After the Fall* and *Incident at Vichy*," said Elia Kazan recently, defending his record. "From any standard, if you have two successes in one year, it can't be waved aside." Mr. Kazan's standards are obvious enough from this statement, the language of which speaks volumes. Under his guidance, the group has finally discovered its own level, which is precisely that of a conventional Broadway operation, grinding out "hits."

And the situation is getting worse. At the moment, the Repertory Theatre is in a state of chaos and confusion as a result of the bungled—and rather ruthless—attempt by the Theatre Board to replace Robert Whitehead without his knowledge. That the whole burden of blame has fallen on Mr. Whitehead is itself extremely depressing, for it shows that this Board of lawyers, bankers, businessmen, and television executives is more upset by the company's financial condition than by its artistic inadequacies, and is reluctant to support a deficit operation. In crisis, Lincoln Center exposes its naked heart, where the old money motives are still pumping beneath the surface of the cultural cant, and we are right back where we were, in the midst of a familiar commercial anatomy.

Well, it was naïve to expect the traditional system to be

revolutionized merely on the basis of a new building and a few high-sounding press releases, especially when Lincoln Center has always remained closely tied to the actors, directors, playwrights, and audiences of the conventional theatre. The company may still continue to produce its occasional "hits," but it is a wreck which can probably never be salvaged no matter who takes over its leadership: the system seems too powerful and too firmly entrenched. Where we may still look for revolutionary ferment is in the minority theatre—perhaps even on that small experimental stage being built at Lincoln Center, providing that can be an operation completely independent of the so-called Repertory Theatre, and providing it is placed in capable and deserving hands.

(1964)

HEALTH IN
AN AILING PROFESSION

The Actor's Workshop in San Francisco; The APA; TARTUFFE by Molière at The Repertory Theatre of Lincoln Center

■ A group of Russian actors visited New York some months ago to discuss the Stanislavsky system as practiced by the Moscow Art Theatre; but the most lasting impression they left me was of their pleasant personalities, ebullient good health, and sense of common purpose. The West, with its modern tradition of experimental art and bohemian artists, does not take kindly to the Soviet notion of the "artist-citizen," and our attitude is vindicated by the sterility of most Soviet-sponsored literature and drama. Still, the anarchic freedom necessary to our creative artists has now been expropriated by many interpretive artists, particularly those engaged in the collaborative enterprise of the theatre, and I am beginning to think this a serious obstacle to genuine histrionic achievement. The most conspicuous American acting method—one, ironically, linked here with the name of Stanislavsky—has functioned primarily for the manufacture of star personalities. Worse, it has encouraged a neurotic, even pathological mode of performance with the actor's personal problems displacing the objective problems of the role. How many times have we been prevented from seeing a theatrical character by an actor more interested in exhibiting himself? And how many complex roles have been destroyed by a performer's narcissistic quirks and private eccentricities, whether in the form of glowering masculinity or of fussy effeminacy, whether of uncontrolled hysteria or of adolescent self-consciousness?

These reflections are prompted by a recent visit to the Actor's Workshop in San Francisco, a company I had seen before with pleasure, but which I now had an opportunity to observe at leisure. I had already been struck by the unusual intelligence of the group, a rare enough quality in our theatre; now I was struck by something even rarer, its healthy instinct and powerful discipline. To watch these actors rehearse is to watch a close-knit family group co-operating in a common pursuit; to see them perform is to see an ensemble functioning not only with precision but also with dedication, sensitivity, and joy. Unlike New York and Hollywood actors, these performers are gypsies no longer, devitalized by the uncertain conditions of their work and depressed by the unsatisfying quality of it. They have found a permanent home, and, settling down to develop their personal and artistic lives, have become an essential part of the landscape.

The confidence that results is absorbed into their work. During my stay in San Francisco, I saw a rehearsal of Chekhov's Uncle Vanya, a production of Wycherly's The Country Wife, and a revival of Pinter's The Caretaker: each was marked by the same lucidity of conception and deftness of execution. Even in its early stages, the Uncle Vanya was shaping up as a clarifying experience, the title character being played with such extraordinary force (by Robert Symonds) that I understood, for the first time, why Chekhov named the play after him. Seeing *The Caretaker* again reinforced my initial opinion that its ambiguities are sterile, and its development dull, but this production, nevertheless, uncovered new values in the text, and the setting, a small room surrounded by lathing and piled high with junk, enhanced Pinter's motif of claustrophobic dread.

As for *The Country Wife*—another play that is rather tiresome on the stage (though fascinating in the study)—this turned out to be one of the finest Restoration productions I have ever seen, especially interesting because it managed to remain indigenously American without sacrificing a sense of high style. The director wisely elected to dispense with the usual fluttering fans, baroque bows, and foppish intonations, and to sweep through the play in a bouncy, virile, semi-farcical manner, aided by an organic design which worked almost like a character in the action (the Workshop is especially fortunate in its scenic artists) and by vigorous men and handsome women who spoke admirably, and who were not afraid to be brutal on the stage. Nor was there any timidity about introducing the unexpected. In an opening tableau, the entire company appeared in costume, smiling at the audience—but in the crowd was a young man in a business suit, presumably the father of one of the children in the cast. This insinuation of contemporary life into the Restoration world was entirely natural and unobtrusive, but it had the interesting effect of collapsing time—as did the bridge music, consisting mainly of the Swingle Singers doing jazz vocal versions of Handel and Bach.

Such production concepts seem to grow out of the play instead of being artificially imposed upon it: the Workshop directors are devoted, first and foremost, to illuminating the texts. It is this kind of artistic disinterestedness that has made the Actor's Workshop, under the inspirational leadership of Herbert Blau and Jules Irving, such an important theatre institution. The notes on the programs are a little too self-conscious and pedagogical; and the theatre, as a whole, does not possess that fanatical revolutionary thrust that used to animate The

Living Theatre (because of this, Ronnie Davis, a former Workshop actor, broke with the company to form his own experimental troupe). But if the Actor's Workshop is not likely to unearth new playwriting talent, it brilliantly serves what already exists. For works of the classical and modern repertory, and of the Anglo-European avant-garde, there are few permanent companies as good, and none as healthy, vital and devoted.

It is a pity that the Actor's Workshop has not brought a three- or four-play repertory to New York, for then the local reviewers would have some standards to judge by, and the APA would not have been so vastly overrated. As individuals, the actors in Ellis Rabb's troupe are mostly competent performers—and Rosemary Harris is an actress of dazzling charm and versatility—but the company lacks a sense of unity, either in its productions or in its over-all purpose. I admit to irresponsibility here, but I saw only two acts of the currently celebrated *Man and Superman*. Although I think the play is beginning to creak a bit in the joints, I am still sufficiently fond of it to have been annoyed by the APA production, for it was perversely miscast. Mr. Rabb played John Tanner in a mode of high camp, converting Shaw's genial wit into mincing peeves and sulky humors, while Rosemary Harris, who would have been ideally cast as Ann Whitefield, was relegated to the role of Viola. This she proceeded to play with such elegance and *esprit* that Nancy Marchand, playing Ann, seemed leaden by comparison—and the production was thrown out of balance. Then, the staging was so gluey, and the settings so tacky, that I saw no alternative but to take up my coat at the first intermission and depart.

I stayed through all of *War and Peace*, attracted by its flashy theatricality, but this ultimately proved a profitless evening too. The adaptation, first of all, would be more suitable for the movies than the stage, since it has an essentially cinematic structure, not to mention a certain Hollywood superficiality. The German adapters—Alfred Neumann, Erwin Piscator, and Guntram Prufer—have turned Tolstoy's well-fleshed novel into a skeleton scenario of love stories, battles, and death scenes, employing a garrulous narrator (in evening clothes) to introduce the characters, advance the plot, bridge time, analyze war

strategy, and announce the Theme. This Theme is only occasionally Tolstoy's (the conflict between Chance and Will in the
creation of history); most of the time, the authors are more
interested in pushing their own rather gratuitous anti-war propaganda. I am inclined to doubt that there are still many theatre
audiences bristling with militancy, but if so, it is extremely
doubtful that they will be converted to peaceful purposes by
such crude exhortations and clumsy techniques.

If the theme of the play reminds one of agit-prop, so does the
form—this is Epic theatre without the epic talent of Brecht.
Ellis Rabb, who directed, takes full advantage of the play's
visual opportunities, staging it on levels, through scrims, and
inside picture frames, while maneuvering toy soldiers around a
miniature battlefield which smokes with exploding cannon and
burning bridges. Unfortunately, the entire action is drenched in
a constant spray of background music. This proved a mistake
for three reasons: 1) the music is often inappropriate, 2) it is
badly amplified, and 3) it tempts the spectator to listen to the
tunes instead of attending to the play. This, at least, was my
temptation, particularly because the musical performers seemed
better trained than the theatrical ones. Rosemary Harris, ravish-
ing in an Empire style, gives a charming performance as
Natasha, and Keene Curtis is strong and masterful as Napoleon;
but the rest of the acting tends to be rather routine, and many
of the more intimate scenes are stagy. In short, this is a worthy
production in its externals—including a striking setting by Peter
Wexler and handsome period costumes by Nancy Potts—but
whenever this company gets down to essentials, it is without
real cohesiveness, authenticity, or depth.

The majority of the actors appearing in *Tartuffe* have been
imported especially for that production. But since they have
often worked together before—and since they are seasoned classical performers—this pickup cast is far superior to any previously seen at Lincoln Center. This sounds like a grudging com-
pliment, so let me strike the comparison—it is a brilliant company by any standard, and a tribute to the regional and Off
Broadway theatres where most of these actors developed. By
using his own people instead of those recruited for Lincoln

Center by Kazan and Whitehead, William Ball has shown New York that the great drama of the past is not at all beyond the reach of American performers, provided they can be guided by a capable directorial hand, and are prepared for the classics by education, commitment, and training. He has shown us, in brief, what the Repertory Theatre might have been had it not betrayed its own dreams.

This production of *Tartuffe* is, without question, the most exciting work yet seen at Lincoln Center—if not a total triumph, then, at least, a qualified one. The direction, to be sure, is just a little flossy, in that Ball's numerous interpolations tend to be sometimes distracting and sometimes irrelevant. Then, a few of the actors left over from Kazan's original company are rather stiff and awkward in lesser roles; the setting may be too substantial for such a stylized mode of performance; and I am not certain that the second half of the production lives up to the extraordinary promise of the first. Still, there is an irresistible quality about this *Tartuffe* which makes me disinclined to quibble with it. It makes for an extremely happy evening, bubbling with high spirits, and running over with creative joy.

Let me try to list some excellences, starting with the translation. Richard Wilbur's rendering of *Tartuffe*—like Robert Lowell's adaptation of *Phèdre*—is an artwork in itself: crisp, idiomatic, fresh, and funny, a rhyming play to which the untrained American ear can adapt almost instantly and without strain. Then there is the acting. Almost all of it is strongly defined, from Claude Woolman's stalwart *raisonneur* to Hal Holbrook's delightfully evil Bailiff, but three performances deserve particular praise: Sada Thompson's saucy, bustling, raucous Dorine, bursting with good health; Larry Gates's gullible, splenetic, semi-hypnotized Orgon (a real breakthrough for an actor hitherto mired in dreary roles); and, best of all, the splendid Tartuffe of Michael O'Sullivan.

O'Sullivan's performance is audacious in the extreme; it is chimerical; it is almost surreal. Flailing his spindly arms and flapping his rubbery legs like a scarecrow in a high wind, he scowls, squints, pouts, and leers with lightning adjustments of his horselike countenance, snarling and gnashing his huge teeth near a beautiful bosom as if he were about to make a meal of it. O'Sullivan doesn't so much represent the character as transform it into a fantastic dream. Always preserving the mask of the clown, he heightens the comic possibilities of the role by distorting and exaggerating its serious values: whether pious or lecherous, animalistic, menacing, or wheedling, his Tartuffe remains firmly tied to an ecstatic world of fun. This is not exactly the intention of Molière, who saw this hypocritical impostor as an extremist threatening an essentially moderate society, but it is a pleasure, nevertheless, to watch such an imaginative actor at work, and the way he uses a stoup of holy water— blessing with it, throwing it at enemies, simulating tears with it, or merely washing his face—is a lesson in stage business alone. This is a magnificent farce performance, which proceeds along a plane of inspiration very rare in our theatre.

The production, too, is consistently ingenious, and—except for occasional, and inexplicable, dark patches throughout—consistently sunny and sprightly. Locating the play in the period it was written (the characters—and especially Orgon, who looks like Dumas' Aramis—would be very much at home in a farce version of *The Three Musketeers*), Ball has directed the action as if the floor were tilted, with the actors rolling from one side to the other. The stage is in constant motion, and alive with perpetual invention: this is an evening dedicated wholly to delight. But the greatest delight lies in the sense of possibility the production awakens for the health of the theatre, and of those who work in it. It is by abandoning themselves entirely to such collaborative imaginative acts that performers redeem their profession from all its vices—the exhibitionism and vulgarity, the pretentiousness, tawdry glamour, and self-indulgence—and revive our flagging expectations of the histrionic art.

(1965)

RUSSIAN EVENINGS

DEAD SOULS *adapted by Mikhail Bulgakov from the novel of Nikolai Gogol;* THE CHERRY ORCHARD *by Anton Chekhov;* THE THREE SISTERS *by Anton Chekhov: Moscow Art Theatre*

■ The New York visit of the Moscow Art Theatre, last seen on these shores in 1924, is probably one of the most eagerly awaited events of recent American theatre history. Founded by Stanislavsky and Nemirovich-Danchenko in 1898, this celebrated company became, as everyone knows, the parent body of such influential American theatrical institutions as the Group Theatre and the Actors Studio, while the Stanislavsky system of acting has long functioned as the cornerstone of our own realistic school. Ever since the thirties, however, a good deal of controversy has collected around Lee Strasberg's interpretations of Stanislavsky's techniques, a controversy that has split the American theatre right down the middle. Would Stanislavsky have approved Strasberg's emphasis on emotional memory, his concern with "private moments," or his concentration on the actor at the expense of the play? Would he have sanctioned Strasberg's tendency to probe the psyches of his students, his encouragement of personal exposure, his linking of psychoanalysis and the stage? These questions, technical quibbles to the layman, have by now assumed as much importance among theatre practitioners as the heresies of Jung and Adler have among orthodox Freudians. And as Paul Gray points out in an illuminating article recently published in the *Tulane Drama Review*, such questions underly the continuing professional antagonisms between Strasberg and the Studio, on the one hand, and Stella Adler, Elia Kazan, Sanford Meisner, Robert Lewis, Harold Clurman, and many alumni of the Group on the other.

The visit of the M.A.T., therefore, is significant not only for itself but also as a way of resolving these plaguey problems once and for all. And it is clear enough now that, as far as results are concerned, the Stanislavsky system bears about as much relation to the Strasberg Method as caviar does to hot dogs. Russian performing, as a matter of fact, forms a distinct contrast with American naturalistic acting, for it is firm, open, direct, and clearly articulated. The actors attain a high level of emotion without ever spilling over into hysteria; they are never eccentric or neurasthenic; they change personality radically from role to role instead of repeating personal mannerisms; and although they are closely identified with their characters, they are not lost in them. While the Strasberg actor is listening most intently to himself, furthermore, the Stanislavsky actor is most intently listening to others: the M.A.T. obviously tolerates no star personalities, and all the actors play as if there were no such thing as minor roles.

These virtues being listed, it must be added that there is something old-fashioned about the Moscow Art Theatre, something a little musty and museum-like. It is ironic, for example, when we remember that Stanislavsky revolutionized Russian stage design, to find the M.A.T. reverting, in *Dead Souls*, to wing-and-border draperies. Aside from V. V. Dmitriev's handsome décor for *The Three Sisters*, none of the settings escapes looking antique or unattractive: interiors consist of shaky flats, buckling canvas, and fading colors, and exteriors of fake grass and badly painted perspective backdrops. Then, the company acting—for all its emotional generosity, physical vitality, and intelligence—is in the style of another era. In gesture, it sometimes reminded me of our silent films; in pacing and intonation, of our early talkies—I could imagine Sylvia Sidney in this company, or Margo, giving her performance in *Winterset*. The men brood and pace; the women bat their eyelids, posture, and wring their hands with grief. Performances seem to take place within cameos or picture frames. When the actress playing Masha in *The Three Sisters* expressed a dawning love for Vershinin by tilting her head, smiling gently to herself, and gazing into the distance, I half expected a camera to iris in on her, with mist blurring the edges. That this style of acting—considered naturalistic a few decades ago—should now seem stagy and artificial demonstrates how much our notions of stage "reality" are subject to change.

There is something clumsy and archaic, too, in Mikhail Bulgakov's adaptation of Gogol's *Dead Souls*, a rendering which reduces that sharp bureaucratic satire to a series of disconnected, repetitious scenes with no forward movement: the play, which does not contain a single sentence not to be found in the novel, simply cries out for more adventurousness on the part of the adapter. As for the production, it is full of variety and charm, but not much lightness of spirit. First directed by Stanislavsky in 1932, it is said to reveal the marked theatricalist influences of Meyerhold and Vakhtangov. I saw evidence, too, of the influence of Dickens novels and Chaplin movies. The actors, made up in the heavily underlined manner of such Chaplin regulars as Mack Swain, Chester Conklin, and Eric Campbell, ambulate in jerky, puppet-like maneuvers; the characters have the exaggerated beefiness of animal caricatures, especially the bearish landowner Sobakevich, played by Alexei Gribov with just the right touch of hugeness, hypocrisy, and greed; and the banquet and crowd scenes are wonderfully precise vignettes of early nineteenth-century Russian society. But the evening somehow fails to rise off the ground.

Victor Stanitsyn's restaging of the original Stanislavsky version of *The Cherry Orchard* also lacks deftness. The production relies too heavily on Stanislavsky's famous off-stage noises (which used to drive Chekhov wild); it mutes the farcical values of the play; and it suffers from an excessively literal setting at odds with the author's symbolic poetry (the second-act exterior, for example, is now less an abandoned shrine than a picnic area). Then, a few of the central roles are either misplayed or miscast: Mikhail Zimin's Lopakhin is inexplicably elegant and incomprehensibly forlorn; Pavel Massalsky's Gaev, while very noble, captures little of the escapism implicit in his caramel-eating and imaginary billiard game; the actors playing Yasha and Epikhodov would have been more effective had they exchanged roles; and Ranevskaya, enacted by the celebrated Soviet artist, Alla Tarassova, is overly melodramatic. Miss Tarassova, who played Anya in the same play when the company last visited the United States (and who is now chairman of the M.A.T. Board), demonstrates how glacial must be the progress of the older members of the company: I doubt if her acting style has changed much in the past thirty years. Gribov's Firs, though, is a wonderfully doddering presence, both in speech and silence, and the entire ensemble functions with poise and ease; but this production frankly doesn't hold a candle to the sparkling Gielgud-directed *Cherry Orchard* I saw in London in 1955.

The Three Sisters, however, a Nemirovich-Danchenko production, revised later by Iosef Raevsky, is a much more impressive event—crammed with detail, beautifully cast, and sensitively performed. The archaism I sensed in the other two productions here takes a more meaningful direction, as a truthful evocation of the past, and all the lyric beauties of the play are made strikingly manifest. The sisters, a doleful frieze in white, blue, and black, constitute a poignant family group; Natasha is played with a developing crudity, which shows the physical and spiritual coarsening of this malevolent despoiler; and Vladimir Belokurov as a complacent Kulygin, Pavel Massalsky as a romantic Vershinin, and Alexei Gribov (again) as a nihilistic Tchebutykin are outstanding in a splendid ensemble. But even this fine performance failed to be definitive. The ending of the play, I am sorry to report, has been changed for more "positive" effect (Tchebutykin is no longer in the last scene, adding his "It doesn't matter" to the desperate affirmations of the sisters) and the Chekhovian subtext is made a little more obvious than necessary (Tusenbach's final leave-taking of Irina, for example, is now rather operatic, while the hostility between Natasha and the sisters is much too open).

With many of Stanislavsky's original intentions thus preserved, one begins to understand Chekhov's continued grumbling about the Moscow Art Theatre as well as his continued devotion to it: it is a company in which great virtues alternate with substantial defects. Chief among its defects today, to judge from the current repertory, is an incapacity to develop with the times. While the best contemporary theatre has moved beyond realism, both in writing and in playing (even in the playing of Chekhov), the M.A.T. is still mired in the glories, as well as in the techniques, of its past. Stanislavsky will undoubtedly be considered always one of the great revolutionary modern artists, whose theatrical reforms have affected every theatre in the West. But another swing of the pendulum has put his company in the rear guard. Perhaps it is time we stopped arguing over who is Stanislavsky's legitimate heir, and founded a totally different family. It is always a difficult thing to reject a father, especially a powerful and brilliant one, but until the American theatre can break the bonds of naturalistic truth and psychological reality, there will be no real advance.

(1965)

GENERAL

.

.

.

SCORN
NOT THE PROSCENIUM,
CRITIC

■ Like the sonnet in the nineteenth century, the proscenium
stage in our time has been frowned upon, scorned, vilified, and
condemned by the country's most influential critics; and, lacking a Wordsworth to take up cudgels in its defense, it is now in
process of being battered and broken by the abuse. "How did
the hoax begin?" queries Brooks Atkinson at the beginning of a
recent article in which he agreed with William Poel and Tyrone
Guthrie that the proscenium stage is "the principal cause of
staleness in the modern theatre." For Walter Kerr, who is generally quite sanguine about Broadway products and productions,
the proscenium is that "jam-packed peephole stage that was
wished upon us by the nineteenth-century realists," and leads
inexorably to bad imitations of unpopular "minority" playwrights like Ibsen and Chekhov. As for Thornton Wilder, he
has often concluded that the proscenium—and especially the

275

box set (the proscenium's most frequent tenant)—is the main enemy of theatrical truth, since it "stifles the life of the drama" and "militates against belief." It is true that these critics rarely agree on precisely what kind of "staleness" the proscenium is responsible for—for Atkinson, picture-frame plays are "violent and sensational," while for Wilder, they are "soothing," "evasive," and distrustful of the passions—but they all shake hands in blaming it for practically every shortcoming of American drama and dramatic production.

Now it is easy enough to agree with one of these critical assumptions—that contemporary American theatre has its failings. Weary, stale, flat (though not always unprofitable), flabby, dishonest, dull, slushy, sentimental, and soporific while belching with occasional bursts of energy, it alternates between somnolence and hysteria like a beatnik hopped up on Benzedrine. Since most of our plays sound as if they were written by the same dramatist, staged by the same director, and performed by the same actors, let us also agree that the American theatre is in real danger of drying up in its own juiceless and dreary conformity. But now let our pleasant harmony with the critics come to an end. For while Atkinson, Kerr, and Wilder all show a real awareness of the need for some radical change in the theatre, they have not convinced me that they have any effective idea of the direction this change should take.

Which is not to say that, on a purely formalistic level, their anti-proscenium arguments are unsound or unperceptive. I am easily persuaded that the picture-frame stage is partially responsible for many dramatic excesses of a purely technical nature: that it "boxes a performance in" (Atkinson), that it tends to force the playwright into "contriving, curtailing, and distorting" (Kerr), and that it sometimes "fixes and narrows the action to one moment in time and space" (Wilder). I have also heard and do in part believe actors who swear that the proscenium arch cuts off their communication with the audience, leaving them with the sensation of dropping their emotion into a great dark mouth which swallows it up without sending anything back. And from my own observation, I am becoming convinced that the proscenium permits the secondary talents of the theatre—the scenic artists, costumers, and lighting designers—to usurp the stage from the playwright by introducing opulent and irrelevant "effects" which often distract attention from the main dramatic action. While none of these seems to me a problem which smaller theatres, firmer playwriting, or more modest designers could not solve, I will certainly not deny that the open stage would solve them more effectually. So let us grant that the open stage is a more flexible instrument than the proscenium and that it helps establish a more intimate relationship between the actor and his audience.

Now if our critics had had nothing more extravagant than this in mind, there would have been little need to quarrel with them. But their animadversions upon the proscenium extend a good deal further. And what begins as a perceptive technical argument almost invariably leads to an aesthetic conclusion of the most extreme and illogical kind: that if the theatre would only reject the proscenium stage, dispense with the box set, and get rid of the curtain, the general spinelessness of American drama would somehow magically disappear.

What is more, this idea (if one can call it that) is now hardening into dogma even in the most sophisticated theatre circles. The Ford Foundation is currently awarding huge sums of money to stage and theatre designers (all of them charter members of the Broadway Establishment) in the expectation that architectural innovations will have some effect on the quality of American drama; and, with the same hope, other philanthropists are underwriting the open-stage Lincoln Center theatre, even though the whole project is already controlled by the same people who now bring such dubious distinction to the commercial stage. We have precedents enough to doubt the efficacy of such back-door approaches to excellence. After a disastrous opening season, attributed by most of the reviewers to the theatre's conventional proscenium stage and settings, the American Shakespeare Company at Stratford completely redesigned their house so that it featured a wider apron, downstage exit areas, and scenery which moved in and out on mechanical dollies. Result? Overwhelming physical productions but no appreciable improvement in the interpretation of Shakespeare's plays. The Phoenix Theatre, whose offerings have been plagued by unevenness and failure primarily because the company has never developed a firm and courageous artistic policy, now produces all its plays on a raked apron stage, using open curtains and unlocalized scenery. Result? No appreciable improvement in the quality of their productions. And, as for Broadway itself, the huge apron stages, introduced by such designers as Jo Mielziner and Will Steven Armstrong to mollify the critics, have had absolutely no effect on the quality of the plays or production techniques, except to call unnecessary attention to the sets.

I do not mean to imply that there is any harm in all this enthusiasm for architectural reform; *externally*, it may do a lot of good. What *is* harmful is the assumption that such reform will solve any internal problems. The danger is one of false emphasis, for by blaming the proscenium for all the evils of American theatre, the real source of these evils remains unexplored. Let us examine some of the critical objections to the picture-frame stage to see if there is any justification for all the abuse.

1) *The picture-frame stage "confines the theatre as an art to variations on a standard mode of performance."* Wrong. What makes Broadway performances so standardized, unimaginative, incoherent, and inaudible is simply that no other kind of performance is taught or tolerated—and experiment is probably impossible anyway given the inadequate rehearsal time and the pickup quality of the cast. Our dominant schools of acting, led by the Actors Studio (whose members hold classes as well), have chosen to confine their instruction to the most narrowly realistic techniques, and—dedicated to internal "truth" even when faced with non-illusionistic plays—have reduced acting to mere imitation, turning out actors who all look and behave alike. Anyone who saw the Piccolo Teatro di Milano during its recent visit to the City Center (a great barn of a theatre with a huge picture-frame stage) could observe for himself that authentic histrionic imagination survives very well within proscenium walls when the actors are audacious and well trained, the director conversant with other than Method techniques, and the company as a whole equipped to break out of the conven-

tional molds. (If you missed this group, take a trip down to The Living Theatre, where another kind of histrionic experimentation is being attempted with real success—and on a picture-frame stage.)

2) *The picture-frame stage "confines the theatre as an art . . . to variations on the styles of plays written by Ibsen and Chekhov."* Although we would have a healthy theatre indeed if our dramatists wrote as well as Ibsen and Chekhov, wrong again. Over the past eighty years, the proscenium has proved perfectly hospitable to the plays of Strindberg, Wedekind, Brecht, Lorca, Pirandello, Synge, O'Casey, Kaiser, Toller, O'Neill, Camus, Behan, Beckett, and Ionesco to name only a handful of the playwrights who composed non-realistic, and sometimes non-illusionistic, plays for the picture-frame stage without any loss of imaginative power. If Broadway has never seen their plays, I would suggest the reason has less to do with the poor proscenium than with uncourageous producers and unresponsive audiences. Similarly, though the works of Sophocles and Shakespeare were obviously designed for open stages, they do not suffer so much from proscenium treatment as the critical theorizing would have us believe (remember the Old Vic productions of *Oedipus* and *Henry IV*?), and the plays of Ibsen and Chekhov have proved perfectly viable in the round and on the apron. Whenever you feel inclined to blame the proscenium, remember Eric Bentley's valuable rule of thumb: "No play will succeed on an apron stage for which it was written unless it has qualities that would make it a success on all types of stage for which it was *not* written." In other words, if the play is sound and the production appropriate, an effective performance could be staged on a leaky raft in the middle of the China Sea.

3) *The picture-frame stage, and particularly the box set, leads to "soothing" and "evasive" drama.* This charge simply makes no sense to me at all. I do not wish to defend Ibsen's realism here (it retains a good deal more vitality than its detractors acknowledge), but "soothing" is the last epithet I would apply to it. To be sure, some American plays in the realistic mode— like those of Inge and Chayefsky, for example—are indeed

"soothing" and "evasive" because, despite their fidelity to surface authenticity, they are much closer to romance; but the realism of Ibsen, Chekhov, Shaw, and O'Neill is designed to cut below the flattering surface to the harsh and rock-ribbed reality beneath. I suspect, in fact, that one of the reasons Ibsen is never performed on Broadway is that he is never soothing enough for the audience, while the elaborate formal experiments of Wilder and MacLeish have become popular because underneath the unconventional surface you often find thick sentiment and easy affirmations. In short, the determination of the dramatist to confront or evade a specific problem is a question of conscience and vision and has almost nothing to do with the stage for which he writes.

The whole proscenium controversy, then, strikes me as an elaborate evasion of the real problems of our theatre, shifting our attention to purely formal considerations when we should be examining Broadway economics, Broadway timidity, Broadway opportunism, the hit-flop mystique, the general imitation of what is current and fashionable, and the absence of any commitment to anything higher than mere survival and success. Chekhov—who is now almost as maligned by the critics as the theatre he wrote for—probably had the last word to offer the detractors of the proscenium when, sixty-four years ago, he had his Treplev say, "I come more and more to the conviction that it is not a question of new or old forms, but that what matters is that a man should write without thinking about forms at all, write because it springs freely from his soul." It is this urge of the spirit and strength of conviction alone—and not formal experimentation or new theatre buildings—which will turn our theatre at last from a cheap and gaudy sideshow into a temple of enduring art.

(1960)

OFF-STAGE NOISES

■ Every year, Broadway celebrates the silly season with a ponderous ritual of self-praise called the Antoinette Perry ("Tony") Presentation Ceremonies. In the course of this spring rite, while TV cameras dolly back and forth between the glittering celebrities on the rostrum and the dutiful claque at the tables, the theatre Establishment awards itself a number of merit badges for its own plays and performances. Although it is also an occasion for the speakers to make superior digs at the Academy Awards, the Tony is really the exact theatrical equivalent of the Oscar. Both the film and theatre industries like to disguise their enormous devotion to money and popular success under the pretense of rewarding artistic achievement; yet, in both cases, the sole criterion of excellence is the box office. It is true that Hollywood, unlike Broadway, will occasionally permit a notable work to reach the nomination stage (this year *Wild Strawberries* contended with *Pillow Talk* in the category of Best Original Screenplay—and lost!), but I suspect that Broadway would also make such a feeble gesture if it had any artworks available to nominate. Anyhow, the Tony operation is as mechanical as a National Cash Register and nobody but the winners takes the awards very seriously. So I will not bother to tell you who collected them, except to mention that most of the prizes went to a musical too treacly even for the daily reviewers to keep down their throats, a work distinguished only for having had the largest advance sale in the history of the theatre.

What has become extremely offensive, however, is the insincerity, meretriciousness, and sheer vulgarity of the ceremony. My stomach began to turn when Helen Hayes announced that Broadway actors were the most glamorous, witty, and charming people in the world; flipped over on its side when Helen Menken, her voice quivering with emotion, handed a special award to John D. Rockefeller III, presumably in tribute to his bank account; and yielded its contents completely when Mary Martin *recited*, as an inspirational guide to career success for the drama students in the gallery, the entire lyric of Oscar Hammerstein's "Climb Every Mountain." Broadway luminaries have never been famous for their intelligence, modesty, or good taste, but before the mass media cultivated a national craving for idiocy we were generally spared any lengthy exposure to their minds. Now that the American acting profession seems to have lost its dedication to anything higher than fame and fortune, perhaps it is appropriately represented by the bejewelled, befurred, and benighted creatures who participated in this tasteless charade; but I cannot completely suppress my nostalgia for the time when acting was a calling and not merely a form of self-aggrandizement. The Tony ceremony gives truth to the old bromide that "the great big wunnerful heart of show biz" is composed entirely of gold, studded here and there with rhinestones and sequins.

If the Tony awards indicate that players, to use Hamlet's words, should "speak no more than is set down for them," the latest utterances of Tennessee Williams suggest that extra-dramatic silences might be requested from playwrights as well. Mr. Williams' public pronouncements have multiplied as his fame has spread, becoming—like his plays—increasingly exhibitionistic with each passing year. His latest exposure of his private life took the form of an interview published in the New York *Times* where, among other personal confessions, Williams both publicized and interpreted his recent breach with Elia Kazan. "The fact is," said Williams, "Kazan has been falsely blamed for my own desire for success. . . . It's quite true that I want to reach a mass audience. I feel it can dig what I have to say, perhaps better than a lot of intellectuals can. I'm not an intellectual. And perhaps, at times, I've exceeded the dignified limits in trying to hold an audience, but it's wrong to blame Kazan for this. My cornpone melodrama is all my own. I want excitement in the theatre."

The confused and contradictory manner in which all this is expressed signifies that Williams is less confident of his position than the bald surface of his words would indicate; and I do not doubt that he still retains a good deal more understanding about the nature of Broadway compromise than almost anyone who works for our commercial stage. Yet, he has chosen to advertise a considered decision to conform to popular taste. What he is saying, once you remove the cant from his language, is that he prefers the easy admiration of the mink matrons and the expense-account executives (Broadway's "mass audience") to the respect of that smaller group which demands that his art be uncompromisingly honest (the "intellectuals"), and that his work is frequently shaped accordingly. Where he differs from Kazan in this respect is that while Kazan's choice is much the same, it is far less conscious, for Kazan possesses an instinctive rapport with the popular audience which Williams, a former highbrow, has always lacked. Thus, although Kazan seems more sympathetic to the social humanitarianism of Miller than to the sexual existentialism of Williams, he has always held the key to Williams' popular success, and it is in this light that Williams' agony over the "breach" must be regarded.

We shall never know, until an unauthorized biography appears, at what point Williams stopped trying to be an artist and settled down to becoming a corporation, but I suspect the decision came right after the critical and commercial failure of *Camino Real*. It may still be too early to conclude that Williams reinforces Fitzgerald's sad insight that there are no second acts in American lives—like Fitzgerald, he may yet realize the talent he has abused—but his current career demonstrates that the greatest enemy against which the American artist has to defend himself is his own insatiable appetite for universal love.

(1960)

ASPIRIN AND SURGERY

■ A few months ago, I was abruptly confronted by a gifted but highly effusive actress, intensely devoted to an inspirational Broadway play in which she was then starring. Having learned that the work had failed to inspire me, she proceeded to defend its merits, especially emphasizing its effect on audiences. "You don't seem to realize," she announced, flourishing her expressive hands a hairsbreadth from my nose, "that every night someone leaves our theatre a completely changed person!" When I raised an eyebrow, she added, "You don't know! Every week I receive letters from people who say our show has given them a more mature outlook on life!" I ventured—somewhat timidly in view of her evangelistic fervor—to express my doubts that three hours in the theatre could work wonders that eight years on the couch sometimes fail to achieve. She chided me for my skepticism about the curative powers of the drama, and, unreconstructed, we went our separate ways.

It struck me later that what she had been voicing was not just an eccentric personal opinion, but a growing conviction of the Broadway stage. Clearly, the newer American playwrights often confuse themselves with psychological counselors, for deeply imbedded in their plays you will generally find an object lesson about the diagnosis and treatment of romantic, emotional, family, or social disorders. William Gibson affirms that by charitably helping others you may absolve your own guilt; Robert Anderson tells us that adulterous encounters can be considered a form of self-sacrifice and sympathy; William Inge plumps for "maturity" in love and family relationships; and Paddy Chayefsky suggests that romantic passion will conquer psychosis, neurosis, and evil spirits. There is an unwritten law in our theatre, countersigned by producers, directors, and critics alike, that a play must illustrate a significant forward development in the lives of its characters, so that the audience may depart with hope in their hearts and a renewed conviction about the possibilities of change.

As a consequence, our younger dramatists invariably see man in relation to his "problems"; and, sharing a warmhearted belief in progress and human perfectibility inherited from the social dramatists of the thirties, they tend to view existence as a temporary ailment which can be easily cured if you find the proper medicine. In the past, the recommended medical reference books were the writings of Karl Marx. Today—with "love" and psychological adjustment the inevitable prescription—they are the cheery chapbooks of the Neo-Freudian revisionists. The "cures" outlined in present-day drama are, of course, only nostrums—or, at best, sedatives—packaged in pleasant-tasting pills to be swallowed painlessly by the audience. But it seems to me that even some of the older and tougher dramatists, who recommended social rather than psychological change, were confusing their function and getting the drama all mixed up with the social sciences. For most American playwrights, past and present, have a tendency to define man exclusively in relation to his institutions, implying that man finds health through integration with a real or ideal society. In America, Utopia is invariably confounded with Levittown.

Compare the modern French dramatists who, far from emphasizing integration, seem obsessively concerned with disintegration. You will find, in advanced French drama, few attempts at therapy, uplift, or improvement, little belief in the "infinite perfectibility of man," and no conviction that humans realize themselves through togetherness and community living. Quite the contrary, the younger French writers seem to create on the (truly Freudian) assumption that it is civilization itself that has caused the discontents of man. Consider their attitudes toward the social unit. For Samuel Beckett, whose world consists of impotent old creatures, sitting and listening to their organs decay, society is no more than a noise in the street; for Eugene Ionesco, it is a source of planned inhumanity, its language a species of absurdities, clichés, and gibberish; and for Jean Genet, the social world is an enormous brothel, presided over by whoremasters impersonating Authority. Liberal critics have severely censured these writers for assaulting the "dignity of man," but the French might reply, and sometimes do, that man surrendered his dignity long ago when he capitulated to debased institutions and permitted himself to be dehumanized in a mass culture. But although these playwrights may focus on the spiritually diminished man, implicit in most of their works—and explicit in the plays of Camus and Sartre—is a desire to rediscover the last outpost of man's dignity, that existential quality in man's spirit which is irrational and ecstatic and which cannot be defined away by social, psychological, or scientific theory.

If the function of art—like that of the social sciences—is to create co-operative citizens, then the French drama should be burned and the playwrights banished. A good case could probably be made for the argument that French nihilism has been partially responsible for the instability of French government. On the other hand, our government is relatively stable and our public arts soothing. We are never disturbed by revolutions; our students spend their leisure chasing girls rather than demonstrating against regimes; and even our bohemians are "beat." Yet, we have paid for our surface calm by becoming a notably docile, passive, and uneasy people—overly addicted to such anodynes as alcohol, drugs, tranquilizers, and TV, and plagued by startling increases in homosexuality, insanity, delinquency, and divorce. You would never suspect, for all the sociology in our drama, that payola and the fix have become a national way of life; nor would you guess, for all the therapy, that a "well-adjusted citizen" is not necessarily a more honest one. Instead of trying to preserve man's unfathomable mystery, our playwrights have delivered man over to the uses of society; and Broadway has now become another branch of what Brecht once called the "bourgeois narcotics factory." As long as the American dramatist continues to feed us aspirin fantasies instead of performing radical surgery, he will be not the physician of man's distemper but merely another symptom of an advanced disease.

(1960)

WHY I WRITE

■ A few weeks ago, an indignant subscriber wrote a letter to this magazine, hotly protesting my "uninformed comments" on the theatre, which he proceeded to characterize, in a flamboyant Augustan manner, as "unadulterated tripe." The stimulus for this wholly unsolicited flattery was a negative notice I had written of the Phoenix's *She Stoops to Conquer*. Observing that most of the "competent" drama critics on the newspapers had confirmed him in his enthusiasm for the production, this correspondent enclosed a rave review from the *Times* as incontrovertible proof of my professional "incompetence." After stating that all who love the theatre should support ambitious groups like the Phoenix, he concluded his note with a demand for an "apology" or, at least, a "reasonable explanation" of my outrageous conduct.

Confound your infernal impudence, I roared, eagerly dipping my pen in formaldehyde and framing a reply in my most poisonous style—but as I paused to consider the implications of this letter my belligerency vaporized into astonishment. Clearly, this correspondent had assumed 1) that I am accountable for correctly anticipating *his* response to a play, 2) that critical "competence" is measured by the writings of newspaper reporters, and 3) that a drama critic has a duty to love the theatre! Where had he picked up such outlandish notions? Had I inadvertently put them into his head? Quailing at the thought that others might be nourishing similar delusions, I determined to make my critical purposes—clear enough to me—explicit to the more benighted of my readers. So here, in lieu of an apology, is an explanation of why I do and do not write.

First, dear reader, let me assure you that I do not write in order to arbitrate your theatregoing activities. I confess to the darkest ignorance about who you are, how much you know, or what you consider a good play, so it would be the sheerest impertinence for me to try to guide your taste. I have a further confession to make—I am not even sure that you exist. So to be perfectly safe, I imagine you as an ideal spectator, one who responds only to the best in the theatre, and who therefore visits it very seldom, generally with a profound distaste for what you see. If it depended on you and me, the Broadway box office would close tomorrow, and all the producers would go back into the real estate business—if, indeed, they ever left it. For while we share a fanatical devotion to dramatic art, we suspect the "theatre" is very rarely a place where this is displayed.

Now if you find this character fits you, then we shall be friends and communicants; but I grant that you may wish to dissociate yourself from such a rigid description. Perhaps you are a "common" spectator, and for the sake of a few hours of relaxation are willing to accept considerably less than perfection. If so, depart from me, along with your brethren the "common" reader and the "common" man, and go consult a "common" reviewer. You will find him in your newspaper, especially hired to cater to your taste, his virtue being that he knows just as little as you, and sometimes even less, having qualified for his present job by his supreme averageness. What he practices is called journalism, a technique created in the eighteenth century with the rise of democracy, the lowering of standards, and the growth of a large lay public which wanted to be informed quickly without troubling its brains too much. He is your man, if your demands are not too severe, for he is much more eager than I to proclaim new masterpieces—inflating reputations, publicizing personalities, and boosting the economy of the theatre along the way. But do not, like our indignant Augustan, confuse his work with criticism, which was invented by Aristotle, designed for experts, dedicated to absolute standards, and practiced today by very few.

For the function of criticism does not lie in the designation of some trumpery piece as "the best damn show I've seen in years." It is, in the language of a modern Aristotelian named

T. S. Eliot, "the commentation and analysis of works of art . . . for the elucidation of art and the correction of taste." By this definition, to be sure, we all stand condemned of non-critical, if not journalistic, practices, because in an age of bad literature like our own there is little else to be written on a regular basis—unless you would prefer a depth analysis of *Under the Yum Yum Tree*. A drama critic working in a journalistic capacity, unwilling to lower his standards, and continually confronted with the spurious, the mediocre, and the false, can become a social philosopher like Bernard Shaw, an aesthetician of the stage like Stark Young, or an analyst of dramatic technique like Eric Bentley—if he works for a mass magazine, he is more likely to become an entertaining stylist like Kenneth Tynan. But he establishes his claim to serious criticism when discussing a genuine work of art, bringing his whole experience and expertise into the service of analysis, illumination, and interpretation. And this is why I bite with such obvious relish into the occasional masterpieces that come my way; and why, lacking these, I often choose to belabor you with extra-critical lectures on the dismal state of our culture, our theatre, and our national spirit. For if the critic is the humble servant of genuine art, he is the implacable enemy of pseudo art, waging war on all the conditions which produce it, including the writer's cynicism, the producer's greed, the actor's ambition, and the spectator's spiritual emptiness.

As for the correcting of taste, this function every true critic guards as jealously as if it were his own personal property—not for the sake of a contemporary theatregoer's ephemeral pleasure but for the sake of a harsh posterity much less inclined to charitable opinions than our own age. It is under the cold, impersonal eye of the future that the dramatic artist writes, suppressing his natural desire for fame, love, success, and money in order to communicate his vision truly in eternal aesthetic form. And under the glare of this eye, the critic, too, must make his judgments, always conscious that he will ultimately be judged himself. Can you imagine the mordant laughter with which twenty-first-century man, picking up a rotting copy of a play like *J. B.*, will note that someone once considered it "one

of the most memorable works of the century"? This laughter is
what terrifies us in our sleep, and nudges us forward in the
ruthless pursuit of art.

(1961)

THE LESSON
OF THE MOISEYEV

MOISEYEV DANCE COMPANY

■ After witnessing a thrilling program of dance by Moscow's
Moiseyev company the other night, I was pressed by an anxious
crowd into the lurid phantasmagoria of Times Square, where I
stopped to observe the local attractions. Ads for movies called
Geisha Playmates, Virgin Sacrifice, and *Woman Bait* were
graphically displayed on the pornographic marquees of 42nd
Street grind houses. Fatuous situation comedies blared from
blinding TV sets in dark, gloomy bars. From loudspeakers
above record shops floated the hollow moans of teen-age croon-
ers, wailing in echo chambers about the tortures of frustrated
love. In front of dance halls, strollers were examining glossy
photos of peroxide girls in the full ebb of defeated sexuality.
And on the side streets, overdressed Broadway audiences were
exhaustedly emerging from gaudy musical fantasies celebrating
the triumph of money over mind. Is it by some sinister design
that the Moiseyev troupe has been installed at the Met, just a
stone's throw from these rotting citadels of our degenerate mass
arts? Is it mere coincidence that the first thing a spectator encounters, after admiring the bursting health and animal exuber-
ance of these Soviet dancers, is the general deadness of life and
desperation of spirit among the masses of this grim metropolis?

Whatever the motive, the effect is disheartening: the simple geographical placement of the Moiseyev troupe next to these soulless American diversions evokes comparisons which make us reek of decay.

In a sense, such comparisons are somewhat invidious, since it is doubtful if Moiseyev dance is typical of Russian mass culture—which I suspect is pretty much as dreary as ours. For one thing, the company is too accomplished; for another, the evening, though full of fervent patriotic pride, is almost totally free from tendency or propaganda. Aside from an occasional wooing scene, in fact, the dances contain hardly any programmatic content at all, not even in the famous *Partisans* sequence, where one expects a chauvinistic tribute to Russia's gallant resistance to Nazi aggression, but gets instead a series of fiercely beautiful sword dances and horsemanlike maneuvers, performed in voluminous Cossack cloaks. Leaning heavily toward the abstract, the entire repertoire of the Moiseyev seems like an open affront to Soviet realism, if not to Soviet unity. The company performs regional folk dances from the various Soviet republics, each executed—in appropriate, tasteful local costumes—through graceful glides, formal monograms, swirling turns, wild abandoned leaps, occasional acrobatics, and even (in a dance-cum-balancing act from Uzbekistan called *The Platter*) a touch of local vaudeville. Clearly, this is not the usual Soviet mash, flavored by the stale gravy of political didacticism. The appeal of the Moiseyev can be found rather in its extraordinary precision, virtuosity, and energy, and, above all, in its bubbling, wholesome, infectious good nature.

Yet, we must inevitably compare the Moiseyev with our own mass arts because its program is so clearly designed as popular entertainment and not as high culture. One would like to measure the work of this troupe against the more profound creations of Martha Graham or George Balanchine, but its ambitions are much too modest. Communist totalitarianism has effectively suppressed that individual freedom essential to serious art, and the choreography of Igor Moiseyev, like most Soviet creative expressions, is without psychological depth, a tragic sense of life, intellectual and spiritual content—in short, the qualities we usually associate with the finest Western dance. (It is also free from the major defects of so much American choreography, namely that obsessive sexual emphasis, chorus-boy effeminacy, and slick sophistication.) But then the function of the Moiseyev is quite simple and unpretentious. The company is content merely to celebrate community differences within the Soviet, communicating—through a kind of transcendent joyousness and virility—the deepest energies of the various Russian peoples. That these energies remain so triumphantly vital suggests that, despite Soviet meddling with most forms of expression, the ethnic cultural diversity of Russia has somehow been preserved, and, with it, the art of the folk which prevents a people from becoming a mass.

It is a fact tinged with irony and melancholy that here—where cultural freedom has no real enemy but the profit motive—this naïve, rich, direct expression of the people has petrified and died, as the people themselves have begun to stiffen, turning to lumpen stone before the Medusa head of uniformity. The death of a genuine people's art is heralded by the pseudo-folksy guitar strumming of a Greenwich Village bohemian, but the mass media pay for the funeral, graciously supplying cemetery plot, headstone, and gravediggers. Observers less apologetic toward democratic culture than sanguine sociologists have yet to measure how severely our degraded mass arts have degraded our masses, but the coarsening of both is sufficiently obvious to the Moiseyev company which concludes its program with a hair-raising parody of American teen-age dance. To watch these vigorous men and apple-cheeked girls—who have just been demonstrating their perfect discipline, dignity, and agility—collapse into the absurd postures of American adolescents, their faces going slack, their behinds protruding obscenely, their lips wrapped loosely around dangling cigarettes, their gaudily costumed bodies plastered together and swaying narcotically to the idiot rhythms of rock-and-roll, is to see the tragedy of our culture enacted in scarifying terms. But then one needs only walk a few steps up from the Met to see this tragedy even more horribly confirmed.

For let there be no mistake about it: The culture of a people is not just a reflection of their aesthetic tastes, but an accurate index of their hearts and minds. And the American mass arts— now manipulated solely by profiteers and salesmen—shamefully display to all the world the devitalization of the American masses. "We had fed the heart on fantasies," wrote Yeats. "The heart's grown brutal from the fare." The brutalization of the people's hearts by the fantasies of mass culture is something for which no amount of social or economic progress can provide much comfort, for it signifies the systematic deterioration of the American spirit. To judge from the Moiseyev company, the Russian spirit is still vibrant, despite the deadening weight of totalitarianism, and the Russian heart is still pulsing with life. What, then, is the lesson to be learned from this rich dividend from the cultural exchange? It is that we must somehow un-massify our people and their culture if either is ever to live again.

(1961)

THE KEYNES
OF TIMES SQUARE

Lee Strasberg

■ In a country without plays, the public's attention fastens on the player. Improvising from his own character, creating his own script, the actor has become the subject of countless inter-views in newspapers, magazines, and books. In Hollywood, which also has no dramatic art, such interviews are common-places—Sidney Skolsky and the gossip columnists have always been dependable sources of information about the eating, sleep-ing, and coupling habits of the stars. Today, however, in a more dignified format, Broadway actors are conversing freely not only about their private lives but also about their professional lives—about what everyone has agreed to call their "art." Since there are as few genuinely creative spirits among contemporary players as among contemporary playwrights, I find it significant that the word "artist" is so promiscuously applied to the one, so chastely to the other (playwrights are more frequently called "craftsmen"). For this, I suspect, we have the Actors Studio to thank—an institution which has inflated the importance of the actor's calling at the expense of the author's. Very few interpretive performers are intellectuals, but Method actors are especially famous for their ignorance of, and indifference to, that higher art which actors have traditionally served. Like most products of professional education (teachers college graduates, for example), they are much more concerned with techniques of communication than with the objects to be communicated. If you want this documented, consult the index of an interview book like Lillian and Helen Ross's *The Player: A Profile of an Art*, and count the number of references to Ibsen (two), Brecht (three), and Shakespeare (none), as compared with the number to Lee Strasberg, Elia Kazan, and the Actors Studio (forty-three).

Reviewing the book, and observing the numerous testimonials to Strasberg, Norman Podhoretz draws this conclusion: "Considering how many bad plays have been saved by actors who did indeed turn themselves into the characters they were portraying, one might say that Lee Strasberg has done for the commercial theatre in America what Lord Keynes did for capitalism." The comparison is apt enough, though I doubt that history will thank either man. Like the economic reforms of Keynes, the histrionic reforms of Strasberg reinvigorated a sick institution which was threatening to expire from its own fakery, inadequacy, and incompetence. Keynes's innovations, however, seem to have been rather more effective, for while capitalism still retains a certain energy, Broadway has now shriveled away, the Method having become just another of its feeble stereotypes. The last Broadway play I saw, primarily staffed by Studio people, was *The Fun Couple*—a performance so agonizingly amateurish that I began to feel nostalgia for the pre-Method artificialities of Guthrie McClintic.

I hear the objection that it is unfair to arraign the Actors Studio for the felonies of its individual members; after all, the Studio is not a producing unit, but a place where actors are supposed to perfect their craft. I am, however, getting rather bored with this argument, and I no longer find it convincing. The Studio takes refuge in pedagogical disinterestedness when its members fail, but it has never been reluctant to exploit their successes. Then one must ask, Why has the Studio been satisfied, all these years, to feed its members into a debased commercial system where such failures become inevitable? What is the purpose of histrionic truth when it serves nothing but dramatic falsehood? The fact is that Strasberg's reforms have all been too limited, too timid, too superficial—like those of a prose stylist who raises the quality of advertising copy. Unlike Stanislavsky, who invented a new acting technique in order to mount dramatic masterworks, thereby transforming the Russian theatre, Strasberg has been the interior decorator of a crumbling structure whose foundations he has done nothing to change. The Actors Studio is now about fifteen years old, and world famous. But can its achievements be seriously compared with those of Joan Littlewood, Jean Vilar, or Bertolt Brecht? Has it become identified either with a new approach to classical repertory or with a radical new modern dramatic movement?

Quite the contrary, it has become identified with Broadway, for which its well-publicized Method seems to be tailor-made. As I remarked two years ago: "The Studio actor, confined to his own psychic biography, has been unable to make the essential imaginative leap into another's life, with the result that he tends to play himself over and over again. Thus, the Studio Method is most appropriate to the commercial theatre, where type casters seize on a single salable commodity for merciless exploitation." This accounts for the multitude of Studio actors in Hollywood, the land of personality-mongers; and like the Group Theatre, the Actors Studio has been unable or unwilling to help its members resist the blandishments of the West Coast. I am quite aware that the actor, one of the most unfulfilled workers in our culture, has little to choose between Broadway and Hollywood. Since neither medium offers artistic satisfaction, he might as well accept the greater money, fame, and power. Still, one wonders about the more influential Studio associates, past and present. Marlon Brando, by returning to Broadway in carefully selected roles, could revolutionize our theatre overnight: his mutinies remain confined to the Bounty. Elia Kazan has the power to direct any play he chooses: he chooses *Splendor in the Grass*, while no doubt preparing to bring the same vernal glory to Lincoln Square. As for the actors who have remained in New York, none (shall we except Strasberg's daughter, Susan, who wants to play Camille?) have shown any inclination toward any but narrow naturalistic roles; and really gifted performers like Geraldine Page and Kim Stanley are continually repeating themselves with nervously mannered portrayals.

One must conclude that the Actors Studio, instead of being a temple of high theatrical ideals, has come to reflect the most pernicious qualities of our theatre: the glamour and pretentiousness, the fear of risk, the lust for fame, the quick success. The Studio is now at the height of its notoriety—the object of benefits, testimonials, and Kulchural winks from the White House—but this testifies less to its appetite for art than to its passion for publicity. Lee Strasberg, a monastic figure with tremendous charisma, has attracted a fanatical following; but a great teacher sets a great example, and little that is exemplary in the way of selflessness and humility has recently been seen from that quarter. Strasberg's insulted snit over Lincoln Center is a case in point—a real man of the theatre would have been proud to be excluded from that cultural frou-frou—and the way in which the Studio exploited the tragic aspirations of Marilyn Monroe was nothing short of scandalous. Well, the Studio is preparing to inaugurate its own theatre; I wish it godspeed. In the meantime, I am looking around for a much more revolutionary figure than Lee Strasberg to bring the theatre back to life. Keynes succeeded in reforming our economic system through melioration and compromise, for politics, as we are always told, is the art of the possible. But art is the politics of the impossible, and compromise is not enough. What Broadway needs is not a Keynes but a Marx—not one who will trim its toenails, but one who will lop off its malignant limbs.

(1962)

A BUCCANEER
ON BROADWAY

David Merrick

■ Though it is impossible to extend this feeling to the shows he produces, I have always nursed a grudging admiration for David Merrick. In a season as slack as an idiot's jaw, the unconscionable activities of this theatrical freebooter have proved by far the most lively events on Broadway: somebody ought to package *him*, and send him off on tour. Merrick has brought, to a gray profession eager to look respectable, the shameless hucksterism of a modern Barnum, including a colorful personal style and boundless contempt for all those who do not help to push his products. Chief among these malefactors, of course, are the reviewers; and while most producers are bowing and scraping before these hallowed figures, Merrick is barring them from his theatres, damning them as fools or knaves, and even dispensing with them entirely as cultural middlemen. To Merrick, the best appeal to the public's pocketbook is through publicity, and, aided by the New York newspaper strike, he has gradually been converting all other available means of communication into house organs for his shows. When *Oliver!* was previewing, for example, a bevy of disc jockeys not only flooded the ether with Lionel Bart's undistinguished tunes, but even began adding their own enthusiastic testimonials to the musical. This sudden zest for culture on the part of DJ's was supplemented—the day after the work opened to sour notices from Kerr and Taubman—by a rave review from Merrick himself on WNEW, and by a radio voice, identified as "your theatre reviewer," which announced on most local networks that *Oliver!* was the greatest musical hit since *My Fair Lady*. Since the voice neglected to mention that it was participating in a commercial announcement, one heard it dimly, as it were, through the snores of the F.C.C.

Tactics like these may indeed have turned *Oliver!* into the biggest moneymaker since *My Fair Lady*, even though it is a totally synthetic, vapid, and opportunistic work, not interesting enough to discuss. More interesting to me are the motives of its sponsor, and the kind of image he is fashioning for the contemporary Broadway theatre. For Merrick is the embodiment of pure, disinterested commercialism—his motto might be that of Shaw's Undershaft: Unashamed. As a producer, he has about as much identification with his products as a manufacturer of trusses—even less, since his shows are usually imported from abroad, already packaged, with a built-in success factor. Merrick's open dedication to profit, and his indifference to promoting his own tastes, are an outrage to his "stage-struck" brethren in production who like to think that they are altruistically advancing culture; but his seems to me the more honest attitude, considering the state of our current theatre. If we exclude Alexander Cohen, who has shown consistent courage and good taste, none of the producers who "believe" in their plays has a better record than Merrick; and there is even a slim possibility that, if foreign tastes improve, he will eventually bring in something of value, as he once brought in (and quickly closed) the Osborne-Creighton *Epitaph for George Dillon*. Merrick discriminates neither against the good nor the bad, so long as it makes money. But the effect is refreshingly subversive. By reducing every theatrical function, including reviewing, to a link in the cash nexus, he is discrediting Broadway more effectively than a battalion of minority critics. Perhaps, deep down within his press agent's heart, he is as bored with the commercial theatre as all the rest of us.

(1963)

ARTISTS AND
BUREAUCRATS

THE HARASSING OF THE PACIFICA FOUNDATION
by the Federal Communications Commission
THE CLOSING OF THE LIVING THEATRE *by the
Internal Revenue Service*

■ There is only one TV program I watch with regularity, a
thoroughly illogical and thoroughly engrossing horror series
called *The Outer Limits*—but tonight's show was canceled on
behalf of the United States Government. The network, always
vigilant in the service of the public, had decided to substitute
one of those behind-the-scenes-of-a-crisis extravaganzas—this
one revolved around school desegregation in Alabama, and
featured Bobby Kennedy as the hero, Governor Wallace as the
villain, and President Kennedy in a supporting role. During the
ten minutes I watched this artificial pseudo event, I could not
help but admire the acting. Our professional theatre has a lot to
learn from such amateur performers as these who can, with
television cameras looking on, improvise so convincingly a
drama of state: rattling papers, conferring worriedly with aides,
sweating through shirt sleeves, gripping phones with an air of
grim expectancy. It occurred to me, of course, that the Ken-
nedys were using public-relations devices to improve their image, and I could even foresee a day when they might stage a
crisis if their TV ratings declined. But I don't complain that
American officialdom is becoming an arm of show business;
after all, what's good for M.C.A. is good for the country, and
why shouldn't the Executive reflect our basic national values?

The thing that really annoyed me was having one of my favorite programs canceled by the government.

For I am getting rather depressed by these cancellations. It was bad enough when the Narcotics Bureau and the Vice Squad began to interrupt Lenny Bruce in the middle of his act, finally hauling him off to face charges of obscenity and addiction. It grew worse when the F.C.C. mysteriously began to stall on the license applications of the Pacifica Foundation, a system of three FM stations which comprise the only non-commercial, listener-supported radio network in the land. And it has now passed the limits of toleration with the closing down of New York's Living Theatre and the arrest of twenty-five of its members and spectators, by the Internal Revenue Service. I realize, of course, that free expression and free art continue unabated in the alleys of Broadway, in David Susskind's conversations with eight-year-olds, and on all the major networks. I also take consolation in the fact that the State Department really adores the theatre (didn't it send Helen Hayes and Mary Martin abroad?), and that the Administration occasionally invites *Esquire*'s hot center to a hot dinner. But in the light of all these splendid manifestations of our exploding interest in art and intellect, why do I have the uncanny feeling that our few truly free organs of intellect are being impounded, and our only non-faddist, non-ersatz art is being interrupted, as it were, on behalf of the government?

I am under no illusions about the innocence of the victims; each of them collaborated, to some extent, in his own victimization. Lenny Bruce's comedy, being rooted in the unconscious, is always blasphemous or obscene; the Pacifica Foundation has sometimes been irresponsible in its programming, giving political platforms even to crackpots; and The Living Theatre owes $23,000 in back taxes, besides having broken government locks in order to stage a last, unauthorized performance of *The Brig* for the financial benefit of the actors (this enterprise netted $16). It was, furthermore, extremely negligent of The Living Theatre not to apply for tax-exempt status when it was already eligible: to commit such an oversight, surely, is to court martyrdom. Still, in view of the uncompromising stand of the various government bureaus, one begins to suspect that the cases are more political than legal, especially when we note that the culprits are all identified with some unpopular cause, movement, or posture: peace marches, civil rights demonstrations, opposition to capital punishment, anti-clericalism, Cuba, etc. What is worse, I think, is that all of them are extremely unpredictable—both in the quality and the kind of their offerings—and there is nothing more offensive to the bureaucratic mind than unpredictability. I suspect, for example, that the F.C.C. might have been happier with a Communist radio station than with one capable of encompassing all shades of political opinion. And I suspect, too, that The Living Theatre might be functioning today if it had not followed its program of experimental dramas with a documentary on the brutality of the Marine Corps.

I am suggesting, in short, the possibility of bureaucratic conspiracy. And in the case of the Pacifica Foundation, this is more than a possibility. There, difficulties arose immediately after WBAI ran a program attacking J. Edgar Hoover and the F.B.I. This aroused the interest of a Senate watchdog committee, and, inevitably, of the John Birch society which now monitors Pacifica daily for evidence of obscenity and subversion, and deluges the F.C.C. with complaints. It is to such pressures that this rubber-spined agency is yielding, but isn't it ironic that the F.C.C., which came to public attention when its last chairman attacked the "wasteland" of the networks, should choose to harass the one oasis in this communications desert? If some of us are beginning to think that the present administration typically holds the right opinions while sanctioning the wrong actions, it is because of such paradoxes as these. Network programming is more inane, more commercial, and more restrictive than ever, but the F.C.C. invokes its authority only against a free minority station like WBAI.

The case of The Living Theatre is similar, though more complicated. There, legal culpability can be proved, since the group is bankrupt. Bankruptcy is usually taken as a sign of failure in America, so perhaps I should mention that The Living Theatre, for all its erraticism, is the best—indeed the only—

experimental repertory troupe in New York, and one of the very
few American companies to receive acclaim abroad. It is not, to
be sure, in the main stream of the official culture, it has not
attracted the friendship of the newspaper reviewers, it has not
drawn a large audience—but theatrical advance has always been
made at the cost of critical hostility and losses at the gate, and
no American repertory company functions today without substantial financial help. This help has not been forthcoming to
The Living Theatre, despite scattered donations from individuals and the smaller foundations. The New York State
Council on the Arts prefers to subsidize productions of Kismet
and Plain and Fancy, while the large foundations pour their
money into such semi-commercial ventures as Lincoln Center
and the Actors Studio Repertory—groups which are already
supported by Broadway angels and the Broadway public. It
finally becomes obvious that the real issue here is free expression, and it is an issue which legal and economic questions only
obscure. In a commercial society, everyone is permitted to speak
his piece if he can afford to buy a platform; but as the platforms
become more expensive, all non-official opinion ceases to be
heard.

If this legal muzzling of everything radical, dangerous, or
difficult continues, the alternatives will not be pleasant. Madness may be one of them—to judge by the Birchers' influence
on the F.C.C., the mad, at least, can command the attention of
bureaucrats. Another alternative was unwittingly suggested
when The Living Theatre committed an act of civil disobedience to stage its last performance, the spectators climbing over
roofs and through windows in order to see it. Jean Genet once
imagined "a clandestine theatre, to which one would go in
secret, at night, and masked, a theatre in the catacombs. . . ."
Will this be the theatre of the future when every other possibility has been harried into oblivion? Will this be our last
underground refuge when art and entertainment are totally
dominated by Broadway and the wunnerful world of show
biz—with an occasional guest appearance by Bobby Kennedy on
a crisis of our time?

(1963)

Postcript:
THE DEATH OF
THE LIVING THEATRE

■ Having been found guilty of interfering with the Internal Revenue Service when that agency was padlocking their theatre, Julian Beck and Judith Malina have been given prison terms— six weeks and three weeks, respectively—and The Living Theatre is now defunct. These consequences I find to be deplorable in the extreme. It is true that the behavior of the Becks in the courtroom was far from praiseworthy. In an effort to "humanize" their case, they proceeded to conduct their own defense in a manner that sometimes seemed to court martyrdom; and they severely tried the patience of a friendly judge through arrogant antics and provocative outbursts. It may be that the Becks are self-destructive. Still, they should never have found themselves in court in the first place; the case should never have come to trial.

It is hard to comprehend why the I.R.S. chose to close down The Living Theatre and sell its meager assets when the customary way to recover delinquent taxes is to keep a plant in operation; and it is harder still to understand why the government pressed such a severe indictment against the Becks after their unfortunate, but understandable, attempt to keep their theatre running. By launching its heavy legal machinery against this frail couple, the United States has actually injured itself, for it has silenced one of the few American theatrical troupes to win substantial acclaim abroad. Indeed, the United States has profited directly from this acclaim, since, in spite of its refusal either to support or recognize The Living Theatre on its trip to

Paris, it was, ironically, the United States government which received the Grand Prix when the group took acting honors in an international competition. Is it an American custom to exploit cultural triumphs while badgering those who achieved them?

The virtues of The Living Theatre—its artistic dedication and uncompromising idealism—are the very qualities for which the Becks were prosecuted: the same fanatical single-mindedness that kept this company going for thirteen difficult years resulted in an act of civil disobedience, designed to perpetuate the theatre's life. Could not this act have been tolerated and forgiven? In view of the fact that we are less in danger today from anarchic individualism than from bureaucratic interference with the rights of individuals, the prosecution of the Becks served no purpose whatsoever, except to achieve a hollow legal victory at the cost of a resounding cultural defeat. I am sure there are more pressing things for the government to do than to pound into dust one of the very few theatrical institutions of which Americans can justly be proud.

(1964)

THREE PLAYWRIGHTS
AND A PROTEST

Slow Dance on the Killing Ground by William Hanley; The Slave and The Toilet by LeRoi Jones; Tiny Alice by Edward Albee

■ Three new plays by the younger generation of American dramatists compel a protest from me.

Slow Dance on the Killing Ground. William Hanley's melodrama has one arresting moment, which occurs right after the rise of the curtain. The scene is a neighborhood candy store on a dark, deserted street; the proprietor, a middle-aged German, is taking inventory. Suddenly, a Negro enters, obviously eluding pursuers, dressed in a black cape, string tie, sneakers, and dark glasses. As played by the gifted Clarence Williams III, he is a sinister figure, hunched like a monkey, and ambulating with the balletic grace of a junkie Charlie Chaplin. The most conspicuous element in his costume is an umbrella, the point of which has been sharpened for a kill, and it is not long before he is menacing the storekeeper with this improvised weapon, muttering wild irrelevancies in a hip, auto-didactic verbal style. Accounts of the psychopathic killer known as the Umbrella Man have prepared us for the brutal attack which must follow—but the expected blow never falls. Instead, the Negro sits down, removes his glasses, changes his ominous tone, and—employing a highly eloquent vocabulary (he has, he tells us, an IQ of 187)—initiates a three-hour talkathon, quoting from Gide and Kafka, and analyzing the roots of his own behavior: he suffers from insufficient mother love!

Mr. Hanley's game might be called Truth without Consequences; his rules are to evoke an evil reality, culled from some recent headline, and then to soften this reality with psychological bromides, self-conscious motive-mongering, and sentimental evasions. This technique he applies not only to Negro crime but to a large number of our current theatrical obsessions: Jewish victimization, German guilt, Appearance versus Reality, the Need for Commitment to Something Higher than the Self, and (with the entrance later of a young girl in search of an abortion) the Importance of Loving the Life Inside Your Body. Mr. Hanley's play, in short, is like a catalogue of contemporary Broadway themes and conventions, but in order to include them all, the playwright is forced to sacrifice consistency of character, unity of form, and logical continuity. What begins as a melodrama eventually becomes a disquisitory debate, a sex comedy, and a soap opera; each of the three acts seems totally independent of the other two; and the characters must function in a host of different roles, the Umbrella Man, for example, acting as confessor, confidant, orator, psychological counselor, social worker, and judge, in sequence. At the end, he returns to his original role as menace, when he reveals that he has murdered his mother. But by this time, all credibility has been swallowed up in the drama's sententious molasses, where every speech is italicized, and every line is a curtain line. This is Mr. Hanley's first Broadway effort, and the significant thing about it is how a dramatist so new to the street could have so quickly become privy to all its commercial secrets.

The Slave and *The Toilet*. While Hanley's play reveals a jaded talent, these two karate blows by LeRoi Jones display no talent at all—they are inspired primarily by race hatred. Larry Rivers' set for *The Toilet* consists of seven urinals; the scene is the boys' john of a predominantly Negro high school. There students congregate, during pauses in the educational process, to exchange insults and obscenities, and to gang up on unprotected students, usually "whiteys." The major victim of *The Toilet* is a Puerto Rican homosexual who, having sent a love letter to one of the Negroes, is brutally beaten, and then tossed, bleeding and unconscious, into one of the urinals. The Negro he loves—and who helped to mug him—returns surreptitiously at the end to cradle the victim's head in his lap and to sob over his prostrate form. This maudlin conclusion reveals a soft chink in the author's spiky armor, but still the play is not a drama but a psychodrama, designed for the acting out of sado-masochistic racial fantasies.

The Slave projects these fantasies into a Genet-like war between White and Black, which the Negroes are on the verge of winning. The play concerns the visit of the Negro military leader, once a poet and intellectual, to the home of his former (white) wife and her present husband, a white university professor. Before long, the Negro has, predictably, maligned the professor's liberalism and his manhood ("Professor No-Dick"), rabbit-punched him to the ground, and emptied his revolver into his body, while leaving the woman lying dead under the debris of her exploded home. The play, to say the least, is out of control, and its language is full of semi-literate blather ("I have killed for all times any creative impulse I will ever have by the depravity of my murderous philosophies"). The decay of Western culture—to which the playwright frequently alludes in *The Slave*—is nowhere better exemplified than in the unwarranted favor this culture has lavished on LeRoi Jones, because he has shown little theatrical purpose beyond the expression of a raging chauvinism, and few theatrical gifts beyond a capacity to record the graffiti scrawled on men's room walls.

Tiny Alice. Edward Albee has called his new play a "mystery story," a description which applies as well to its content as to its genre. The work is certainly very mystifying, full of dark hints and riddling allusions, but since it is also clumsy and contrived, and specious in the extreme, the mystery that interested me most was whether the author was kidding his audience or kidding himself. *Tiny Alice* may well turn out to be a huge joke on the American culture industry; then again, it may turn out to be a typical product of that industry. The hardest thing to determine about "camp" literature, movies, and painting is the extent of the author's sincerity. A hoax is being perpetrated, no doubt of that, but is this intentional or not? Is the contriver inside or outside his own fraudulent creation? Does Andy Warhol really believe in the artistic validity of his Brillo boxes? *Tiny Alice* is a much more ambitious work than the usual variety of camp, but it shares the same ambiguity of motive. For while some of Albee's obscurity is pure playfulness, designed to con the spectator into looking for nonexistent meanings, some is obviously there for the sake of a sham profundity in which the author apparently believes.

My complaint is that Albee has not created profundity, he has only borrowed the appearance of it. In *Tiny Alice*, he is once again dealing with impersonation—this time as a metaphor for religious faith—and once again is doing most of the impersonating himself. The central idea of the play—which treats religious ritual as a form of stagecraft and play-acting—comes from Jean Genet's *The Balcony*; its initial device—which involves a wealthy woman handing over a fortune in return for the sacrifice of a man's life—comes from Duerrenmatt's *The Visit*; its symbolism—revolving around mysterious castles, the union of sacred and profane, and the agony of modern Christ figures—is largely taken from Strindberg's *A Dream Play*; and its basic tone—a metaphysical rumble arising out of libations, litanies, and ceremonies created by a shadowy hieratic trio—is directly stolen from T. S. Eliot's *The Cocktail Party*. The play, in short, is virtually a theatrical echo chamber, with reverberations of Graham Greene, Enid Bagnold, and Tennessee Williams being heard as well; but Albee's manipulation of these sources owes more to literature than to life, while his metaphysical enigmas contribute less to thematic perception than to atmospheric fakery.

To approach *Tiny Alice* as a coherent work of art, therefore, would be a mistake, since, in my opinion, most of it is meaningless—a frozen portent without an animating event. There are thematic arrows, to be sure, planted throughout the play: allusions to the imperfectibility of human knowledge, appearance and reality, the unreachableness of God, but all these ultimately point down dead-end streets, or are bent and twisted by leaden paradoxes. Let me, in consequence, try to discharge my duties to the play simply by outlining the plot.

In return for a bequest of two billion dollars—presented to a waspish Cardinal by a bitchy Lawyer who used to be his schoolfellow—a lay brother in the Roman church named Julian is sent to the home of Alice, the millionairess who donated the money. Alice later turns out to be a priestess in the service of a god (or goddess) named Alice, for whom she is acting as surrogate. She is also identified with the Virgin Mother (the Lawyer has suggestions of Satan), even though she seems to have slept with everybody, including her butler (named Butler), who functions as a kind of hierophant. Alice, Lawyer, and Butler all live in a gigantic castle, which represents the universe. Inside one room is a perfect miniature model of this castle, called "The Wonders of the World," and inside the "Wonders," presumably, is another miniature—and so forth, on the principle of Chinese boxes. The possibility arises that the actual castle is merely a model within an even larger room, which is itself only a miniature, *ad infinitum*. The "Wonders," however, is not only a symbol of the expanding universe, but also an altar, to which the mysterious threesome pray, and inside which the god Alice may reside (thus, "tiny" Alice).

THREE PLAYWRIGHTS AND A PROTEST / 309

Slowly, it is revealed that this priestly trio is preparing Julian for a ritual sacrifice. He will eventually be forced to re-enact the death of Christ, a role for which he qualifies not by virtue of any moral beauty, visionary power, or special sanctity, but rather because of certain pathological attributes. He longs to debase himself, is subject to hallucinations, and enjoys masochistic fantasies of being bloodied by gladiators and eaten by lions. His martyrdom, however, comes in quite a different way. First, he is seduced by Alice; then she marries him; then deserts him; and finally the Lawyer shoots him. Now the Passion begins, accompanied by a hailstorm of religious symbols. Julian, dying, is held, like Jesus in the Pietà, by a blue-cloaked Alice, who begs him to accept the godhead of Alice. Julian refuses at first, and is left in isolation. Then, in what may be one of the longest death scenes on record (it is surely among the dullest), he cries "Alice, oh Alice, why hast thou forsaken me?" and stumbles—arms outstretched in crucifixion—against the "Wonders of the World." Accepting Alice at the last, he expires, to the accompaniment of heartbeats and breathing amplified over a loudspeaker.

The only thing that might redeem a concept like this from its own pretentiousness is some kind of theatrical adroitness; but I regret to say that Albee's customary ingenuity has deserted him here. The language, first of all, is surprisingly windy, slack, sodden, and repetitive; the jokes are childishly prurient ("The organ is in need of use," says the sexually undernourished Julian upon visiting the chapel); and the usual electricity of an Albee quarrel has degenerated—when it is employed in the opening scene between the Cardinal and the Lawyer—into mere nagging. Furthermore, Albee has not been able to exploit his own devices sufficiently. The miniature castle is a good conceit; but it functions more for obfuscation than for theatrical effect, being used to good advantage only once (when the chapel catches fire). And finally, the play vacillates between excessive fruitiness and excessive staginess, whether Julian is being enfolded within the wrapper of the naked Alice (and disappearing somewhere near her genital region), or being gunned down by the Lawyer in a manner reminiscent of Victorian melodrama.

As for the production, it staggers under the ponderousness of the play. John Gielgud is probably one of the few actors in the world capable of disguising the ludicrousness of his role; but he is forced to maintain a pitch of exaltation, bordering on hysteria, throughout the entire evening, and even he cannot prevent his speeches from sounding montonous. Irene Worth, the most charming of actresses, is warm and compassionate as Alice, and John Heffernan has a wry, laconic quality as the butler, but the production, as a whole, does not work, for the director, Alan Schneider, has been unable to find a convincing histrionic equivalent for the portentous style of the writing. Only William Ritman's setting, a massive affair with huge wooden doors and expansive playing areas, is really very satisfying, for it supplies that sense of solidity and substantiality that the play so sorely lacks.

These three plays are fairly representative of the kind of theatre being produced by our younger dramatists, and therein lies my protest: Whatever their superficial differences, they are all possessed by a subterranean nihilism. Hanley, Jones, and Albee seem to be preoccupied with important contemporary concerns—the position of minority groups, the Negro revolution, Existential *Angst*, the loss of faith—but some essential commitment is seriously lacking, and the central questions are invariably skirted. What results is less an artistic quest than a fashionable posture or personal exhibition, with the playwright producing not masterpieces but conversation pieces. This, to be sure, is the characteristic art of our time. Now that the cultural revolution has become an arm of big business, the mass media, and the fashion magazines, values have all but disappeared from artistic creation, and a crowd of hipsters and their agents are cynically exploiting the fears and pretensions of a semi-educated public. But while the nihilism of Pop Art, for example, is relatively open, the theatre continues to simulate values and feign commitments: it will not be long before these masks fall too. The collapse of the original Lincoln Center Repertory Company signifies the end of the theatre of the thirties, and the extinction of its dreams—but I dread the nightmare that is coming to take its place. Must we choose between a discredited

Establishment and a careerist avant-garde? Are the only alternatives to be between the collapsed idealism of the old and the secret cynicism of the new?

(1965)

AFTERWORD

■ My book closes on a question, the answer to which must remain, of course, problematical. One thing is certain: Our drama is in a process of radical change, the old forms altering their outlines, the new ones struggling for definition. In this process, two insurgent movements are beginning to figure prominently—the one racial, the other sexual. The tradition of American political drama, which once found expression in the social realism of Clifford Odets, Lillian Hellman, and Arthur Miller, has now been captured by the Civil Rights movement, while the bohemian strain in our drama, which previously entered the experimental plays of Eugene O'Neill and the lurid fantasies of Tennessee Williams, is now being cultivated in that fashionable brand of artificial friskiness known as "camp."

These two revolutions—the Negro and the Sexual (or Homosexual)—are now supplying the central issues of our time, but neither has yet produced a first-rate dramatic work. The tremendous energies behind the Negro's drive for fuller freedom have been poured into a large number of militant plays, including those of James Baldwin, Ossie Davis, and LeRoi Jones; but for all the nobility of the cause itself, such plays have thus far tended to be self-righteous, melodramatic, and shrill. The "camp" playwrights, on the other hand, though often more sophisticated writers, have been much too preoccupied with exploring bizarre, clandestine, and arcane experience, as if sexual erraticism were an automatic guarantee of theatrical unconventionality; but since the stage is many moonshines lag of the novel in frankness, even this issue has been cryptically approached or seriously evaded.

Were I to attempt a prognosis, however, I would guess that the Negro and the Sexual revolutions will eventually determine the two basic postures of our theatre, for although they occasionally merge and overlap—as in Baldwin's *Blues for Mr. Charlie*, LeRoi Jones's *The Toilet*, or Albee's *The Death of Bessie Smith*—they are more often responsible for clearly contrasted forms of drama. Thus, the Negro protest play—like previous protest drama—is essentially realistic, fervent, hortatory, affirmative, and political, while the bohemian "camp" play—like much avant-garde drama—tends to be formally experimental, playful, exhibitionist, pessimistic, and personal (or sometimes, as with *The Zoo Story* or *Tiny Alice*, even pseudoreligious).

The important plays of the future American stage may be created out of one or the other of these genres; perhaps, as I am more inclined to believe, they will issue from the pen of an artist who remains unattached to movements and independent of schools. But my prognosis must stop short of prognostication. What remains certain is that no lasting dramatic improvement will take place until certain obstacles impeding growth are burned and purged away. For there is nothing more constant in our changing theatre than the impediments it throws into the path of the aspiring playwright or performer—unless it be the impediments this playwright or performer places there himself. To remove these blights on the landscape is still a cardinal necessity of the American theatre. Only when they are gone will our discontented seasons finally yield some abundant harvest days.

INDEX